PRAISE FOR
HATING PERFECTION

"Astonishing! . . . Lively, highly original, tightly argued, and a joy to read. . . . An electrifying achievement."

> —**HUBERT DREYFUS**, professor of philosophy,
> University of California, Berkeley

"Adds an argument to those used by Leibniz for the claim that this is the best of all possible worlds and one that is more persuasive than his."

> —**NELSON POLE**, professor of philosophy, emeritus,
> Cleveland State University; developer of the
> LogicCoach family of computer programs

In some ways God exists and in some ways God does not exist, I claim. Religious people have taken just as much exception to *Hating Perfection* as atheists.

—JFW

"A passionate and perceptive challenge to some of our most deep-seated and cherished philosophical and personal assumptions about human happiness and progress."

> —**LARRY S. HAUSER**, Alma College,
> frequent contributor to *Mind and Machines*,
> *Mind and Behavior, Behavior and Philosophy*,
> *The Internet Encyclopedia of Philosophy*,
> and other peer-reviewed journals

"A startling new perspective on existence."

> —**PIOTR HOFFMAN**, professor of philosophy,
> University of Nevada, Reno

"Williams provides us with a fascinating new way of seeing the world, and thus living in it, that might reconcile us to existence."

> —**TYLER KRUPP**, University of California, Berkeley,
> post grad and lecturer

"This engaging and eloquently written work tackles life's biggest questions of meaning, free will, and why this world rather than another. The answers will surprise you."

> —**MATTHEW LIEBERMAN**,
> professor of social psychology,
> University of California, Los Angeles

"Engaging, thoughtful, and eloquent. The fundamental ideas are often surprising, but always deeply considered and deeply felt. I highly recommend [*Hating Perfection*]."

> —**JOSHUA BEATTIE**,
> Stanford University Online High School

"Devastating and exhilarating."

> —**DAVID PARK**, reviewer for Bolerium Books

"A pretty good slant on things."

> —**STEVE JASPER**, illustrator

"Fascinating, sustained, thorough, and careful."

> —**SCOTT RAGLAND**, associate professor of philosophy, St. Louis University

"These short meditations on the richness and variety of the world illustrate Leonardo's idea that details make perfection, but perfection is not a detail."

HATING PERFECTION

*A Subtle Search for
the Best Possible World*

Revised Edition

JOHN F. WILLIAMS

Humanity
Books

an imprint of Prometheus Books
59 John Glenn Drive, Amherst, New York 14228-2119

Published 2013 by Humanity Books, an imprint of Prometheus Books

Inquiries should be addressed to
Humanity Books
59 John Glenn Drive
Amherst, New York 14228–2119
VOICE: 716–691–0133
FAX: 716–691–0137
WWW.PROMETHEUSBOOKS.COM

17 16 15 14 13   5 4 3 2 1

Library of Congress Cataloging-in-Publication Data

Williams, John F., 1947–
     Hating perfection : a subtle search for the best possible world / by John Williams
          p.   cm.
     ISBN 978-1-61614-875-1 (pbk.: alk. paper)
     ISBN 978-1-61614-876-8 (ebook)
     1. Life. I. Title.

BD431.W5157 2009
128—dc22

                                                                2009018778

Printed in the United States of America on acid-free paper

With gratitude to
Hubert L. Dreyfus and Lee Ming Williams

Artists

The author invites professional analytic philosophers to begin *Hating Perfection* with the Postscript, page 361. Continental philosophers and "lay" readers who like storytelling will likely prefer to begin at the beginning.

CONTENTS

THE UPPER LIMIT TO THE
VALUE OF POSSIBLE WORLDS

Part One

WHISKEY LAO

The Handbag

For a thousand years the pleasant old capital of Laos, called Luang Prabang, has been a holy city. In its placid streets, in its many temples, in its perfumed gardens overlooking the Mekong River, languid Buddhist monks live and die in peace. But the Mekong wanders away into the feverish jungle and into a world far from holy. Here the secretive hill tribes still practice the ancient, terrible rites. Here strange old witches toil grimly over bubbling cauldrons, toil without rest, and mutter their dark incantations. As the vapors rise, demons inhabit the bodies of men. Far from the holy city, lost in their jungle fastness, the legions of the damned offer madness for sale at one dollar per bottle. They call it "Whiskey Lao."

Exploring the world for something new, turns up just as much evil as good. But the good and the evil are new.

This is a true story. It happened exactly as stated. Some people look at a river and immediately dream about its destiny. A river combines mystery, yearning, and harmony; soothes and excites; travels unpredictably, yet always for a reason. The river was our addiction. It beckoned and we followed.

Inconclusive reports filtered back to us in Luang Prabang. Two hours by sampan up the Mekong River, a certain Lao village, population perhaps sixty souls, produced a notorious moonshine. Visitors newly returned from the scene, haggard and reticent, would do no more than mumble a few disjointed comments. One man furtively described the production method as ". . . primitive but interesting." Then he hurried away.

We had no premonitions. Overcome by innocent curiosity, we embarked from the city quay at ten o'clock of a fine, temperate, January day. The morning mist had just begun to burn away. Since our wooden battleship of a sampan could accommodate eight passengers in its comfortable interior and another twenty on the sturdy roof, wife and self teamed up with Denise, a fellow guest at our hotel. This polished young Australian had chanced to overhear our conversation the previous evening. Having no pressing engagements for the next six months, she proposed a joint expedition. And so it happened that Denise from Brisbane, self from San Francisco, and wife Lee Ming from Beijing, three harmless tourists, ventured together into the jungle. We had no premonitions. We only wanted to have a bit of fun.

Denise proved to be an entertaining companion. As the holy city receded behind us, she gossiped knowingly about the game of cricket. Neither San Francisco nor Beijing enjoys this sport, but Brisbane knows it well. Yes, Australia's aborigines enrich humanity with many unique rituals. Lee Ming and I grabbed our chance for enlightenment. During the three previous evenings, while confined to our city hotel with limited English-language programming selection, we had watched cricket "test matches" on Rupert Murdoch's Star TV, beamed via satellite from Australia. This arcane sport does not yield up its secrets easily to the uninitiated. Several hours of close observation had left us still groping. But Denise gave us a brilliantly lucid explanation of batsmen, bowlers, overs, innings, outs, runs, and wickets. We learned that the batsman guards his wicket, much as the muskrat guards his musk. Surprisingly, cricket turns out to be a protracted variant of American baseball. Indeed, a cricket match continues for days on end. The "test match"—a truncated form of the game, concocted to accommodate the frantic modern age—sometimes begins and ends on the same calendar date. Still, even today, baseball's seventh-inning stretch, which lasts about forty seconds, corresponds in cricket to afternoon tea.

We talked without concern. This section of the Mekong has a deceptive serenity. Beneath the broad and brown sun-sparkled surface lies a multitude of dangerous rocks, like sharp teeth concealed by a friendly smile. Our Lao boatman—an enormously likable man—sat far forward in the bow and kept his eyes constantly on the eddies ahead, reading every menacing swirl. While his wife tended the motor in the stern, he navigated a zigzag course with easy skill, now nearing the left bank, now the right, planning all his moves in advance and putting us completely at ease in rather treacherous waters. At the end of the day, when we paid him twenty American dollars, he beamed like a searchlight. In our travel experience of Asian countries, Laos is both the most beautiful and the most impoverished.

Yes, to be sure, the journey upriver was stunningly gorgeous, as expected, with each bend bringing on a fascinating new vista of riverside cliffs and caves, jagged green hills arranged in receding layers and still clinging to vestiges of the morning mist, water buffalo disporting themselves in the shallows without a care in their tiny brains, and all generally right with the world. No need to make a song and dance about it. How could the boatmen make a living on an ugly river? Finally and at last we disembarked on the wide muddy banks at the foot of our target village, directly in front of the sinister stills boiling with the legendary brew. We were the only guests at the party.

The Lao people suffer their poverty with cheerful tolerance. Much of their economy is growing rice, we were told, but even so, the disastrously poor soil dictates that rice be imported. Away from the river we sometimes observed the bald patches evidencing slash-and-burn agriculture. In Laos one does not stand up in the boat, in full view of one's gentle companions, and waste his fertilizer on the Mekong River. Instead, one scrambles off the vessel at the first opportunity, marches straight past the stills, straight through the village, and directly into the jungle beyond, there to do one's bit, however insignificant, to relieve the people's burden. Lee Ming and Denise followed me closely on this arrow-straight course, brushing aside the villagers' frantic efforts to divert us into more genteel facilities. And so it happened that we began our inspection of the village from the rear, working our way back to the river and the secretive rituals it supports. The inhabitants may not have expected this development.

In the village we found about forty women and children and two men. For the benefit of those bland visitors having no enthusiasm for epic benders, some of the women weave colorful cotton purses and shawls. Using string and polished sticks of wood, they construct their complicated looms on site. These fragile monstrosities, like giant misshapen spiders made of found objects, improbably standing on their rickety stick legs, somehow function as precision machinery. I watched a pretty young woman at her loom, on the sunny porch of her house. She was making a handbag. Similar handbags hung for sale from the porch railing. At the speed of Three-Card Monte she manipulated her shuttle and threads. The clever loom relied on two foot pedals placed closely together, each a long sturdy stick hanging by strings tied at both ends. With her bare right foot placed just at the two balancing points, the weaver moved her heel and toes back and forth between these pedals, dancing an intricate little jig, always keeping the strings taut and each pedal controlled, and depressing first one and then the other at two-second intervals. The handbag progressed rapidly.

After thirty seconds of me watching her, she began to talk in Lao as she worked. I responded in English. Separated by language, we had a conversation by tone of voice. Each of us elaborated our remarks, as if talking to a puzzled pet dog. And we talked over each other, sending and receiving at the same time. But we definitely had a conversation. It seemed to go this way:

— So buy a purse. Just reach into your fat wallet and fork over the cash, you stuck-up rich foreign moron.

— I don't use a purse. What would I do with a purse? My wife makes these decisions. She doesn't happen to be here just at the moment. Excuse me for living.

— Yeah, you like to stand around and watch the colorful native people busting their butts, but you're too cheap to buy anything.

— Hey, it's not my fault you're sunk in poverty. But maybe I'll bring my wife around later. Maybe she wants a purse.

— Okay, yeah, you do that. I'm not going anywhere.

— Nice loom you have. Works pretty well. You're weaving up a storm here.

— I get cramps. What a life. It's boring, making purses every day by myself. Not to mention lonely.

— Yeah, it must be lonely. But what can you do?

Yes, I had grown numb from caring about all the unfortunates who hadn't the foresight to get themselves born into a wealthy society. As I left her without making a purchase, she kept on talking in confidential tones, as if I were still standing next to her. I walked away slowly, with bowed head, listening to her voice gradually fade away.

Other women tended the brewing process, performing heavy lifting and constant labor. Still others cooked or vended or looked after the babies, often balancing all three tasks at once. The small children looked after themselves. One handsome young man with a rakish smile undertook the leisurely assignment of selling a special, milder brew, made from the dregs of the mash. And I spotted one elderly gentleman as he tottered out of his house and down the dirt path, his eyes completely bloodshot and his gaze carefully averted from mine.

The houses were partly of stone construction, painted and well maintained. No waste or garbage was visible. The largest and most colorful structure in the village was the Buddhist temple. But no monks resided there.

Just off the little town's central square, near the jungle border where visitors were perhaps not anticipated, Lee Ming and I discovered an unfamiliar plant material carefully set out in shallow boxes to dry in the sun. A very old woman kept watch over this vegetation, and she watched us approach with bright eyes. The plants were slender green shoots about eight inches long, tied up into little bundles. I bent down to smell them. The old woman picked up a bundle and held it in front of me. I leaned forward to sniff. Immediately she shoved the whole mess into my nose, then cackled uproariously at my surprise. Her open mouth revealed a single incisor standing lonely vigil. We cackled along with her. Travelers quickly learn to take the rough with the smooth. At this reaction she shoved the same mess into her own nose. Her cackle increased to a nearly deranged level, as if this event were the high point of the month for her, but her sharp eyes held no amusement and they remained fixed on mine. Still gamely sharing the merriment, we edged away from her and continued our inspection elsewhere. She had distracted us from examining the green bundles.

Later, down by the stills, we saw similar green bundles, but these were steaming, freshly cooked, and not easily identified. Women mashed them in enamel basins, using jagged baseball-sized rocks. These women did not look up as we approached. When I raised my camera, they turned their heads away, indicating displeasure.

The central feature of the brewery was thirty large trash barrels, rusty on the outside, divided into five groups of six. Each family of six sat neatly in twin rows of three under a simple thatch roof. Under each barrel a narrow trench was carved into the dried riverbank mud. These trenches, uniformly sized, had perfectly flat floors and precisely vertical walls. In most of them an efficient, slow-burning wood fire heated the barrel above, causing vapors to rise. Peripheral equipment included many large, cheap, identical pottery jugs with plastic wrap coverings, and large, transparent, plastic gasoline containers, all these with liquid inside. None of the women fell idle for even one second; none so much as paused to wipe the sweat from her brow. They worked with studied concentration. They were aware of us, inconspicuously but shrewdly. No one chatted or smiled. We watched a woman transfer liquid from a gasoline container to a pottery jug positioned below; she used a plastic hose and sucked on one end to get the flow started. Some of the jugs rested under heavy groundcloths, others sat in the sun, implying different stages of fermentation and aging. We watched as two women, using all their strength and coordination, lifted a heavy jug and poured the white liquid contents into a heated barrel. Another woman used a large, flat metal bowl, held with two hands like a big spoon with no handle, to skim off white mash from a boiling barrel and discard it onto the riverbank. We surmise that rice, the green plants, and river water were three of the ingredients. The finished product was sold in quart-sized, clunky, cheap glass bottles, each sealed with a bit of plastic wrap and a tiny rubber band.

We paused, trying to discern the Master Plan. More was happening than met the eye. The trash barrels all looked the same on the outside, but at least three different steps were executed in parallel on the inside. Among the peripheral equipment, one fermentation and two aging steps were apparent. Although the equipment was indeed primitive, the brewing process was quite sophisticated. The Heinekens may have consulted here.

A number of steps were *not* performed under the gaze of outsiders. As with cricket on Star TV, we could discover no connecting unity. The women deflected us subtly from approaching the barrels, like batsmen guarding their wickets. The Master Plan remained hidden.

Suddenly our concentration was interrupted. An older woman shoved a bottle of "Whiskey Lao" into my hands and demanded one thousand "kip"—about one dollar. I put on a mildly puzzled face. She produced a large enameled cup, white on the outside and stained a dirty brown on the inside. No matter, the alcohol would surely annihilate any germs present. Lowering this vessel into a nearby jug, she filled it with about one inch of clear, yellowish liquor. Our moment had come. I took a dainty sip. The choking reflex kicked in at once. Determination to swallow wrestled with asphyxiation. Just in time, just before the onset of wheezes and tears, the swallow came. Lee Ming, noticing my distress, took an even daintier sip. Lee Ming can be a keen observer of human behavior. My turn again, this time with better preparation in the mind. The stuff was fiery but surprisingly tasty. Lee Ming had a determined second go, but that was enough for her. Three-fourths of the liquid still remained. I threw back my head and drained it off at one long gulp. The Lao woman's face congealed into a watchful mask. The delicious, dangerous fire traveled down the esophagus and spread itself in the stomach. Interesting to feel the exact shape and position of these organs in the body. The first alterations to consciousness came in seconds. Within three minutes I was transmogrified from nimble biped to heavy machinery. Basic ambulation now required heightened awareness. Evidently, the one-dollar bottle contained enough Mekong madness to stupefy several adult elephants. Lee Ming and I, aggregating less than three hundred pounds, declined the purchase. Remnants of reason estimated Whiskey Lao to be roughly twice as potent as Chinese mao tai. And the alcoholic buzz had a warm, unusual edge. The ensuing afternoon was most pleasant—a friendly smile of an afternoon concealing sharp teeth.

Since we were not buying their kickapoo joy juice, I took Lee Ming back to the woman of the loom. Lee Ming was only moderately plastered. She carried out a coherent negotiation and bought a handbag. The seller's grousing turned to gratitude: She threw me the most brilliant smile I have ever seen. What a mercurial young woman, I thought.

By now my body felt like a Caterpillar backhoe operated by a novice. Which way to the river and the sampan was hopelessly obscure. This predicament amused me. A kind of optimistic, animal cunning took shape in the fog. By dint of intense concentration, I stayed close behind Lee Ming. I copied her movements. Where she put her feet, I put mine. Unwittingly, she led me all the way back to the sampan. We arrived just behind Denise. I crossed the makeshift gangplank without falling into the river. Denise and Lee Ming began to giggle.

Yes, the afternoon was pleasant enough in its strange way. The world shrugged off the bondage of time passing and took on a vivid intensity, as if some unseen hand had turned up the Bright knob and punched the Slow Motion button. The three explorers luxuriated in a leafy pavilion floating above the river, eating lunch and discussing the luminous inner life of cricket. Baseball can focus on one white-knuckled, all-important swing of the bat; cricket smoothes away the chance and fluke of the single moment, to test the more interesting idiosyncrasies of the man. We clambered around some candlelit caves—magical to me and mundane to Lee Ming—containing images of the Buddha. I learned to operate the heavy machinery with tolerable grace. And finally we began the return journey.

The alcoholic buzz dwindled to insignificance after ninety minutes. For five hours by the clock, the psychotropic buzz persisted at the full. Our boat seemed suspended on the river. The green hills gently pulsed and throbbed. Dazzling diamonds danced in bright swarms on the water. Heaven itself, vivid blue and billowing white, radiated soft enervation and tranquillity. Scattered thoughts drifted with the current. At the quay, we paid the boatman and he threw me the second most brilliant smile I have ever seen.

Denise smiled also, but more discreetly. She looked sideways, out of the corners of her eyes, first at Lee Ming and then at me. After a moment of mutual silence, she took her leave.

That evening, back in our snug hotel room, my little pink American toes tucked safely into the coverlet, I dozed and dreamed, dreamed and dozed. . . .

Suffocating night was descended on the Lao village. No moon shone, no stars twinkled, but the flames under the boiling barrels leaped like the very fires of Hell. The women toiled doggedly, adding the secret steps no outsider might witness. Urging them on, an aged crone capered maniacally in the firelight, casting fantastic shadows across the vast muddy flats, her eyes and razor-sharp incisor gleaming redly, her exultant cackle filling up the night, one bony fist held defiantly aloft, and brandished therein her mesmerizing Satanic bundle of green. From a hut close by, an elderly man, clutching a cheap glass bottle, peeped out from a window. In the flickering succession of shadow and dancing light, his features reflected wonder, horror, groveling worship, and bleary-eyed bafflement. No one took notice. If only none would notice me! But amid the hot flames and ceaseless toil, a face began to turn. Slowly, a reddened glowing face turned full to mine. It was the woman of the loom! By her brilliant Siren smile transfixed, that tenacious part of me trembled and yielded. Fear and desire became one. Beautiful destruction, sweet oblivion, finally and at last, I longed to go to her. But we had come away with no bottle. All we had was the handbag.

The Siren

C ame the sober morning, as usual. The cravings lingered. I could still go back to the Lao village and their whiskey. But some part of my tenacity failed to function. A painful knowledge, a fearful apprehension long pushed aside, came forward.

For many years I had played the restless nomad. How far do our lives focus on the single place or the single day? What use to visit the same village a second time? Could the familiar give us refuge? We have refuge and we have no refuge.

We know what will happen this day and we do not know. We have control and we are helpless. We are vital and we decay. We can change the world and we cannot change it.

All of the universe, every corner of it, conspires to keep us tantalized but unsatisfied. The world cunningly appears as order and as chaos. Deliberate mystery takes the disguise of accident. We know how to proceed and we do not know. We can predict and we cannot predict. No virtue and no vice is the key that faithfully unlocks the universe. Every approach has successes and every approach is flawed. All of us have answers and none of us have answers.

Our own desires mutually contradict. We want certitude, achievement, challenge, surprise, risk, and peace. We want peace without too much monotony, triumph not quite spoiled by fear, joy not yet overshadowed by despair, light with just enough darkness, high mountains and shallow valleys.

Satisfaction eludes us, and therefore we strive for satisfaction. Animated solely by our predicament, we seek to escape it. Driven finally to love life by the death that waits, we crave immortality: some form of immortality, something left behind, someone to remember us, some gesture of defiance, some measure of relief from the final penalty.

All of us are different and all of us are the same. Satisfaction eludes us, and therefore we struggle and create wonders for a time. We make looms from sticks and sophisticated breweries from trash barrels. Wondrously do we struggle. Fleetingly we are saved. Always and at last we are lost.

That which makes us ourselves defeats us. We ourselves join the conspiracy against us. We cannot do otherwise. Heaven and hell, embracing, indissoluble, transfixing, indomitable, brief, deadly, the timeless ritual inalterable, are one and the same perfection, the same Siren smile.

Hating Perfection

Those two days in Laos were good news and bad news. Now ten years later their impact has worn off a bit. I won't conceal the bad news behind euphoria, as the whiskey did. Here it is.

Good reader, the best possible world might have features that you and I hate. It might even resemble our own world: painful, unjust, ruthless, and fatal. To see why, I ask you to consider your life and mine from an unconventional perspective.

The "trial analysis" below has 565 words. Without stopping to justify every particular, it quickly sketches in a big picture.

At first, you may find the picture mocking and repugnant. Nevertheless, I ask you to perform this exercise: Can you identify a sentence below that you *know* to be false?

If all the sentences might be true, then our hateful world might be perfection.

TRIAL ANALYSIS

Living forever just can't work out. Any story can go on too long. The best possible world must therefore solve a key problem: how best to terminate the inhabitants.

Our own world—the universe around us—has its own answer. Gentle reader, you and I will be dead, and in time all we do brought to nothing. And yet, we have excellent reason to go forward with our lives.

To keep us interested, our world is a paradox. To keep us interested, the world gives and it takes away. Each day we know

24

what will happen and we do not know. That mixture draws us in. We know how to proceed and we do not know. We can change the world and we cannot change it. We understand the world and it shows us something new. Our most piercing satisfactions we fail to anticipate, desire, or even imagine in advance. The world transcends our plodding ambition. It moves us. It fascinates. It lies before us lethal and seductive. Though our final end is visible, we still want to go forward. Such is the world's hold on us. We the addicted are terminated well.

Nor can our addiction be more pleasant. The reason lies not in the world, but in our perception of it. Whether or not you want it to, your mind automatically organizes the world into balances. You and I don't understand good luck except by comparison to bad luck. We don't understand certainty unless confusion has meaning also. We cannot perceive triumph except as the converse of defeat.

Perception so organized implies this general balance: Optimism and pessimism felt throughout the world and throughout its history, have equal size. If the world is wonderful, it must also be horrible.

And this general balance: Modern people experience the same ratio of satisfaction to dissatisfaction, as people living in ancient Rome or Han Dynasty China or the Pleistocene. In every era, fifty percent of human experience falls below average.

But *how* our experience falls above or below average—that's where our world excels. Its ways are legion. This world in its subtle variety, cultivates our dependence on comparisons. This cunning world addicts us. It alternates good fortune and bad, advantage and disadvantage, the expected and the unexpected, justice and injustice, virtue and vice, beauty and ugliness, clarity and confusion, health and sickness, youth and old age, triumph and defeat, delight and despair—the multifarious mirrored facets in our minds, of good and evil subtly elusive to our control. The world disturbs, entices, and sounds us. We want to act. We want to find out what happens next. We want to move forward with our lives. Skillful and versatile, the world plays on our facility to compare.

In any era, fifty percent of human experience must fall below average. But *how* our experience falls above or below average—that's where our world excels.

Living forever just can't work out. For us who are terminated well, the death that waits has mirrored effects. We feel both sorrow and exaltation. Each gives size to the other. The sorrow being quite large, we turn our faces away; we believe we are mortal and we don't believe it. But the measure of our doom, the balance to our misery, sometimes rises to the ineffable and the sublime. Though our final end is visible, this world gives us excellent reason to go forward.

Such is the trial analysis. If it's not clearly wrong, then we have an open question. Our world *might* be flawless.

Beer at Joe's

This book claims that our frequently vile world has no flaws; that any alternative world would be worse. Not entirely good news, if true.

By the end of this book, we will be radically disciplined and rigorous about those claims. Right now we're still informal. Quite informal. We're loafing about, getting the lay of the land, spotting hazards, spying out the true direction to perfection. Which way it is, might be unexpected.

Let's repair to Joe's Bar and Grill. We don't want to overwork ourselves on the first day.

God and Satan happen to run into each other at Joe's. They fall into conversation. One topic leads to another. God confides that He has been thinking about creating a world with people.

"You want to create people?" says Satan. He looks interested. "Of course I can't conjure up a world like You can, but sometimes I get ideas."

God pauses. He frowns. He looks Satan in the eye. Then He says, "I wonder how our ideas would compare."

The two worthies agree that each of them will work up a detailed proposal for a world with people, and meet again the following evening at Joe's Bar to compare notes.

The next evening, when God shows up at Joe's, He finds Satan already waiting. They greet each other and make polite small talk. They walk together to the corner of the bar and climb up onto adjacent barstools. Joe, without being asked, brings them two lite beers, then retires discreetly to his conversation at the far end of the bar. The other patrons leave the distinguished visitors in peace to discuss their important business. God and Satan rest their elbows comfortably on the bar. Their small talk dies away. Satan takes a sip of his beer, pulls over a dish of salted peanuts, and pops one into his mouth. He waits for God to speak first.

"The goal of My world," God begins, "is bliss and profound satisfaction."

Satan allows his eyelids to droop restfully. "How inspiring."

"Yes. It is. Satisfaction and bliss. I want a lot of the satisfaction to be subtle, because that's the best kind." God sips His own beer. Satan's eyelids have returned to the moderately alert position. "To make My world subtle," God continues, "I'm going to need a periodic table of elements and DNA chemistry."

Satan munches another peanut. "Curious." he says. "I also came up with atomic elements and DNA chemistry. I want my little creatures to have the worst agonies imaginable. I'm talking *subtle* agony. I'm talking pitiless evolution, no rules except survival, a thousand cunning ways to shove the other guy aside." Satan chugs a healthy slug of beer and smiles to himself.

God's eye has acquired an odd look. "It seems we both want a subtle world, but for different reasons." He sips again. "I have a biological evolution also. In My world, tiny seeds grow into beautiful trees."

"And in mine!" says Satan brightly. "But not always. Not even most of the time." Satan is warming to the subject. He takes another big swallow. "Beautiful dreams are made to be shattered!"

"Yes, you have a point there." God takes a ponderous breath, then slowly intones, "The most wonderful dreams must be fragile. How else can they be valuable?"

Satan chuckles. "I let my little buggers succeed now and then, temporarily of course, just to keep them interested. How can I shatter their dreams if they don't have any?" A third peanut disappears into his mouth.

Satan has begun to try God's patience. On the specific details of a created world, they have disagreed on nothing, but that fact doesn't seem to bother Satan. Can the Prince of Darkness really be this dense? God decides to be more direct. "In My world . . ." He pauses for a time, to capture Satan's full attention, then spits out His words with the precision of a machine gun: "On September 25, 1997, at 6:03 in the morning, Elaine Fenster Throckmorton puts on blue socks."

The smooth upward motion of Satan's hand, holding yet another peanut destined for oblivion, halts abruptly. The hand freezes in the halfway position. Satan stares at God. "Elaine Fenster . . . !" For several heartbeats he cannot speak. Then he manages to say, "Does she have 16,241 hairs on her head?"

"If you count the shortest hair. It's only fourteen angstroms long."

"Her shortest hair is fourteen angstroms?!" Satan is still staring. Waiting calmly for Satan to digest the implications, God holds his gaze. At last Satan looks away. "Well, I'll be damned!"

God rolls His eyes heavenward. Satan chews on the forgotten peanut. At length, a grin comes to Satan's face. God finds His annoyance fading. He shakes His head and permits Himself an answering grin.

"Let's do it!" says Satan.

"You're on!" says God.

They shake hands, and in that instant, both of them disappear completely.

Joe's paying customers have mostly accepted these events with stolid indifference. They never quite understood either God or Satan anyway. However, the familiar figures actually vanishing causes sharp intake of breath. For a moment no one knows what to do or say. Then Joe recovers. He shouts out with a hearty voice, "That gets rid of them! My special whiskey on the house!" And a great cheer rises from the bar patrons.

But presently the faces turn pensive. As Joe clears away the beer mugs and tidies up the bar where the two visitors lately seemed so real, a silent room looks on.

The hour being well advanced, Joe has long since closed his bar. The room stands empty and still. The nighttime lighting shines only on the spot where God and Satan were talking. Suddenly they reappear, sitting on their barstools. Satan has a question.

"What about virtue and vice?" he says. "Maybe I can corrupt some people, while You try to turn them onto virtuous pathways, don't You know."

"Well, so what?" answers God. "I want virtue to withstand temptation, and you want vice to resist enlightenment. We still agree on the composition of the world."

"Hmm." says Satan. He eyes the dish of peanuts. "But which of us will be more effective? Do I corrupt more souls or do You enlighten more?"

"Neither. Virtue and vice get graded on the curve. They measure each other, just like delight and despair."

"What?!" says Satan. He sputters a bit and his face turns red. "Tell me it ain't so!"

"Look," says God, "other bartenders don't serve peanuts, but Joe has the virtue to offer them free with our beer. Joe has that virtue by comparison. He does something other people don't do. If all the bartenders gave us peanuts, we wouldn't be so impressed with Joe."

"But I can well imagine a world where all the people are vicious! I have my standards, and I know viciousness when I see it!"

"That's only half a world you're imagining. First you imagined a world with virtue and vice mixed up together. Then you subtracted out the virtue. If you were thinking only of the vicious world and no other, some of the people in it would seem virtuous!"

Satan winces. Then he has a happy thought. "So the world must have vicious people if it has virtuous people?"

"Um, yes, that's one way to look at it. People will always be vicious or virtuous by comparison. Comparison with someone, somewhere, sometime. The comparisons can be complicated, but comparisons they still be." God pauses. He looks into the middle distance. His tone turns confidential. "I have to admit, a subtle world with vicious people holds a certain fascination for Me. That's where virtue gets really interesting."

"Isn't that a kick in the head!" says Satan. "That's the same world where viciousness gets interesting." But now a shadow crosses Satan's face. He sighs. "I just can't find any ground to compete with You or mess up Your world."

"No." God's face becomes a mask. "We don't have to fight. Both of us want a subtle mixture of virtue and vice in the world. Just like we want a subtle mixture of delight and despair. We agree on every detail, because both of us want the most subtle world possible."

Satan's grin has returned. He has a dreamy, faraway look. "The most subtle world possible. . . ." After a moment, he comes to the surface. He almost wants to slap God on the back. "You're not such a bad fellow! We do agree on every detail!" With slow and studied deliberation, Satan picks up the dish of peanuts. "But I feel like the winner. The winner of Your game. Subtlety must be transitory. Everything we give to them, we take away."

The two worthies sit side by side in the room's single pool of light. God makes no response. His mask remains, but He glances at Satan from the corners of His eyes. Satan has the peanuts and a smile as he and God disappear together again.

The Black Death

Does the best possible world have bubonic plague?

For untreated cases of plague, the mortality rate runs to about ninety percent. Some victims die quickly, others linger. The initial infection of the blood may cause death in just three or four days. But most victims survive that attack. For them, the bacteria gradually spread, bringing very high fever, chills, prostration, delirium, and enlarged painful lymph nodes, called "buboes." Should the victim live on, the lymph nodes burst and discharge pus. Blood may ooze out all over the body and turn black. Hence the name "Black Death."

Parallel to that progression of symptoms, the plague organism might at any time invade the lungs. Pneumonic plague proves rapidly fatal. It produces airborne droplet sprays that spread to other people, rather like the common cold.

Pasteurella pestis, as some people like to call it, smolders for centuries among rats. When the bacterium flares up in rat-infested sewers, fleas can transmit it to humans, who have suffered periodic outbreaks.

The worst epidemic rose up from Constantinople's rats in 1334. It spread unchecked. During the next twenty years, perhaps three-fourths of all the people in Europe and Asia died from the plague. That period of human history was so dark, that afterward we rarely talked about it.

Pasteurella pestis cut down the wicked and the righteous alike. The victims included children far too young to understand any rational reason why they suffered. Yet they died in torment.

Modern science and modern garbage collection services have learned to prevent many infectious scourges, including the plague. In consequence, human populations have exploded. Today we overuse our resources, our pollution accumulates, biological weapons threaten a planet lousy with people, and many of us hold life cheap. We have no assurance of a glorious future.

Gentle reader, you may have a number of complaints against the world. You may have serious doubts that our universe can only be the very best of all possible worlds. You may believe that nothing I can say will convince you.

Part Two

FAIR WARNING

The Exaltation of Growing Weeds

Does a perfect world inflict pain on the innocent? Does it raise up wicked people? Does it take away life held precious? Does it crush the inhabitants at random?

Here's what I'm going to tell you, summed up in two paragraphs.

Perfection has its own unkind agenda, as if it were an alien presence in the world. What the inhabitants strive to have, the best possible world keeps elusive. Satisfaction, justice, triumph flicker subtly in and out of our reach. That's why we care about them. We get neither absolute satisfaction nor total justice nor unlimited life nor final triumph. We don't always reach our aspirations. If we did, we could not value them.

The best world diverts our strivings to its own ends. It moves beyond our banal wishes and our incoherent ideals. The best world surprises us. It sounds us. Sometimes it gives us superior moments we cannot desire, strive to have, or even imagine in advance. We have banal wishes, but subtle lives.

Good reader, if you are anything like me, you will have a thousand doubts and objections. You will not like the world's tactics, if that's what they are, nor my defense of them. I don't like those tactics either.

I will offer you some logic, some evidence, and some "psychological stories." I plan to change your perspective. Your sufferings will still be your sufferings, but maybe possibly the world will be a little bit more than it was.

You deserve first to know who I am.

One of my ancestors was hanged for stealing horses. Another died by Tommy gun in Detroit. Still another fell off a tall building without explanation. But I was born anyway.

Most of my lineage escaped death at the hands of their angry fellow beings. Consider the tenacity of an earlier ancestor. He made his first crossing to America in 1609, aboard the *Sea Venture*. That expedition met with shipwreck off the coast of Virginia, and starvation ashore; the survivors accepted rescue and went home. However, my ancestor had learned much. His prospects in England remaining ordinary, he tried again for a new life. In 1620 he attached himself to a group of cultists unhappy with Europe. They believed in never making love except when fully clothed. But they did have enough money to buy an ocean-going vessel. My ancestor returned to America with his new friends on the *Mayflower*. This time he knew to seek help. And the previous inhabitants did not foresee the consequences of helping him. They attended their first Thanksgiving all unaware of what they had done. Too late they wanted my people dead.

Sometimes we have wanted each other dead.

My wife also made a desperate journey to the New World. Lee Ming was born in Beijing, to a family politically incorrect. Before the communist revolution in China, her grandfather grew rich trading with foreign devils. He kept a sizable stable of wives and concubines, all of them gorgeous in family photographs. The revolutionaries, after prevailing on the mainland, quickly put him to death behind prison walls, along with Lee Ming's older paternal uncles. Her father spent four months in a re-education camp. There he aroused suspicion by failing to confess. Before she was born, Lee Ming's family was tainted.

Lee Ming did not go to prison, but shortly after she turned eighteen, the revolutionaries put her to hard labor for three years. In a cast iron factory with a dirt floor, little equipment, and no furniture, she struggled to make the casings for large electrical generators.

Fortunately, Chairman Mao was soon to die. And Madame Mao had poor political instincts. One of her fighting slogans: "We would rather grow socialist weeds than capitalist wheat!" Many Chinese preferred not to lose themselves in the exaltation of growing weeds. Two years after her husband's death, Madame Mao and all her allies fell from power. A general amnesty ensued. The factory released Lee Ming. She came to America on a student visa, to a little attic room, with fifty dollars in her plastic purse. Five years later she had a degree in chemistry from the University of California at Berkeley.

Lee Ming considers me incompetent to manage my life. She married me eighteen years ago. We have no children, but we have traveled. Sometimes we live in the United States, and sometimes in China.

Lee Ming's mother and father feel patriotism toward their country, and devotion to its communist ideology. They view human beings as noble deep down. Unfortunately, confused thinking does sometimes obscure our inherent nobility. Capitalist thinking, for example, obscures my own nobility. When I told Lee Ming's mother, "People ought to have their own opinions," she said, "You have a tendency toward selfish individualism." She was trying to help me.

Just at the crack of dawn one day in Beijing, my mother-in-law visited Lee Ming and me at our apartment. She found us with documents spread out all over the floor. Immediately she feared the worst and began asking questions, using Lee Ming as translator.

— You are under investigation?

— Um, you could say that, yes. The US authorities want to adjust our tax payment.

— Why don't you pay them what you owe?

— Well, what we owe is under dispute. I don't think we owe anything.

— Then why does your government investigate you?

— They do that sometimes. I suppose they want to collect as much money as they can.

— No, they don't. People are basically good. They give you
problems only when you bring them on yourself. You must
look first to your own faults, before you criticize others. If you
don't want to pay what you owe, then I will pay it for you.

My mother-in-law was a conscientious communist. She
wanted my true and finer self to emerge. If everyone summoned
the resolve to see the world as golden, it would be golden.

Alas, I could not have her faith. Her daughter also felt skeptical.

When Lee Ming and I spent our first lengthy period in Beijing,
much of the city wanted us to leave. We had to put on psychic armor
just to go outside. We encountered anger against foreigners and
anger against a mixed marriage. Lee Ming understood the cutting
remarks in Mandarin all around us. Her Western husband had
stolen a Chinese woman. Lee Ming had sold out to the capitalist barbarians, and legitimized them. She heard herself called "slut" and
"whore." I heard "white ghost," the Chinese N-word. Strangers
routinely deflated the tires, after we parked our bicycles. Strangers
shouted their rage at us in the streets. Lee Ming's own parents tried
to sting our sense of shame. "Why do you stay in China? What can
we say to our friends, when they ask about our daughter? They will
think she failed in America. Why else would she come back?"

And yet, both of us felt strangely attracted to Beijing. For eight
months we persevered under pressure. One day during the second
month, in a crowded hotel lobby, as the hotel staff and divers
bystanders plied us with their smirking insults, Lee Ming and I
went berserk together. For fifteen minutes we shouted at the tops
of our voices, at no one in particular, before hundreds of blank
staring faces. Our passion finally spent, we walked to the bus stop
and rode home like zombies. But later that night, we could not stop
laughing. No one had known what to do with us!

Beijing's hostility was impersonal. We made up our minds to
prevail. Gradually we learned to handle each and every weapon
arrayed against us. We became deceptive and skillful.

Sometimes, to get cooperation, Lee Ming played the part of my
state-sponsored guide, hired by the gullible American tourist, at a fat
price accruing to the Chinese. Her compatriots hastened to assist her.

Sometimes Lee Ming was a stranger. On occasion I found myself surrounded by a hostile crowd, unwilling to let me pass without a substantial tariff. Lee Ming would walk up to me and ask in English, "May I help you, sir?" and then pretend to take upon herself the process desired by all: parting me from my money. Her compatriots hastened to assist her.

Sometimes Lee Ming and I disagreed publicly. When directions or helpful information was refused us, sometimes the guide could not smooth down her disgusted client. Feeling solidarity with the beleaguered guide, Lee Ming's compatriots hastened to share with her their particular satisfactions. "Don't tell the foreigner!" they said with glee, and told her everything.

I learned to deflect angry greed with Chinese humor and halting Mandarin: "I don't carry money. I'm a good husband. My wife says a good husband doesn't carry money."

Lee Ming became expert at bestowing the discreet carton of cigarettes, the fat little envelope. We could go almost anywhere.

And the open warfare with her parents ended after we said, "Let's agree to disagree." Sensing our resolve to ruin ourselves, they backed away and bided their time.

The turning point came on a bright winter afternoon. We lived in a concrete-slab building, along with eight hundred other families. They were the wheat, we were the weeds. Snow had piled up on the access sidewalks. Soon it would melt underfoot and freeze again as ice. Every year, we were later told, a number of residents slip on the ice and injure themselves. The building has limited maintenance. That afternoon, in the best Maoist tradition, without being asked, I spent three hours shoveling all the sidewalks. Some of the neighbors came to watch, with narrowed eyes. Two days later, they started saying hello.

At that time, Beijing had giant construction cranes everywhere. The city we knew was vanishing. During our eight months, new buildings sprouted up on all sides of us. Heavy trucks replaced the donkey carts. Limousines crowded the bicycles. Modern skyscrapers appeared where ancient little shops had been. Open-air vendors gave way to Western-style shopping malls. The dirt road in front of our building abruptly changed into an eight-lane

freeway. We seemed to live inside a filmed image set on Fast Forward. And the physical changes brought psychological change.
Hostility to the foreigner lessened. Western popular music could be
heard in restaurants and stores. The occasional waiter or clerk
smiled and asked us to come back. During our last two weeks in
1994, as we bicycled and taxied around the metropolis, we were
astonished at our own feelings: actual tears on our faces, intense
regret and sorrow, that something was ending forever, that we
could never again struggle almost unbearably in that exotic city.
And indeed, we have several times returned to my parents-in-law
now sweetly accepting our strange ways, to a city far more tolerant
and comfortable but in our view much diminished, to a Beijing
proud and excited to be Beijing no longer.

Must we regret the passing of implacable obstacles? Shall we
rejoice that life harasses us? Does a mule have the best approach to
his problems?

Good reader, even if I had an opinion, you would be unwise
to follow it. Some of my ancestors, and some of Lee Ming's, have
been justly executed for thievery and murder.

Even worse: my ambitions have always been simplistic, and
my wishes banal.

This book won't give direct answers to your practical questions. But it might shed light on them. I will ask you to view
human struggle from a particular perspective.

Gentle reader, you and I have unwelcome problems. What we
want and what we get are different. The reason why they are different, has a certain splendor. I don't advise you to cope with the
world as I have. That's not my purpose. I do ask you to stand next
to me for a time, and look in the direction I am looking.

Lee Ming and I believed we had no comfortable niche in the
world. We were restless yet everywhere abraded. To begin, I want
you to know who we are; why we felt out of place; why we started
poking our noses into isolated backwaters of China and vicinity;
why we hated the collective aspiration, and searched for our own
unique destruction.

Heaven and Hell Together

Many trial readers of *Hating Perfection* had these first reactions: ridicule, then anger and shock. No one wanted to believe that human beings have already gone to their highest heaven. But those reactions gave way to something better, and different for each reader.

Planet Earth has large amounts of suffering, injustice, and deliberate cruelty. Nevertheless, I make these claims: Our universe is the best possible world. Everything in it happens for the best. Not the smallest detail anywhere can be improved. And that perfection explains why we exist. Understanding it allows us to view our universe and our lives from a new perspective.

For human beings, the best heaven and the worst hell are the same place. Our own essential nature makes them the same place. We cannot have one without the other. Our most exalted experience must be founded on anguish, and on the shrouded awareness that we will perish.

This book investigates two principal issues:

1. What ought to exist? Among all the logically possible states of existence, which one ought to be the actual state?

2. What evidence do you and I have, that what ought to exist does exist?

My answers will go like this:

What ought to exist is the most subtle world possible, alone and solitary.

A substantial body of evidence indicates that the actual state of existence is in fact just that: the most subtle world possible. Substantial evidence does indicate that actual experience in the actual world, from the beginning to the end of our universe, has higher, more valuable subtlety as a collection, than any possible alternative collection of experience in a world. On that evidence, ours is the most subtle world.

To make said evidence more vivid and personal, I will be talking a lot about the unique human style of subtle experience.

Living as we humans must in heaven and hell together, opens a door to high subtlety. Our intricate and incessant comparisons open the door. This world takes advantage. This ingenious world plays on our comparisons. An undeniable pattern of evidence reveals an entire cosmos working hard to give its inhabitants subtle experience. On that evidence, the actual world is the most subtle world possible, the world that ought to exist.

Those are my claims. I don't expect you to believe me right away.

Short stories appear often in *Hating Perfection*. They illustrate the argument. The stories have their settings in Southeast Asia, where I lived for six years.

Good reader, you already have a strong idea of the world's evils. I will not minimize them or pretend they don't happen. They do happen. But none of them are gratuitous.

Some of the evils are more than human sanity can bear. *Next* section begins the argument for best possible world. This section gives fair warning.

Rain in Wuhan

Chinese culture has a polite ritual, where an offer must be made three times before it may be accepted. For example, if I happen to be sitting on a park bench next to a stranger, and wish to share my bag of peanuts with him, I will urge him three times to take some peanuts. Even if he is hungry, he will decline twice.

In 1991 Lee Ming and I spent several days in the city of Wuhan, on the Yangtze River. One morning we crossed Wuhan's East Lake on our way to a scenic area beyond. The East Lake being comfortably spacious, our crossing took forty-five minutes at its narrowest point. For twelve yuan, a goodly sum in China, we hired a large wooden gondola propelled by an old woman. She was at least sixty but quite vigorous. Her occupation gives her good exercise, and she may live to be a hundred. She stood high in the stern facing forward, one foot braced behind the other, and pushed two long oars, each running through an iron ring attached to the gondola's side. She rowed strongly in a continuous rhythmic motion, leaning forward and thrusting the oar handles before her, then dipping the handles and drawing them back again. Because the oars were long and their handles overlapped, her hands crossed one over the other during the forward thrust, uncrossed toward the end of the thrust, then crossed and uncrossed again at a lower level on the way back. The complete motion was complicated and skillful. She shoved us along at a good clip, her breathing elevated only slightly. She enclosed herself in her own thoughts, paying little heed to us; as if she would see many more like us. After forty-five minutes of healthy exercise, she brought us to the far side, where we intended to spend the day. We stepped ashore. Immediately she turned her boat around and rowed away. We were left alone in an isolated area.

Clouds had gathered during our crossing. The old woman had just passed out of earshot when the temperature seemed to drop, the wind stiffened, and a light rain began. Both of us were dressed for hot weather. Lee Ming was the most vulnerable. She was wearing only thin cotton shorts and a flimsy short-sleeved blouse. Within a minute she was soaked to the skin and exposed to serious illness. No shelter and no other people were visible. We ran up the wide sloping bank of the lake and discovered a highway just a hundred yards away. It had some traffic. I stuck out my thumb. Two passenger cars drove on by. Then nothing for ninety long seconds. But the third vehicle stopped, a heavy truck painted blue all over and fully loaded under a brown tarpaulin. The driver reached across the cab and opened the passenger door. We scrambled in. Lee Ming sat in the middle, shivering. The driver turned the heat way up for us. He was a personable man, about thirty-five, not especially handsome. We learned that he worked hard for a small salary. He drove us right to the door of our hotel in the city, twenty minutes out of his way. Lee Ming stopped shivering after the first five minutes. The driver had saved her health. She thanked him and trotted off toward the warm clothing in our hotel room. I remained to settle up with him.

The driver climbed down from his truck to cool off. He walked around to the passenger side, where I had exited to make way for Lee Ming. When he came close to me, I felt good. We stood together companionably, our shoulders forming a right angle. I fished in my pocket and quickly produced a one-hundred yuan note. His face broke into a happy smile. I held the note out to him. In my broken Mandarin, I asked him to take it. He pushed my hand away, but remained standing beside me on the passenger side. I made a more elaborate little speech and offered the note again. He pushed my hand away a second time, but stayed next to me. I made the third offer and expressed my sincere desire that he take the money. The ritual had reached its culmination. He looked into my eyes, his expression friendly but odd. The rain dripped from our faces. Then, for a moment, I saw him as impervious to all human supplication. Gone was his counterfeit interest in my one hundred yuan. Gone was my illusion of safety. He vanished into his truck and drove away.

Red and White

The human iris comes in many different colors, but never red. In Western horror films, the demon sometimes stares with inhuman red eyes, the better to thrill our fear of dying.

Chinese people almost universally have a black iris, matching their black hair. In certain parts of China, the inhabitants have never seen a human eye of any other color. They have never seen a foreigner. Indeed, some citizens remain unaware that the world is round, the sun considerably larger than the Earth, or that any other country exists except China. But they have another awareness that we lack. They live side by side with disembodied spirits and apparitions. A malignant ghost might look like me. I have brown hair, pink skin, yellow eyebrows, giant bulk, a typically generous Caucasian nose—and demonic green eyes flecked with eerie brown and yellow.

In the civilized West, children generally fear ghosts more than adults fear them. In China's remote enclaves, the reverse can be true. The children of reclusive societies are sometimes emancipated. They escape both schooling and grinding labor. Where their parents seldom stop working, these children have the freedom to play most every day. Their parents have anxieties and enemies; they have friendly curiosity. Their parents fend off the unknown; they enjoy a degree of privilege among strangers and apparitions.

In China, the dominant civilization proudly call themselves "Han," after their earliest enduring dynasty in recorded times. But scattered among the Han people are some fifty minority ethnic groups, each with its own distinctive flavor. One of these is the Li people, living near the southern fringe of Hainan Island—the large island south of the Chinese mainland.

Relations between the Li and Han peoples have long been guarded. The Li people keep firearms handy, and Han people rarely venture into their area.

The two societies have a common feature. Shrouded awareness of death permeates life. But sometimes the particulars are very different.

Early in 1994, Lee Ming and I escaped the Beijing winter. Lee Ming has a black iris. She has seen enough Beijing winter. We spent four months at an isolated, primitive hotel near the southern tip of Hainan—the warmest spot in China. During the first few days, we poisoned the mice in our room, disposed of their corpses, cleaned everywhere, made paper maché repairs to the broken windows, added new pencil drawings to the white and pastel green walls, and then looked around for new worlds to conquer.

About one mile from us, a river marked the boundary between Li and Han. We crossed the river over long, narrow logs, worn shiny by long use, and loosely supported on wooden stilts: Crossties were lashed to the stilts by some fibrous plant material; on the crossties rested the poles, cradled between the stilts. This footbridge was six feet above the river, about thirty feet long and one foot wide—that is, three to four poles wide. No nails secured anything. The slippery poles tended to rotate under our feet. At first, Lee Ming and I had to crawl across on our hands and knees. But eventually we learned to saunter over the bridge just like the nonchalant Li children.

The hotel staff warned us against intruding into the Li area. The Li people were primitive, intolerant, and violent, they said. Of course we could not resist that description. Being a foreigner, and therefore having no part in any animosity between the Han and the Li, I went first, and crawled across the bridge, armed only with a canteen of water.

The Li domain might have been the Jungle of Oz. The sunny hills and low mountains abounded with wildflowers, butterflies, odd shrubs and trees, and colorful snakes. I found a long stick and beat the tall grass ahead of me, giving the snakes fair warning not to mess with me. To my relief, they acted responsibly. Most of them slithered away. The more belligerent snakes, by hissing, gave me ample opportunity to go around them. We adopted a sensible policy of live and let live.

The Li people had no plumbing or electricity. They resided in the valleys, mostly away from the snakes. Here the well trodden footpaths were shared alike by humans and animals: pigs, chickens, geese, and small Brahman cattle. Each species showed elaborate courtesy. No one littered anywhere or pooped in the pathways. Whenever I met a cow coming the other way, we each made room for the other to pass.

The water buffalo had close personal relations with the humans. They may have believed they *were* human. Man and beast labored together all day in the rice paddies. The buffalo knew exactly how far to pull the plow, before turning to the next furrow. During the cool mornings and evenings, each buffalo had a human guardian, who pulled up plants from the river bottom to feed him, or led him to a succulent swampy place and watched over him, while he stuffed himself and grunted with pleasure.

However, on my first day in the Li area, all of the tidy mud-and-thatch huts seemed unoccupied. Only the animals were visible. I paused eight feet away from a water buffalo, off duty at the time, standing in his rice paddy. He was big and his horns were big. He stretched out his muzzle toward me. I could almost read his mind: "Here's something you don't see every day." We stood motionless, watching each other. For thirty seconds the tension mounted. I'm a city boy, and my nerves were no match for a buffalo's. My sudden retreat startled him. He retreated also. But we had moved apart only two steps when, simultaneously, he and I understood the situation. We looked back at each other sheepishly. I relaxed. He nuzzled the ground—a non-threatening posture.

I resolved somehow to appear less dangerous. But where were the people?

After wandering for an hour among the hills and empty huts, I heard uncanny music in the distance. Never have I heard anything like that music. I went toward it, and discovered some two hundred people gathered together. They were eating and drinking. The alien symphony came from a four-person band: two tootle horns with finger holes, one drum, and one pair of gongs. The players sat on stools shaded by a small canopy. They faced each other in a circle. Next to them stood a sumptuous artificial bower, twenty feet high and fifteen wide at the base, covered with red and white paper decorations that resembled delicate flowers, the whole exquisitely proportioned, and wondrously vivid in the sunlight.

I stopped fifty yards away, just on the far side of a little rivulet. Its steep banks formed a natural barrier. Nevertheless, none of the people looked at me. I could feel their suspicion that I was an apparition, and not especially auspicious. Remembering the standoff with the water buffalo, I sat down on the ground—a non-threatening posture. Still no one looked in my direction. Five minutes passed. Then came the response. A tactical unit of forty children had massed under cover on their left flank. I did not see them until they were already charging to the center. They came forward at the dead run, in disciplined formation, uttering no sound. Each child scooted into position on the opposite bank. Shoulder to shoulder they squatted on their haunches, arms resting on knees. Rather suddenly I had forty pairs of wide eyes in silent deployment staring across at me.

I could not help smiling. These youngsters had curiosity and confidence. They smiled back. I remained seated. After three more minutes and much mutual grinning, a middle-aged gentleman joined the children. With a friendly gesture, he invited me to cross the little stream.

Both of us spoke a little Mandarin, but neither could understand the other's accent. I walked beside him toward the festivities. With gestures he offered me food and drink. I declined, but indicated my interest in the music. Without invitation, I walked toward the band. Immediately all of the adults relaxed and smiled. The band members welcomed me as if I were the prodigal son. The gong-player rose gracefully and offered me his stool. Someone brought him another stool. He showed me how to position the two gongs in my left hand, and the two mallets in my right hand: The larger gong hangs by a leather strap, below the smaller gong. The two mallets steady each other, when gripped correctly in the right hand. With expressive face and hands, the abdicating gong-player directed me. He taught me the entire gong sequence. But the tootle-horn harmony was so unpredictable, that he always had to show me when to begin. Mesmerized by their music, I played the gongs for nearly two hours, until my hands were raw and my left arm ached. The Li people seemed delighted with my performance. When at last I put the gongs down to take my leave, they motioned me urgently to keep playing. Shaking every hand within reach seemed to placate them. I got back to the hotel barely in time for dinner. Lee Ming had grown anxious about my long absence.

At dinner, the local Han people were astonished that I had not been shot. As to the particulars of my experience, they refused to listen.

The next day, I brought Lee Ming as translator, to thank the Li people. Lee Ming took *her* first journey across the roly poly footbridge. I found the exact spot where the party had been. But the beautiful red and white bower had disappeared, like a magical chimera. The band and their little canopy were gone. The people were gone. In their place, a solitary young man, about thirty years old, slowly carried two large wooden buckets of water, balanced on a pole across his left shoulder. He put down his heavy burden and came toward us. His mood was so strange, that I did not know what to think of him. I became solemn.

Lee Ming said, "My husband wants to thank you. He had a good time yesterday at the party."

The solitary man said, "It wasn't a party. My mother died."

He confessed that he had believed me a malignant ghost. I had appeared out of nowhere, with giant body and greenish eyes, just like a ghost would do. But then I had joined the band. Their task was to scare away evil spirits. And I was truly frightening. He thanked me for protecting his mother's soul.

Among the Li people, red and white are the colors of death.

I had enjoyed myself at his expense. I didn't know what to say.

Instead of expressing sympathy, I gave my opinion that his mother had departed unmolested and in peace. As Lee Ming translated, I watched him closely. For a moment, his face showed intense pain.

Lee Ming and I wandered often on the far side of the footbridge. Every healthy Li adult worked long and hard. Only the children could spend much time with us. Nevertheless, every time we visited, one of the adults greeted us and made us feel welcome. Busy as they were, they took some trouble to brighten our lives. They showed us the safest trails, that led to the tallest mountain peaks. Sometimes they cut down fresh coconuts and gave us to drink from them. They always invited us to eat, but we always declined. They never tried to get money out of us. And they only brought out their guns when posing for their photographs. They seemed almost lonely.

One day, Lee Ming walked alone into a Li village. She surprised twenty children of all ages, playing together. She was wearing enormous brown sunglasses. They took one look and ran for their lives, shrieking in terror, and shrieking with pleasure at being terrified. Lee Ming stood alone, a bug-eyed monster, in the middle of the village. Then she took off her sunglasses. Cautiously, the children crept out of hiding and began to approach her. They had happy faces. Suddenly she put the glasses back on. Again they ran away, shrieking and laughing. Off came the glasses. Out came the children. Lee Ming put the glasses on but immediately removed them, then put them on halfway. The children crowded around her, dancing and laughing.

Every healthy Li adult worked long and hard. The local children knew, both Han and Li: they were living in their golden years.

Our hotel had a senior maid, about sixty years old, obese, and rather formidable. When she climbed just one flight of stairs, her breathing grew painful. Every day she marched around the premises barking her displeasure, while the younger maids scurried to appease her. On the fourth day, the senior maid and I met by chance, in the big beautiful garden that forms the hotel's central courtyard. Standing among the profusion of tropical flowers, we had our one and only direct conversation. I was not yet aware of her no-nonsense style.

"Do you know why foreigners have big noses?" I said, hoping to break the ice. She made no response. She just stared at me with piggy little eyes. Feeling a bit lost, I managed to continue, "Because the air is free!" I inhaled and exhaled the fresh garden. She maintained her severe silence, as if she were Madame Defarge. My discomfort grew. Then she said, "In *my* country, you had better trim down your nose."

The next day she accosted Lee Ming and said, "You married a foreigner. When your parents get old and need help, he won't care. Your mother raised you for nothing."

"Well, my mother doesn't think so."

"What's he doing here anyway?"

"He likes this place."

"'He likes this place.' What about the food? It can't be good enough for him."

"The food's okay. Besides, my husband wants to diet."

"Yes, he *is* pretty fat." She glared at Lee Ming. "Spend your time with your parents. They don't have long to live. Your mother raised you for nothing." She turned her back and walked away.

This maid became increasingly angry at our behavior. Why, against all advice, did we tramp around among the Li people and the snakes? Our conduct was strange and our motives shrouded. She agitated to have us expelled from the hotel. Repeatedly she asked the loaded question, "What's so interesting about this place?" The American might be a newspaper reporter, with ill will toward the Han and sympathy toward the Li. What was more, the staff got paid the same wages, whether or not they had to wash our sheets and cook our food. For a few days, our situation seemed precarious.

Then the manager came down firmly on our side. He saw the Big Picture. His hotel, charming as it was, had only intermittent electricity and running water. It was conveniently close to nothing in particular. It had eighty rooms and a staff of nineteen, but frequently only two paying guests: Lee Ming and her barbarian husband. If the staff were nice to us, we might come back and even bring friends.

In China, the boss must be placated.

But the most telling factor in our favor was the staff's children. Just like the Li children, they could not contain their curiosity about us, whatever their parents' misgivings. The children made their feelings known. We stayed four months. I gobbled down every morsel of my rations and lost fifteen pounds. Our antagonist made a few last attempts to incinerate us with her piercing stare, and then resigned herself to yet another of life's disappointments.

One evening, after another meager dinner, I played "Tag, you're it!" with fifteen Han children. The game was animated. Lee Ming refereed, and gave me a running translation. One boy, nine or ten years old, kept teasing a rather pretty girl just below his own age. I decided to tease him. I said, "You'll probably end up marrying her. Then you'll be under her thumb."

Immediately he shot back, "I still have twenty years before that happens!"

Dry Bones

If our universe turns out to be the best possible world, so what? Will this information put food on your table or clothes on your back? Will you love anyone differently?

On television I once saw a university professor and his top graduate students digging in the desert. The temperature was one hundred and fourteen degrees Fahrenheit. Not a tree or shrub anywhere gave shade from the sun. Most of the group kneeled together and bent down low. They were cleaning the ground with toothbrushes. They brushed slowly, inch by inch. They took pains not to let their dripping sweat fall on the dry bones. Although their dinosaur had been dead some one hundred million years, and therefore had no economic value even as an additive for dog food, they handled it softly, as a treasure beyond all price.

If we discover what the dinosaurs looked like, so what? Will this information put food on the table? Will we love anyone differently?

We might. No one can foretell how that knowledge would affect us. No one can prefigure his own most piercing satisfactions. What will we feel? And in what seductive countenance, does precisely that mystery inflame our longing to find out!

Good reader, in fairness I must warn you: A dinosaur fossil does not rise up from the desert floor, and in her inhuman glory, advance upon the scientist who dared to behold her.

Part Three

RANDOMNESS AT LARGE

"What Then Must We Do?"

One way or another, this question looms large for most humans alive today. It expresses a particular perspective on our lives.

All over the planet, for several hundred years now, in novels, fables, plays, and movies, our fictional stories reflect intense interest in "What Then Must We Do?"

Indeed, modern fiction often follows a well trod formula. It goes something like this:

The protagonist starts out with a particular approach to life. This approach comes under pressure. Circumstances intrude upon it and kick it around. Finding her original ideas unsuccessful, the protagonist revises them. She changes. Now her new approach to life gets tested. The story reveals the new approach as more successful than the old. The protagonist and the audience gain a nugget of insight into the problem, How do we conduct our lives successfully?

Here's a typical, fictional narrative in the modern style:

Mom and Dad work long hours to advance their careers, while missing Junior's soccer games. Junior, feeling unloved and rudderless, starts to go bad. He falls in with unsavory companions. He smokes marijuana. He shoplifts from the video store. His grades decline. Mom and Dad, engrossed by their projects at the office, find time to yell at him now and then, but postpone giving him real attention.

Then comes the crisis that profoundly affects all three characters. Junior goes joyriding in a stolen vehicle. He declines to yield the right-of-way to a telephone pole. The local constabulary intervene with prejudice. The very next day, Mom steps down from her career fast track. Dad does the same. They have learned a Life Lesson. They change. The happy ending finds Mom and Dad and Junior better off with less money and more time together. As the story entertains us, it also gives us advice.

Our stories didn't always have that intense focus. The *Iliad* and the *Odyssey* fail to examine What Then Must We Do? We see an intricate working of destiny, but little change in the characters. They just do what comes naturally. The Greeks land on the beach wanting to conquer Troy. Ten years later, they still want to conquer Troy. At the beginning of his story, Odysseus yearns to be home with his family. Ten years later, he yearns to be home with his family. If the characters change or learn Life Lessons, those details are passed over. Nor do the stories suffer from that omission.

The Chinese history *Three Kingdoms* has a structure similar to the *Iliad*. Again, the characters just do what they do. No Life Lessons.

Three Kingdoms describes the death throes of the Han Dynasty, from about 200 C.E. to 265. It takes up the question, How do human actions reflect the will of Heaven?

Dream of the Red Chamber, a lengthy Chinese novel with only four or five major characters, describes a very personal human tapestry, with just about no advice on what to do about it.

Those two Chinese books are regarded as masterpieces. Neither is the product of a modern society.

Modern fiction is different. Perhaps the most widely viewed movie ever made is *Gone with the Wind*. It follows the ubiquitous formula. Scarlett O'Hara begins the narrative with youthful, foolish ideas about Love, Romance, and her cloud-built dream bunny Ashley Wilkes. Then the brutal American Civil War intrudes and kicks those ideas around. Scarlett changes. She becomes a lot more practical. Just before intermission, with no romance at all, she shakes her fist at the heavens and shouts, "As God is my witness, I'll never be hungry again!"

By film's end, Scarlett changes further. She changes far enough to revise her affections. Exit Ashley, enter a more earthy and capable dream bunny. Although Rhett Butler walks out on her near the final scene, the audience has reasonable confidence that Scarlett will get him back—that a new and wiser Scarlett will at last find happiness.

Circumstances intrude upon the Main Character. She must change her approach to Life. The new approach has more success. We get at least a partial answer to the burning question, How do we best conduct our lives?

The many variations on that formula, show its ubiquity.

Some stories turn the formula inside out. In *Lord Jim*, *The Godfather*, and in *1984*, the brutal circumstances intrude and the protagonist learns a Life Lesson. But the lesson is perverse and negative.

Some stories stand the formula on its head. For Wodehouse's Bertie Wooster, the brutal circumstances are ridiculous and the life lessons absurd.

Charles Dickens shows us Sidney Carton, David Copperfield, and Scrooge changing their ideas for the better. They can learn from experience. By contrast, Madame Defarge and her knitting club feel way too much anger to attain that benefit.

In *King Lear*, *Romeo and Juliet*, and *Othello*, someone learns the life lesson too late.

When Hamlet must revise his youthful enthusiasm about life, he has difficulty finding an appropriate life lesson. For him, What Then Must We Do? is a puzzler.

The postwar Italian films *The Bicycle Thief* and *Nights of Cabiria*, give a dark answer to What Then Must We Do? When the brutal circumstances intrude, there's nothing we can do—except hang on to our humanity.

In *Don Quixote*, the warts and bruises of Spanish society are presented to a lunatic. The crazy guy knows What Must Be Done, but the reader is left groping.

The manifold variations on the formula only highlight our obsession with What Then Must We Do?

And so, imagine an intense chessplayer. He brings enormous personal energy to the game. Yet he loses often. His pieces get captured and his king gets harassed. He says, "I want to be successful at chess. Don't tell me why chess is better than other games. That information has no use. It doesn't help me win. And if chess is so wonderful, why do I wish my position were different?"

Understanding precisely why chess is a wonderful game, exactly why its rules are felicitous to our fertile brains, might help now and then with the problem of winning. But surely the larger effect is this: chess games become a bit more to us than they were.

Understanding precisely why the world is the best possible, exactly why its laws and structure are felicitous to its searching inhabitants, may or may not help with the problem of getting what we want. But this understanding does give, I trust, a new perspective on being alive.

The Human Style of Interpreting the World

To understand why our universe is the best possible world, you and I must first understand what *subtle* experience is and why it has value.

To understand subtle experience in general, we start by understanding subtle experience in the human style.

Human subtle experience rests on a key element: the comparisons we make. In fact we humans do use comparisons to interpret the world.

Human comparisons operate in a particular way, and we came to have them in a particular way.

FLUID COMPARISONS

Our comparisons resemble a fluid mobile-in-progress. We compare our comparisons, and compare those comparisons. My teeth are whiter this week than last week, they have whitened faster than my brother's teeth, and the rate of divergence accelerated after I switched toothpaste. I compare my comparison of comparisons. If my salary increased 3% this year, I can make a positive comparison. But if my salary and all my friends' salaries and all my colleagues' salaries always increase by 3% every year, then the positive comparison has smaller size. The positive comparison gets diluted by comparison to other positive comparisons. If one and only one individual gets a 2% raise, he can still make a positive comparison to last year's salary, but he has reason to be unhappy! If the individual with the 2% raise does better work then anyone else, he has *more* reason to be unhappy. If he's a notorious slacker, he might be overjoyed with a 2% *decrease*. If he regards himself as an artist, not a salaried worker, then a 5% increase might annoy him—until his wife points out how creative he must be to have a salary increase different from everyone else's. However, if his wife always finds a way to put a positive spin on circumstances that annoy him, he might grow more annoyed. On the other hand, if his neighbor's wife more blatantly emphasizes the positive, he might appreciate his wife's subtlety—but resent other people failing to notice his wife's subtlety and his own artistic nature. We humans make comparisons—lots of comparisons.

Here's another little ocean of fluid comparisons. This one edges into daydream territory. If I buy a new Porsche, I might feel satisfaction because my neighbors drive less glamorous cars. But after three days, the happy glow starts to wear off. A new feeling emerges. Impulsively I spent more money than my thrifty, responsible neighbors. Then, after brooding awhile, I get a bright idea: In the whole hidebound neighborhood, only I have the courage to enjoy life with toys I can't afford. Now I'm cocky again. Then my neighbor buys a top-of-the-line Lamborghini. He always has to go me one better. Suddenly my Porsche has pedestrian status. However, where I am courageous, my neighbor is an idiot. His retirement savings won't amount to much until he's ninety. With my Porsche, I can still retire at seventy. But my neighbor tells me, "Enjoy yourself while you can. You might get run over by some old Chevy, long before retirement." My neighbor burns me up. "More likely by a Lamborghini," I say. There I was, living with style in the moment, and to hell with the future, until he put me in his shadow. I should have scorned the Porsche and bought a bus pass. But now my other neighbor trots by in his designer running outfit, complete with blazing bolts of lightning on the arms and legs. In his whole existence he never spent a penny on a car. He rides to work on a bicycle. He's fit and he'll retire at fifty. We wave and smile. My Lamborghini neighbor says, "I pity that stingy tightwad. He'll never understand the thrill of driving a fine machine." I nod agreement with my ally. But I'm thinking, "*You* paid too much for that thrill."

Most comparisons our minds make automatically, without volition, and whether or not we pay attention. But we can also cultivate or emphasize comparisons. My parents once told me, "Eat your broccoli. Children in China are starving." My parents wanted to influence my mobile-in-progress, by pushing forward new comparisons: I was well fed; other children were not. I was disdainful; they would have loved my greasy, flaccid broccoli. Because our comparisons are fluid, they can be influenced.

And because our comparisons are highly fluid, the ways they change often reflect our idiosyncrasies. Lee Ming had a Maoist reaction to "Eat your broccoli." She said, "Wonderful. Children in China are starving, so American children volunteer to eat more food."

MOST EXPERIENCE HAS VARIABLE SIZE

Each of us measures experience by comparison to other experience. If your friend lives in good health to age one hundred, you might perceive him as having long life. But if most people live in good health to age nine hundred, then you would be inclined to see your centenarian friend as dying young.

If your friend has only peanuts to eat, and everyone else in the world has nothing to eat, you might congratulate him on his good fortune. But if everyone else in the world has a smorgasbord, you might feel sorry for your friend eating the very same peanuts.

Depending on the comparisons you happen to make, eating peanuts has variable size, somewhere between enormous satisfaction and abject discontent.

My well-meaning parents wanted eating broccoli to have a different size for me. For that reason, they introduced comparisons to children in China.

When you view someone as immature, you measure him against other people more mature. When you view someone as stingy, you make some manner of comparison to generosity. You see a person as lively by comparison to dullness. A person has a good reputation by comparison to bad reputations. For us humans, optimism and pessimism give size to each other. Simplicity and complexity measure each other. So also do certainty and uncertainty, predictability and unpredictability, experience and inexperience, reluctance and alacrity, competence and incompetence, success and failure, good fortune and bad, fame and obscurity, loyalty and disloyalty, courage and cowardice, grace and awkwardness, beauty and ugliness, delight and despair, a fair wage and an unfair wage, and so on.

A wage might be unfair based on a large system of comparisons, involving: other people's wages, calories needed for better health, other people's cost of living, their lifestyles, their dignity, difficulty of the task, working environment, history of the labor movement, and more. Here we see a master comparison—the fairness of one wage amidst the fairness or unfairness of other wages—deconstructed into a system of subsidiary comparisons, like the tributary balances in a mobile.

However, the variable size of experience does have exceptions. When your dentist drills into your tooth and hits a nerve, that experience bypasses all your fluid comparisons. No matter by what comparisons your mental processes interpret the world, the dental pain has a component of absolute size. No one can influence your landscape of comparisons to reduce that size. The best you can do is distract yourself, try not to notice it, try not to have the experience while you're having it.

Only direct *pain* has an absolute size. None of our *pleasures* have absolute size. Suppose you indulged in the narcotic bliss of heroin every day for ten billion days. The bliss goes right past all your comparisons, just like the direct pain. But direct bliss gets diluted by repetition. It gets old. On the billionth day it has smaller size. It might even go negative. By contrast, if your dentist drills continuously for ten billion days, the pain still has the same absolute size on the billionth day. Gentle reader, may your dentist have a good anesthetic.

This asymmetry between our direct pleasures and our direct pains, obtains for good reason. In logical possibility, human heroin bliss could have continued undiminished forever. But in actual fact it doesn't. Our world did not make a mistake. Absolute pleasures would give us escape from our dilemmas and, paradoxically, lives without value. I'll tell you more about that later.

Absolute pain we do need. Absolute pain acts as foundation and anchor for human comparisons. You can compare the pain of the dentist drilling, to an alternative: the pain of losing your pearly white smile. You can choose between the alternatives. The dental pain is direct and absolute, while the alternative has variable size: If your entire visiting circle have lost their front teeth to rampaging hockey pucks, then harboring a withered tooth might be more bearable than the drill. Direct pains bypass the comparisons we use to interpret the world, yet figure into our comparisons anyway. Their absolute sizes serve as anchor. The mutable sizes need to stand somewhere on solid ground.

With only a few vital exceptions, all our experience has variable and mutable size. This fact is a consequence of how we interpret the world. The mobile-in-progress has elements that grow and shrink.

SCALES OF COMPARISON

Each of our discrete experiences resides within an enormously complicated system of counterparts and comparisons, including not only comparisons to our own experience, but also comparisons to other people's experience as described to us or witnessed by us, and sometimes to fictional experience. Our minds organize and simplify these complications by constructing "scales of comparison." Here is what I mean:

Suppose I take a walk in the park. If my usual occupations consist of mountain climbing, scuba diving, skiing, attending fabulous parties, driving race cars, etc., then I might find walking in the park dull or soothing. But I don't need to think explicitly about those other experiences to find my walk dull. From those previous experiences, my mind has constructed a scale of comparison, such that the walk seems dull *as measured by that scale*. In this way, I measure my walk in the park by comparison to numerous other experiences, without having to think consciously and explicitly about all the comparisons involved. My mind has constructed a convenient simplification: a scale of comparison.

If my usual occupations consist of lying in bed watching TV, or working in a windowless office, or doing time in prison, then my mind constructs a different scale, and the same walk in the park might be quite exciting to me. Again, I can feel this excitement without explicitly and consciously reviewing all the comparisons involved.

We guide, influence, seek out comparisons. One way or another, we often pay attention to how our minds operate. Nevertheless, the vast majority of our comparisons remain automatic and unconscious. The human mind has unconscious methods for organizing and simplifying comparisons. Here are two more examples:

Consider a woman unsatisfied with her boyfriend—but not because she has had better boyfriends. Rather, her girlfriends have told her about *their* boyfriends. She never met the boyfriends described to her. Her girlfriends told her about them long ago. She remembers neither the specifics of the descriptions nor the specific experiences of hearing the descriptions. Nevertheless, when Bozo proposes marriage to her, she views his proposal as distinctly unromantic. She makes no *conscious* comparison to the more romantic proposals reported to her years ago. Yet those descriptions influence her present perceptions; she finds him a lukewarm lover. As her experience accumulates over the years, her mind builds up scales of comparison, a kind of summary by accretion. The specific experiences can fade from memory, without destroying the scales of comparison they influenced. In this manner, the human mind simplifies the unconscious process of comparing experience to experience.

At some point in your life, perhaps while you are still quite young, you reach a fuller awareness that people die, those you love will die, and you will die. Other people's experience of old age, begins to influence the scale by which you measure your own youthful experience—even though you may not actually think about old people when you enjoy the pleasures of youth. Perhaps this point in life marks the end of childhood.

When measuring and evaluating our experience, sometimes we think of the comparisons consciously and explicitly. But mostly we use the convenient simplification of scales prefabricated in our minds. Our mental processes automatically construct and update these scales of comparison, as we have new experience. We need these scales as an intermediary to our comparisons. Otherwise, we would be constantly reviewing an enormous number of comparative relationships between our present experience and all the experiences reported to us, witnessed by us, or directly experienced in the past. Using the scales as an intermediary also allows us to drop a lot of detail from our memories. Only now and then do we review the underlying comparisons explicitly—perhaps when we want to examine or modify the ways they influence us.

Reported experience relates to fiction. Bozo might be unromantic by comparison to fictional accounts of Cyrano de Bergerac. In the fullness of time, we will talk about the effect of fiction on our comparisons. Believing fiction, disbelieving it, believing it halfway, and indeed deceiving ourselves, turn out to be *essential* contributors to *high* subtlety. We rise far above mere calculation.

THE SCOPE OF OUR COMPARISONS

Widely disparate satisfactions are commensurable for us. The satisfactions of running for president, climbing a mountain, eating a gourmet dinner, making love, and walking the dog, are all different yet comparable. We compare such satisfactions and choose among them. We can weigh the pleasure of visiting the art museum, against the pleasure of visiting an old friend, or the pleasure of reading a trashy novel. Many of us can pick out the most satisfying year or the most satisfying day of our lives. Substantially all of our experience, in all its diversity, we compare as satisfaction or dissatisfaction, by one unified, sophisticated, coherent scale. This wide-ranging coherence is complicated, but we feel it. One and the same human being might enjoy food and drink, fall in love, wax lyrical over a sunset, get voted Miss Congeniality, work her way up to CEO of Gigantic Products, Inc., scale dangerous mountain cliffs for the thrill of nearly dying, feel compassion for the victims of Alzheimer's disease, ponder her mortality, travel to exotic lands, fight for justice, ride the abortion issue into the US Senate, bargain at the flea market, write a screenplay, raise children, and go to the racetrack and scream for her horse to pay the rent. One and the same coherent human agent might ask herself, Would I rather watch the sunset or browse the flea market? Would I rather raise children or work my way up to CEO or make more time for sunsets? Each individual human, almost without exception, feels a commensurability and a coherence among *all* the satisfactions and dissatisfactions in the entire jumble of her experience.

Some people believe that our satisfactions cannot all be comparable, because sometimes we have difficulty choosing among them. At times we are torn between our options. Thus, when his girlfriend gives him an ultimatum, a man might be torn between the joy of bachelorhood and the rapture of marriage. When a pleasant stranger offers us the chance to double our money in a week, we might be tempted but suspicious. Mother Teresa felt considerable anguish when choosing between career options: a talented soprano giving pleasure to opera lovers, or a compassionate caregiver to the dying poor.

But our indecision has a clear cause. In each of those cases, we humans cannot entirely predict the outcomes of our choices. We do not always know which options will give us the most satisfaction. How will we feel later about the choice we make now? We have difficulty choosing among our options, because sometimes their outcomes take indistinct forms in the foggy future.

Nevertheless, we are *torn* between such options precisely because we do want to choose the most satisfying outcome. The fact that we might later regret our choice already shows that we are choosing among commensurable satisfactions. The very fact that we are torn, shows that the different satisfactions of each option are commensurable.

We can be torn in complicated ways. The mobile-in-progress has subsidiary balances within its overall balance. Our perceptions of success, virtue, competence, self-esteem, happiness, serenity, maturity, tolerance, adventure, elegance, beauty, fairness, friendship, love—each such category of our perceptions, exhibits its own singular coherence within its own singular diversity. But meanwhile, commensurability among our satisfactions also transcends those limited categories. Thus, in consequence of how we perceive the world, people are straightforward by comparison to people who are devious. That's a subsidiary balance. But meanwhile, we can weigh the pleasure of visiting a straightforward friend, against the pleasure of visiting the art museum, or the pleasure of watching an adventure movie, or the pleasure of reading a trashy novel about lusty men and women, or the pleasure of playing chess against a crafty opponent, or the pleasure of giving the dog a happy tour of the park. The overall balance has a complicated system of interior balances. We are subtle beings.

HOW OUR SATISFACTIONS *BECAME* COMMENSURABLE

Biological evolution on planet Earth, produces subtle agents both highly idiosyncratic and highly coherent. Those properties are difficult to combine in the same agent. Yet manifestly our biological evolution does unite them, in you and in me.

How does evolution join those two properties together? What methods does evolution use that have proved so effective?

Consistent with current widely held views of biological evolution, the combination of high idiosyncrasy and deep coherence in the same human agents, happened like this:

All of our human satisfactions are grounded in the same biological principle of reproduction for survival. The human species evolved from a long series of ancestor species. At each moment during hundreds of millions of years, *exactly one* species alive on this planet, was uniquely *our* ancestor species. Each ancestor species was a successful attempt at effective reproduction. For each of our ancestors, events could be successful or unsuccessful in different ways related to reproduction. The events were different, but all of them correlated to species survival, or to the dominance and survival of specific subsets of the species. As our ancestors gradually gained in complexity, events could go well or poorly for survival, in increasingly varied ways. Finally, when human biological evolution reached the modern species, success and failure had enormous complexity. Events could go well or poorly in very diverse ways. Friendships, parenting, language, hunting strategies, color vision, pattern recognition, curiosity, self-expression, wooing a mate, making sacrifices for love—even killing other human beings—all related to survival. When one of our ancestors courageously gave up his life to protect his fellows from marauding lions, that action advanced his species' survival. When one tribe of humans made frenzied war on another tribe, killing the men and carrying off the women, those actions affected the survival of particular bits of DNA. When a more prudent tribe fled from adversity or from war, those actions also influenced the survival of the human genome in particular forms. For many hundreds of millions of years, the diversity in our experience—almost everything we did, and everything that happened to us—had the underlying coherence of survival. Of course our ancestor species operated successfully among other species for survival. But in addition, the myriad instantiations *within* our ancestor species, with increasing complexity, warred with each other, tolerated each other, and allied with each other, all for survival. As we evolved in biology, and our experience became more varied, it remained directly connected to survival: staying alive and producing offspring. All of the attendant satisfactions and dissatisfactions had that unifying theme. Even killing others and dying for others cohered with staying alive. Biological evolution elaborated and diversified our satisfactions, while keeping them commensurable.

According to recent research, our sense of humor had survival value. Our satisfactions remain commensurable even while our funny bone helps elaborate them and diversify them.

Because the commensurability of our satisfactions evolved for a long time—many hundreds of millions of years—this commensurability has sophistication, detail, and subtlety. Throughout that long period, our ancestor species made decisions and choices affecting their survival. They learned to recognize options increasingly different from each other, and to choose well. They evolved to operate successfully in a long series of unique environments. As biological evolution progressed and varied its pressures against us, a responding sophistication arose, in the ways our ancestors perceived their satisfactions as commensurable. Like a potter that shapes and refines its vessel on the turning wheel, biological evolution refined the subtlety of *how* our species chooses among satisfactions. Under the long, relentless pressure of evolution, commensurability among radically diverse satisfactions became detailed, sophisticated, and subtle—profoundly coherent—very far from arbitrary. Evolution constructed a detailed and idiosyncratic commensurability among human satisfactions. To construct a comparable coherence in the satisfactions of an artificial intelligence, we would scarcely know how to begin.

Thus our biological evolution makes us highly idiosyncratic

yet deeply coherent. Moreover, the coherence continues to work well as we humans build on our biological origins. Human civilizations resonate well to our pursuit of satisfaction. Our biological satisfactions and dissatisfactions resonate in subtle ways within the civilizations we build.

Again consistent with current widely held views in anthropology and sociology, said subtle resonance happens something like this:

After our long, slow evolution as biology, we started to evolve more rapidly as cultures and civilizations. Our satisfactions became more elaborate still, yet remained connected to survival. Thus, we appreciated the tranquil blue of a non-stormy sky, and the exciting red or yellow of a ripe fruit, and perhaps the green safety and distinctive shape of a tree. As successful survivors and propagators, we had emotions about various colors and shapes in nature and in the fertile human body. To enhance our competitiveness as a species, we created artifacts. Apparently, such biological imperatives now find their way into the artistic traditions evolving with our civilizations. We perfected our hunting strategies and now we play chess. We competed for dominance and now we make politics and war, and have selfish feelings. We helped each other survive and now we feel compassion and a sense of justice. Sometimes we prudently kept our tribe out of war, and now we sometimes yield to tolerance. We fought and died to protect our tribe, sometimes with frenzied courage, and now we sometimes feel the fanatic honor of dying for some hypothetical future of humankind. We analyzed the ways and means of successful existence, and now we have sciences, histories, philosophies, and religions. In short, our biological satisfactions appear to be suited quite well to cultural evolution. Their biological coherence conveniently fits a civilized elaboration. Diversity increases, with crosscurrents magnified, yet coherence remains. Human biological satisfactions appear to have that felicity.

Our biological evolution pounding on our satisfactions and making them highly idiosyncratic, quite diverse, yet profoundly commensurable—sets a felicitous table for the evolution of our civilizations.

Our biologically evolved curiosity and analysis now have great scope to manipulate the same physical law that evolved us. The elegance in a ripe fruit or a female breast, or in the song of a bird with no predator near, leads us by subtle stages to the elegance of the physical law that evolved them. We have come to know the potter that shaped us, and from there to know ourselves in a new way.

Our satisfactions being tied together, need not result from immediate causal connections between all our satisfactions and species survival. Many ties to survival can be indirect and subtle. If you walk in the park, enjoying the green trees and the manicured lawns, human existence may be neither threatened nor strengthened. But eons ago, our ancestors probably had emotions about trees as places of refuge, and healthy grasslands as harbingers of plentiful game. Your present enjoyment of the shady green park, winds its way indirectly back to survival. And as you walk, you might muse abstractedly about why you exist. Our ancestors, struggling more directly to survive, may have found similar musings rather more urgent. Our present satisfactions have greater distance from the central focus of survival that unites them, but not yet too much distance.

And our present satisfactions have another kind of distance from the focus of biological survival. Civilization has magnified the conflicting crosscurrents in our evolved satisfactions, sharpening our dilemmas and disturbing our certainties.

Paleolithic humans did not face, for example, the political problems we face. Consider a dedicated FBI agent, assigned to infiltrate and paralyze a dangerous organization of white supremacists. She does successfully infiltrate—by seducing the local Klan leader. He loves her tenderly. She finds herself returning his love. She hates his beliefs and his shrewd plans to destroy non-white peoples. She fears his ability and his resolve. By all that is moral and right for her, this Klan leader fully deserves to die. Society agrees with her. Yet despite herself, she loves him. Somehow, as only a subtle being can do, she finds him at once vile and noble. She would destroy all his works, yet she cannot imagine living in a world without this unique man. And suddenly *she alone* must decide whether he lives or dies. His organization destroyed, no longer able to menace society, facing certain death, the manhunt closing in, but unrepentant—he comes to her and asks her to hide him. She must choose between compassion and duty, between love and justice.

Biological evolution for survival, causally originates both passions: justice and love. *Civilized* evolution has a disturbing aptitude to turn them against each other! Because they do have heightened mutual conflict, many of our civilized satisfactions differ from their forms in biology. Nevertheless, satisfactions remain commensurable, especially when brought directly into opposition. For the FBI agent, the very tension between love and justice, demonstrates their commensurability all too vividly: If she does choose which part of herself to give up, then whether or not she finds her choice clear, she weighs one loss against the other. Only a subtle being, with profoundly commensurable satisfactions, wars profoundly against herself. And if somehow she can reconcile the conflict without giving up a part of herself—if somehow she finds a paradoxical, transcendent resolution—then she finds a *superior* satisfaction, which again has commensurability with the inferior resolutions!

Almost all of us have coherent agency, yet each one of us has many unique idiosyncrasies. We are all the same and we are all different. Our universe does well knitting together diverse satisfactions into one, idiosyncratic, but subtly coherent agency, highly fluid, exposed to profound despair and sublime delight.

Our universe as Siren takes advantage. Rather than mechanically rewarding or failing to reward our specific hopes and dreams, the world sometimes gives us the unexpected and the ineffable: delight and despair we cannot anticipate, fear, desire, or even imagine in advance. In consequence, the comparisons we make take on new dimension. Even the inalterable past can change under the light of new comparisons, when the future arrives in a form we did not foresee.

Our agency does in fact have exquisite dimension and subtle exercise. We do not labor to have them. But the world can be described as laboring to give them to us.

EXPLOITING THE HUMAN STYLE

The world plays on our facility to compare. For us, every sunset is the same and every sunset is different. Every person, every tree, every mountain, every day is the same and not the same.

We have despair more profound and delight more sublime, because the world suffers us to perceive balances like these:

We understand our world and it mystifies us.

We control events and events control us.

We are vital and we decay.

We know what the next sunset will be like and we do not know.

We know what will happen this day and we do not know.

We can protect ourselves and we can never be safe.

We know how best to conduct our lives and we do not know.

We can change the world and we cannot change it.

We have answers to our problems and we do not have answers.

Such is the world's appearance to humans, and the human style of interpreting the world.

Lightness

How our biological evolution shapes our lives, has a commonplace, earthbound interest. How the size and age of our universe shape our lives, has an unearthly beauty.

This chapter begins to explore the causal connections between two facts: our daily lives have subtlety, and our universe has giant dimension.

The present chapter talks about randomness and its property lightness. I'm talking only about *caused* randomness, not uncaused. I'm talking only about randomness that is generated or produced in some way.

Depending on how it is produced, randomness can be fine, high quality, well executed, light—or the randomness can be crude, low quality, poorly executed, heavy, contaminated. This chapter explains how generated randomness can have high quality or low quality, and the role of high quality randomness in human subtle experience.

Both our human agency and our experience have a structured pattern of idiosyncrasy. We may also call it a structured pattern of randomness. Our experience contains a mixture of what we can predict and what we cannot predict, what we can retrodict and what we cannot retrodict, what we can control and what we cannot control, what we do to the world and what the world does to us, what we find intelligible in events and what we find chaotic,

80

and so on. Examples: We know what will happen this day and we do not know. Sometimes we recognize what we are seeing and sometimes we do not. We direct the motions of our bodies and they decay against our wishes. Other people are similar to us but they also have idiosyncrasies contrasting with ours. And so on. All those aspects of our experience derive causally from a pattern of structured randomness. Creating a complicated pattern of randomness within a complicated structure, is the inner significance of our long evolution in the big universe.

Our pattern of structured randomness has a key feature: its "lightness." A succinct definition of "lightness" would be: within a specified structure of randomness, that randomness has no other structures or patterns even faintly detectable. Or we might say: within the specified structure, unusual or atypical patterns are not apparent too often.

Lightness may be a property of any structure of randomness. The game of bridge, for example, has the structure of thirteen cards per hand, and the structure of strict rules of play; but within that rigid structure is a random distribution of the cards dealt. When we play cards, when we construct one of the structured patterns of randomness that constitutes a card game, we introduce lightness into the cards' distribution by shuffling the deck several times. We wish the cards' distribution to conform to the structure defining the card game, *and* we wish to obliterate even faint traces of all other patterns. We want the cards' distribution to be unaffected by what happened during the previous hand. Hence, we shuffle the cards repeatedly to create lightness. We might think of lightness as a measure of the quality of randomness.

Subtle experience is also a pattern of structured randomness. Your experience has the same general structure as mine, but your experience has idiosyncrasies different from mine. The world's evolution of agents and their experience, contains analogies to shuffling the deck and dealing the cards. The actual world has *high quality* randomness: evolved agents are light, their experience is light, and their evolution is light. Lightness in our experience points to the skill of our physical evolution, and to its size. The chapter "Subtlety and Physical Law" (p. 199) examines the ingenuity of actual physical evolution, from the Big Bang to planets and people, as a generator of *light* randomness.

The succinct definition of "lightness," and the card-game example, fail to convey the significance of lightness in our subtle experience. The 1998 film *The Truman Show* raises issues related to lightness, and provides a good point of departure for explaining what the world's lightness does to us.

Truman, the protagonist of the film, has been confined from birth, without his knowledge or consent, to an artificial world. He lives within a gigantic studio building. Thousands of cameras hidden throughout the studio record his every action, even his most private moments, and transmit them continuously as a television show to the world at large. Unknown to Truman, all of his family and friends, and every human being he encounters, is a hired actor. The production company hires an actress to marry Truman, live with him, and simulate loving him. His friends are paid to be his friends. His boss and his rivals on the job and his barber are engaged to act those roles. His mother gives birth to him under contract with the producers. What Truman believes to be the sky is in fact the painted ceiling of the giant structure enclosing his world. He lives in a small artificial town populated by actors. Sophisticated machinery, controlled by the production staff, creates the weather. Truman receives considerable information about the larger world outside. He reads the same books and magazines that outside people read, and watches the same programs on television, except that all such material gets edited to omit any reference to himself or to *The Truman Show*. He believes himself to be a denizen of the larger world just like any other. But *The Truman Show* director finds various excuses and subterfuges to keep Truman always confined to the studio building. For example, Truman lives on an artificial island within the studio. As a child he was deliberately allowed to watch his father "drown," causing Truman to have a pathological fear of crossing open water, including the water standing between his artificial island and any access to the painted walls of the studio. And yet,

Truman's director in his own way tries to give Truman a pleasant life. *The Truman Show* generates revenue when the actors interacting with Truman praise various commercial products on camera. *The Truman Show* has been a huge ratings success right from the birth of its star. Unknown to Truman, a world audience has followed his life through all the rites of childhood and young adulthood. The director has begun to think of himself as God, at least with respect to Truman. However, as the film progresses, the creators of Truman's artificial world start making mistakes in the factitious facade, the adult Truman grows suspicious, and he figures out that he is confined. Having fallen in love with another woman who was written out of the script, Truman decides to escape and find her. The woman returns his love. Along with all the other viewers, she watches on TV his efforts to escape. He succeeds and she flies to meet him. End of story.

The film doesn't quite say that Truman prefers a more dangerous but bigger and more subtle world. The question, Which world is better? gets resolved by special circumstances: If Truman's true love had been one of the actresses assigned a permanent part in the script, instead of a temporary bit part, Truman might not have followed her to the outside world. Moreover, the director of his smaller world gets sufficiently nasty—trying to drown Truman when he attempts escape, separating him from his "dead" father, separating him from the woman he loves, having his "friends" severely abuse Truman's trust to quiet his suspicions, encouraging and exploiting his phobias when convenient, subjecting Truman to dull and gratuitous commercial messages, subjecting him to a dull and gratuitous marriage, letting the entire world be secret voyeurs when he wants privacy—to rival even the big world's disadvantages. Truman clearly got a raw deal in his artificial world, cosseted as he may have been. Doubt about which world is preferable does not arise. The film focuses on a different issue: Playing God with another's life goes awry. The subject doesn't fall in love where indicated, his indomitable spirit fiercely resists manipulation, and "God," being only human, selfishly puts his own interests first. "God" believes he loves Truman, but he really loves the ways he can exploit and control Truman, and keep him forever dependent, like a child. He doesn't love Truman as an adult making his own choices. Yet each of us wants to grow up and run his own life, thank you very much. Quite an interesting film.

The Truman Show declines to address many of the inherent comparisons between the outside world and a smaller, simulated world. But it does illustrate the meaning of "lightness" in our experience. We can think of lightness as a measure of the quality of randomness, analogous to the amount of shuffling in a card game. Many ordinary, everyday events in Truman's experience are mere simulations of spontaneity: "chance" encounters with other people, his wife's daily conversation, even the painted sunsets he watches. In Truman's environment, true spontaneity and serendipity have artificial limits or filters. Without Truman's knowledge, his director orders up certain areas of spontaneity by fiat. For that reason, many events for Truman fit a "heavy" pattern of randomness—his experience has faint traces of incongruous structure—unlike the light pattern we experience in the big world. *The pattern for Truman is heavy even when his director wants it to be light.* The director cannot successfully simulate our world's lightness, even when he tries; the human director just doesn't have a counterpart to the outside world's randomness generator: our long evolution from the Big Bang. As a result, even before the cast and crew start making mistakes, Truman already has the vague, uneasy feeling that something's wrong, that he is "the center of the world" in some creepy fashion. In certain ways he cannot explore his world, as if he were living in a flat painting instead of a three-dimensional landscape.

I want to discuss how lightness affects us, and why the *faint* traces of incongruous structure would *so profoundly* disturb someone in Truman's situation.

We humans like to induct and we are good at induction. We have an excellent nose for sniffing out even faint traces of unintended patterns in various structures. I have a friend who once believed that God was signaling to him through the pattern of automobile license plates he happened to see every day. In fact he *almost could* find the patterns to justify his belief! The world must be careful with the patterns it shows us—and even more careful with not showing us any unintended patterns. Hence the importance of lightness in all the world's many structures of randomness.

When causally generating a randomness structure, reducing the traces of unintended structure can be quite difficult, and the difficulty compounds in *complex* structures of randomness. Agents and environments are very, very complex structures of randomness. Hence a universe with enormous age and size, dedicated to building complex structures of randomness both with patterns and not-patterns. The not-patterns pose far more difficulties than the patterns!

As we will see, our universe must shuffle and shuffle and shuffle "the cards" for billions of years, in myriad different ways, and very cleverly, just to discourage us from saying too often, "Somehow we can practice sorcery successfully," or "Somehow the world feels creepy," or "God speaks to us strangely." Our temptation to say those things can be great enough already with light randomness, in part because we look for induction so well and so thoroughly—because we can sniff out even faint possible failures in the quality of randomness. With less carefully produced randomness, those temptations would increase and materially degrade or distort our ability to find order in the world. Our experience could not be elusive in the best possible way. Hence the *enormous* universe generating *light* randomness in *complex* structures.

The world mystifies us persistently, and we are not easily mystified for long. The world creates *a lot* of complicated high quality idiosyncrasy, conforming to intended patterns and only to those patterns. If the structure of randomness relaxes its vigilance against unintended patterns even in tiny ways, even in just one facet of a complex structure, someone somewhere will find that flaw and tell the rest of us. If the flaw occurs in a man-made randomness, we can recognize it as a flaw. But if the flaw occurs in the world's natural randomness, it will cause our perception of order in the world to deviate from the best possible, and destroy a part of the world's intended elusiveness.

(I do not mean to anthropomorphize our universe by talking about its "intentions." However, I must deal with a curious prejudice in the English language: "ingenuity" and "intention" imply an author, and all their synonyms imply an author.

(According to O'Brien in the novel *1984*, treasonous thoughts can be eliminated by removing from language the words to express them.

(In conformance with English usage, a general may be ingenious. If he formulates a military plan, the plan itself may be ingenious. Conscious beings *and their works* may have the property "ingenious." But our language provides no word to describe ingenuity in a scheme, that does not imply an author of that scheme. And if the plan be directed toward some objective, English again has no word to describe such intent in the plan, without implying intent in an author.

(But I mean to describe ingenuity and intention in our world, and still deny that any agency made it so. "Double plus ungood," as O'Brien might say. Later I will argue that no agency whatsoever can be the author of our world's "ingenuity" and "intention"—on pain of logical contradiction. Thus, in defiance of English usage, we have a goal-oriented, ingenious world that cannot possibly be caused, willed, sustained, or designed.

(But not to worry. We have our existence for a rather more nifty reason. I think you will like the metaphysics of perfection. More on this later.)

Where were we? Oh yes. Our experience combines structure and randomness, predictability and unpredictability. The unpredictability could have been heavy, poorly shuffled, contaminated, of low quality. But instead, the unpredictability in our experience has impeccable lightness.

Even as each hand of bridge is like every other and unlike every other, so each sunset is like and unlike every other sunset. You and I have seen a great many sunsets. They all have the same predictable structure. We know exactly how today's sunset will be just the same as all the others. But today's sunset will have unique, high quality idiosyncrasies, and someone may very well call out to us, "Come and look!"

Lightness is the most problematic feature of an artificial intelligence, far more difficult to instill in a machine than the knowledge and intelligent skills we humans generally share in common. How do we give a machine a light pattern of idiosyncrasies, within the already complex structure of intelligence and knowledge we generally share? How do we erase all discernible traces of unintended heaviness in the idiosyncrasies of a structure so complex? We have an excellent nose for sniffing out the faintest incongruous pattern. Even if we succeed in making a machine that knows what humans know, even if it looks and sounds like a human, even if it has human motives, we will still recognize it as a machine. If such machines were walking around among us, and we got to know them, we would be able to detect something odd and inhuman about them. For similar reasons, Truman could detect a "mechanical" quality in his immediate environment: a faint but easily detectable heaviness in its idiosyncrasies. In like manner, you or I might pick up a hand of bridge and say, "These cards were not shuffled." Within certain kinds of complex structure, such as human agency or Truman's closed environment, good randomness becomes very difficult to generate. The quality of its randomness is the fundamental reason why the big world is better.

For completeness I need to say: Truman's world actually does have quite extensive idiosyncrasy and lightness. Both our world and his have the idiosyncrasy of five digits on the hand, a specific percentage of oxygen in the atmosphere, the force of gravity at a specific level, 365 days in the year, specific species of trees, flowers, and birds, specific organs and hormones in the body, specific kinds of food, specific abilities to recognize other humans by their facial features, the same English language, a specific history of art, music, literature, science, politics, war, and philosophy, specific tastes in manners, love, and humor, etc., etc. Our experience has many thousands of areas or domains of idiosyncrasy. We have relatively specific idiosyncrasies within relatively general idiosyncrasies, and those idiosyncrasies have further idiosyncrasies, and so on, sometimes up to one hundred distinct layers, in my guesstimation. Failures of quality, in the small world's pattern of randomness, occur only in a few areas of idiosyncrasy: whom Truman encounters each day, how they react to him, who wants to be his friend, how his wife feels about him, the vicissitudes of his career, how his actions bring harm or benefit to others, etc. Truman's director fails to simulate lightness only in the few specific pockets of idiosyncrasy that he tries to fill by his fiat. However, even these limited failures of quality, confined to relatively small areas of the randomness pattern, bothered Truman. In certain ways he could not explore his world, as if he were living in a flat painting instead of a three-dimensional landscape. Something about his world did not respond with sufficient depth, with sufficient elusiveness to categorization. We humans want that quality of lightness in *all* areas of idiosyncrasy, or at least in a great many key areas. Lightness in our world gives a unique scope to our idiosyncratic free will.

Toward a large area of our desires and our ideals, our universe exhibits neither visible rejection nor visible acquiescence, but something more elusive. The *thoroughness* or depth of this elusiveness, is one aspect of lightness: a form of resistance to our propensity to find faint contaminating patterns in experience. That the universe can maintain its elusiveness so completely—without even tiny visible traces of systematic rejection or partiality to any strategy we may employ to achieve happiness—constitutes an enormous technical achievement. We know that people who eat generally do better than people who do not eat. We know that people who wear clothes generally do better, by present custom. But we cannot discern that good people are generally happier or less happy than bad people; that practical people generally have better or worse chances for satisfaction than dreamers; that religious people achieve happiness more or less frequently than nonbelievers. We try quite persistently and quite skillfully to find such patterns, but the results can justly be described as inconclusive and unsuccessful. By contrast, the benefits of wearing clothes and eating are vividly apparent. Within a specific limited structure of how to succeed at life, the world reveals to us not even the faintest trace of what strategy we might generally best use to find happiness. The world maintains a large area of enigmatic elusiveness to our struggles for satisfaction. Within this area, our keenest powers of induction fail to reveal the slightest partiality. Said enigmatic elusiveness is a form of lightness. The world presents the intended pattern *and* thoroughly erases the contamination of unintended patterns. No artificial small world like Truman's can come close to that lightness, to that quality of enigmatic elusiveness. Truman understood the responses of his limited world far more effectively than we understand our large world. He knew, for example, that a cheerful "Hello" to the minor players in his life, invariably received a cheerful response. The ways he was befriended were unsubtle. Even before he became suspicious, Truman could already discern certain partialities and tendencies in his world that do not obtain in ours. He could incorporate his knowledge of those heavy, unsubtle contaminations into his search for happiness. As his world could manipulate him, so he could manipulate it. Other small worlds, that differently substitute heavy fiat for some areas of light idiosyncrasy, would also have their weaknesses, perhaps favoring practical people over dreamers, or docile people over their aggressive brothers, and/or giving its inhabitants lives too easy and undifferentiated. But the actual world consistently maintains a very high quality of slippery "no comment" to our initiatives, desires, and ideals. Our world has impeccable lightness. It shows us only the intended structures, with absolutely no contamination from unintended structures. This very high quality of randomness, within the very complex structure of our agency and our experience, required nearly fourteen billion years and staggering ingenuity to achieve.

In the "Physical Law" chapter (p. 199), we will examine the causal origins of our lightness of being. We do not live in a flat painting.

Besides a thoroughly enigmatic response to our strategies in the world, lightness in our experience takes numerous other forms. As a result, we have many profound ways to explore our lives, much to intrigue us, and much to discover. For example, our planet has a variety of climates, terrain, and cultures. If I happen to travel to the other side of the planet, I may find complete new systems of light experience, systems with depth and dimension that could not have been created by heavy fiat. By contrast, the Vulcan and Romulan civilizations, Narnia, the Land of Oz, however fascinating, have no comparable depth or dimension; they *are* flat paintings; they *are* created by fiat. Again, I might join the petroleum industry and spend a lifetime exploring the locations and characteristics of oil deposits in this complicated planet. Or, if I wish, I can become a painter, and explore relationships between complicated physical qualities of paints and complicated human feelings. Because we have a complex, thoroughly shuffled evolution of our agency, the color red does not conform to the heavy pattern of always representing anger.

The glory of our world is its subtle, well designed, well executed mixture of the predictable and the unpredictable in our lives. That mixture requires complex idiosyncrasy and light randomness, which in turn require a very large evolution.

Lee Ming
Crosses the Street

Clouds and conversation often express the world's lightness.

The major streets of Beijing have signal lights on them, just like our traffic lights in America. In Beijing, green means "go." Red means "go for it."

In December 1993, Lee Ming and I crossed a street in downtown Beijing. The day was overcast, dry, windy, and bitterly cold. Both of us were dressed warmly, as innocent sightseers ought to be dressed. I had on my heavy leather Russian-style hat, with mink lining and cozy earflaps, purchased in Beijing. I wore warm leather pants, a sinewy pair of leather gloves, and stout boots, all purchased locally. Lee Ming was hatted and booted in equal comfort. We had spent the morning in Bei Hai Park, admiring the pagodas and the iced-over lake. Walking in the cold had stimulated our appetite for lunch. Across the street was restaurant row.

The skies were grey but our mood sunny. We stood at the crosswalk. The light turned green. Lee Ming started across. A large black passenger car bore down upon her, a luxury German model with smoked glass windows in the rear. The driver ignored the red light against him. He did not slow his speed, about twenty miles per hour. Spotting Lee Ming in the crosswalk, he leaned on his horn. Lee Ming barely had time to leap backward and save herself. Surprise and fear were in her face. She came within a whisker of serious injury or death. Enraged, I reacted without conscious thought. I was walking ten feet to Lee Ming's right and two feet behind her. As the black monster cruised past, I just had time to step forward and bring down my open, gloved hand, hard and true, on the rear fender. The impact traveled up my arm and reverberated through the car. The impact felt good. A moment later, the sinking feeling in my stomach did not feel good.

Lee Ming later told me that slapping the driver's car was equivalent to slapping his face. That car was his identity, the possession that distinguished him from the shabby masses. Unless he took some terrible revenge, and quickly, the story would be told against him for years. The loss of face might well force him into a new line of work.

Immediately the driver slammed on his brakes and threw open his door. I could hear him running toward me. I commended my soul to Whomever and prepared to sell my life dearly.

Fortunately, the driver was six inches shorter and about two-thirds my weight. He was hatless and far too lightly dressed for the cold wind. Clearly he had intended to pummel me senseless, but he took one look and opted for Plan B. If we traded blows, my heavy leather hat would protect most of my head. And I was wearing tough leather gloves. Without his car, he was much diminished. Plan B consisted of standing on tiptoe and yelling up into my face. But I had the advantage also in the verbal battle. Most of his obscenities were lost on me, and he knew it. Mandarin can be quite difficult, when the other person fails to speak calmly. I understood "You take off your pants to fart!" and "You scratch your ass with six fingers!"—dangerous words reflecting on my intelligence. But the rest was just noise. My remarks were rather more clear to him. I began in Mandarin with the phrase "Your mother . . . ," then switched to English and expounded on his mother's habit of greeting every troop train that rolls into town, the uncertainty of his parentage, and the possibility that *I* was his father. The English language lends considerable scope to tones of derision. What he heard was my expressive tone and the repeated Mandarin phrase "Your mother. . . ." He became delirious with rage, but he could neither attack nor retreat, and he was starting to shiver from the biting wind.

Eventually the VIP behind the smoked windows decided that we must all move on with our lives. This decision became manifest when his bodyguard emerged from the front passenger door. The bodyguard was large. His shoulders were broad. He wore an expensive suit that flattered his muscular physique. He straightened his suitcoat to reveal a bulge over his left breast. He remained standing beside the passenger door, leaving the car between him and me, but he smiled at me strangely. At once Lee Ming came up and grabbed my arm. Being a prudent man at heart, I allowed her to lead me away. The driver suddenly had a verbal target who could understand him. He trailed after us across the street and down the sidewalk for fifty yards, shouting at Lee Ming, but abandoning his passenger. Lee Ming shouted back. But now the driver was thoroughly cold. He could not continue. His parting shot at Lee Ming was, "Don't think you're so important just because you're with a foreigner!"

Lee Ming and I continued walking and lost ourselves in the crowd. We calmed down and once more became aware of our appetites. Lee Ming selected a restaurant, we entered, and the waitress pointed to a table by the window.

The waitress was in a bad mood. She scolded the people seated next to us. Lee Ming translated for me. Our neighbors had ordered too little food. "If I had known you would be so stingy," said the waitress, "I wouldn't have seated you at the good table!" She flounced off to the kitchen with their order.

Presently she returned to wait on us. Lee Ming ordered soup and then selected three other dishes. "Maybe that's too much," I said to her in English. Lee Ming gave me a noncommittal look. In Mandarin I said to the waitress, "No soup. We don't want the soup."

"Soup is good for you on a cold day like this!" said the waitress with decision, and turned away just too late to hide her naughty grin.

In our world, the unexpected has lightness. We make the motions of swimming, but sometimes the living sea around us carries us in its own unrevealed directions.

Part Four

WE THE ADDICTED

The Waiter
Brings Linguini

Imagine yourself as a rustic, hardscrabble, honest cowboy. You've just finished a long and exhausting cattle drive. For ten weeks on the trail, you've eaten beans and cornbread out of a tin plate. You decide to reward yourself with your first visit to the big city. You arrive, get a bath and a shave and a haircut, and buy a new suit of clothes. Then you make a beeline for the fanciest restaurant in town. Unfamiliar with the etiquette, you walk up to the first waiter you see, slap him on the back, call him "pardner," and demand a big juicy steak and a pitcher of cold beer. He smiles strangely and says nothing. When he returns, he brings you a bottle of fine Chianti and a plate of delicious linguini. You feel disappointed and disoriented. "What the hell is this crap?" you say. You work hard bringing steak to other people. You deserve to have steak yourself if you want it. But the waiter refuses to bring it.

Ambition in the Big Universe

Our most sublime moments take us by surprise. Those moments we cannot anticipate, desire, or imagine in advance. They lie outside our hopes and outside our ambitions.

And yet, we inhabit a world quite ruthless. The stories you may have heard, that our universe is *indifferent* to our happiness, are a myth. Our universe in fact defeats every form of our happiness. It crushes us completely. It crushes us without compassion and without justice. Nothing and no one we care about survives. In some ways we knew all along that nothing would survive.

By kicking us around and killing us off, the universe achieves a paradoxical result. Good and evil still measure each other. They still balance in our perception. We end up with exactly the same ratio of delight to despair. But our world varies the style of our delight from what we strive to have.

This world toys with our ambitions, keeps them elusive, and finally defeats them all. And there lies its opportunity. We cannot feel our defeat unless defeat has a counterweight. The world does better than honor our plodding hopes and dreams. It clears them away, and gives us instead the ineffable and the sublime. Our best moments take us by surprise.

This tactic fails to give us a better proportion of happiness to unhappiness. But it does give us lives more subtle. With malignant denial and unexpected grace, the world does better than honor our hopes and dreams.

Defeated ambition cannot have a counterweight, unless we do have ambition. This world entices us to strive, explore, and build, even as it finally sweeps away everything we achieve.

Whatever we achieve, we are doomed anyway. For us, all is temporary. Sooner or later, in the cold wind blowing from the future, our footsteps disappear.

How does the world keep us ambitious, while systematically denying our ambition?

The short answer: The world addicts us. One way or another, we want to act, to play the addicting game of being alive. To the phenomenon of What happens next? we are made addicts. This world as Siren lures us on. One way or another, despite the bones littered all over the beach, we mostly want to go forward. We want to know how our ambitions feel as reality. And we want to know all the more, as the world withholds them.

Surely the most sublime works of the human spirit bear the marks of our misery.

Most of us want to find goodness and hope in the world. Most of us feel, and need to feel, some sort of optimism in that direction.

Must the human race really be doomed to its present level of happiness? We do have bright hopes to the contrary. Perhaps we are an adolescent civilization, pimply and awkward and still full of doubts. We may yet reach maturity. Perhaps we can steadily raise our consciousness in pursuit of a just society. Perhaps our ingenuity and creativity, our science and technology, wisely pursued and harnessed, will yet master the challenge of this daunting universe, bring our planet under our control, give us command over information and resources, construct adjuncts to our intelligence, illuminate our nagging problems, overcome poverty and despair, illuminate and overcome our own demons, strengthen our bodies, begin to conquer death itself, bring us closer to immortal gods than to squabbling jungle primates. Must we really be doomed among all these legitimate aspirations? Perhaps we can genuinely change the human condition. Let us rise up, if we can. Let us diminish chaos and replace it with order, if we can. Let us find our way out of darkness, if we can.

We have bright hopes indeed. The Siren calls to us.

We are agents who rise far above mere calculation. We perceive the world as a detailed, coherent, fluid balance. For us, heaven and hell are never to be sundered. If we build a new heaven, we build also a new hell.

To keep us interested, the universe surprises us. The new hells that tag along with our new heavens, often take us by surprise. The world can astonish us with its grace *and* with its malignance. We are made thorough addicts to What happens next? Fifty percent of our experience must fall below average, but *how* it falls above or below average, intrigues us.

Surprising experience relates directly to the world's lightness: to its elusive, high quality randomness. Sometimes our plans have unexpected outcomes. The root cause is randomness in the world. We find quite a lot of randomness in the world.

When we say that an event is "random," we usually just mean that it has labyrinthine causes. In that sense, events are "random" because their convoluted causes defy our powers of prediction. But outside our powers of prediction, each detail has exact causes. Randomness is constructed.

When we produce randomness ourselves, we execute an all-inclusive procedure. To inhabit your orderly game of solitaire with randomness, you shuffle the deck. You inhabit the orderly game with uncertainty, surprise, risk, challenge, by generating randomness, by shuffling the deck, by introducing a convoluted causation into each turn of the card. Your game becomes a mixture of order and chaos. Each turn of the card still has a precise causation, but the causes become so tortuous that you cannot follow them. Hence randomness. What we call "random" and "accidental" in solitaire are really just events with convoluted causes. And so it is with our world.

The randomness in solitaire relates to the predicaments of solitaire. The randomness in solitaire has exact and deliberate causes. All your games of solitaire are alike and all are different. Merely by shuffling fifty-two cards for thirty seconds, you make a particular game different from any other you play.

In solitaire, shuffling the deck shows up in every detail of the game. And so it is with our world.

At last report, this universe is 13.7 billion years old, it has 250 billion galaxies or more, and just the tip of your finger—one tiny piece of just one galaxy—already has at least a trillion billion parts. For a very long time our world has shuffled a very, very large number of cards. With new eyes we can watch this immense and terrible engine of randomness. We can watch the shuffling that infuses our lives with high quality randomness. At least some of it we can watch.

The randomizing begins as the whole universe, we are told, explodes from one tiny point. Three hundred thousand years later, the roiled discharge explodes again. Hydrogen atoms precipitate. Giant hydrogen gas clouds condense. Asymmetries grow; the giant clouds have different sizes and they move in different directions. Idiosyncratic galaxies emerge, spin, generate tides, and collide. These events compress gases together. Stars are born. They burn and ferment heavier elements. They explode. Clouds condense again. New stars are born. Planets evolve with the differently weighted elements mixed into them. A few of the planets happen to be biologically viable—as if the universe threw dice and sometimes got lucky. Such planets emerge as complex coherent structures with high idiosyncrasy. On Planet Earth, this mixture of structure and idiosyncrasy forms a matrix for our long biological evolution. This mixture governs the daily lives of the species evolving. It produces varied and changing habitats. It produces unique but coherent survival strategies with wide variation among species—and considerable variation among individuals of the same species. Our planet's structure-with-idiosyncrasy gets reflected in biological evolution. It gets reflected in our own human personalities. It relates to a certain balance in our experience, where we know what will happen each day and we do not know. And meanwhile, tides and currents operate, climates change, continents drift and buckle, mountains rise and wear away, rivers ramble, cataclysmic meteors fall, calamitous volcanoes erupt, glaciers advance and retreat, elements bubble and cool, bits of DNA couple and uncouple, creatures live and die, eat and breathe, wander all about—the shuffling goes on and on and on. The coherent biological structures become more complicated yet remain highly idiosyncratic. The universe infuses our daily lives with high quality randomness. The universe brews its smooth addicting whiskey.

Unlike solitaire, the game and the shuffling sometimes occur together. Sometimes they are the same. And at times one card changes into another card, so to speak; hydrogen can change into helium. But you get the idea. The size and age of the universe, its evolution by physical law, corresponds to a fantastically enormous reservoir of randomness—with you and me and everyone else swimming in the reservoir.

This randomness is the power the universe holds over us, its power to turn our lives into directions that *we* cannot predict, its power to disguise itself as elusive not-patterns. The world's giant evolution, starting with the Big Bang, makes our lives unpredictable. Events in our lives have convoluted causes. Like the simple game of solitaire, we have both order and chaos in our lives. Our universe makes mountains, thunderstorms, sunsets, stars, trees, and humans. It creates those orderly structures. But the structures have randomness of high quality. No two mountains are the same. No two sunsets. No two human beings. All sunsets are the same and all sunsets are different. No matter how thoroughly I understand the orderly physical laws and preconditions that cause sunsets, no matter how many sunsets I have already watched, I cannot know the next sunset. The next sunset, the next turn of the card, will still be new to me. No matter how thoroughly we manage the processes and preconditions that lead to the Internet, no matter how much experience we have with it, we cannot know who will use it tomorrow, what information they will exchange, how they will react to that information, who will make or lose how much money, what will influence the Internet's evolution, what forms it will take in the future, how much future it has. The Internet may knit us together and it may spread anarchy and it may have more unforeseeable effects on our lives. We know what will happen on the Internet tomorrow and we do not know. We know what it will become and we do not know. We know how the information exchanged will affect us and we do not know. We shape the Internet and it shapes us.

By constructing the Internet, we add structure to the world.

But the structures we add expand the domain of unpredictability, of randomness, of chaos, in our lives. Like many of our technologies and games, the Internet brings order and it brings chaos. Many of our own creations and initiatives exhibit the world's mixture of order and chaos, a mixture balanced in careful detail by the world's big evolution. Our own lives exhibit that balance.

The benefits of the Internet are more visible than its darker implications. That fact is part of our addiction.

The Internet cannot cause delight only. Despair must balance delight. We shape the Internet and it shapes us. The Internet expands and complicates the domain of randomness in our lives. It brings new order and new chaos. It gives callous randomness more power over us. It gives unforeseen scope to our own idiosyncratic demons. Along with all its delights, the Internet breeds new forms of jealousy, treachery, isolation, new ways to lose money, new ways to feel alienated, new ways to be dissatisfied, new ways to hate, new ways to be ambushed, new ways for our plans to fail. Along with delight, the Internet brings new forms of despair, sometimes in unpredictable, indirect, and insidious ways—in complicated ways hidden from our first inspection.

The universe has enough randomness to inhabit and render unpredictable every game played within it—unpredictable to *us*. We ourselves are permeated by randomness and idiosyncrasy. How can we find our way out of darkness? Randomness inhabits our initiatives in the world. As our control and our technologies grow increasingly powerful, skillful, and complete, the consequences grow increasingly unpredictable. Far from diminishing chaos, we devise ever bigger sponges to soak it up.

The vast reservoir of randomness flows into our own creations. Always we will be children swimming in thousand-foot waters.

And indeed, if we become gods, if we overcome pain, disease, injury, decay, and death, if we gain control over all the world, if we wrestle with our own demons and successfully contain them, we will then discover some unexpected way to lose our souls, some relentless new form of darkness, some new and more terrible power of randomness to bend and break us. Such is the structure of the world.

What we value must be uncertain and transient. That fact the world accommodates. It gives, but it also takes away. We humans become *passionate* about justice, virtue, beauty, truth, happiness, life—passionate in the knowledge that these can be withheld, they can elude us, we seek and do not faithfully find, hauntingly they appear and disappear in the flickering engine of randomness. Our predicament animates us. This universe subtly inconstant, disturbs us and motivates us. We build our fortresses to escape for a time, but all of them at last flicker into nothing.

One of our fortresses: we strive to know a beauty and a truth, a justice and a virtue, independent of all material random things, a light that shines steadfastly. But our world defeats us. The knowledge itself flickers, it is lost and found, clear and obscure, it has unexpected consequences, we who view the most steadfast light remain impermanent and fickle. If not the light then the viewer remains caught in the flickering machine, and therefore the most steadfast light still gutters and struggles in this world and finally extinguishes to nothing.

We ourselves are cogs in the flickering machine, temporary but important cogs, strategic cogs. We are key components of the games we play and the games the world plays with us. If we struggle inside the massive random machine, seek to gain control, seek to understand, seek happiness, seek peace, seek in any way, if we want or care about anything, we have predicament. Predicament feeds caring, and caring feeds predicament. We and our world are made for each other. This universe as indomitable engine of randomness, its giant size and age ingeniously deployed, inhabits every facet of our ambition.

Like a skillful matador, the world inflames our desires while it destroys us. We go forward toward our aspiration, only to find it changed into something else.

We cannot feel our defeat, unless defeat has a counterweight. Many people, from time to time, do feel *strangely* glad to be alive. With malignant denial, with unexpected grace, our world does better than honor our incoherent ideals and our banal wishes. The waiter brings linguini.

To keep the progression of ideas orderly, don't you know, I have left something out. Now would be a good time to put it back in.

I have been talking about physical evolution, from the Big Bang to people, as if this evolution explains why we exist. It does not. It fails to account for consciousness and free will—a fact that worries many philosophers. The Big Bang also fails to explain why our world has a Big Bang. And the Big Bang fails to account for another phenomenon. I'm going to tell you about it.

Our world gives us a fine marriage between elusiveness and order: high quality randomness and idiosyncrasy, within an intelligible system of complex patterns. In our daily lives, this elegant marriage has a number of manifestations. For example:

Mountains, thunderstorms, sunsets, stars, trees, and humans are each alike and each unique.

Our satisfactions are profoundly diverse yet profoundly commensurate.

Events for us are expected and unexpected, intelligible and surprising, orderly and random.

We explore our world not as a flat painting, but as a landscape with expandable dimensions.

We control events and events control us.

The world keeps our ambitions enticing but slippery.

No particular approach to life has unmixed success.

The world does better than honor our banal wishes.

We make the motions of swimming, but the living sea around us carries us in its own unrevealed directions.

Physical evolution from the Big Bang to people, cannot account for this felicitous system of interconnected balances. Ingenious as they are, the Big Bang and physical law remain a blunt instrument. But the system of balances seems to be fine-tuned. Very fine-tuned.

Apparently we have in our lives, not just any randomness, but a randomness that does a good job of being elusive, *in just the right ways* for subtle experience. That cannot happen simply because a Big Bang happens.

Understanding a highly coherent physical law and a highly coherent physical evolution, connects together a lot of dots for us. In manifold ways, the Big Bang illuminates our world and our selves. In particular, as we have seen, it does give us useful perspective on balances and idiosyncrasies, on the marriage of order and elusiveness we experience. It gives us perspective—but not a reason why.

The fact of our Big Bang fails to explain why our world has one. In the realm of logical possibility, people could have existed just fine without evolving from anything. Moreover, the Big Bang evolution accounts for neither consciousness, nor free will, nor the ineffable moments that take us by surprise. Physical law and physical evolution illuminate our lives without explaining why we have them.

The section "Moral Responsibility" (p. 265) talks about how free will relates to physical law. In that section, the logic of explanation itself, identifies the reason why we all exist and why we have a Big Bang. But that comes later.

So far, you and I have examined what humans are: ambitious agents, making fluid comparisons, in a structured world, with elusive randomness.

Now we are ready to find the direction to perfection: *who decides* which possible world is the best world, and what is it they decide.

Opinions and Spiders

T his is the key chapter. This chapter gathers up what came before, and it foreshadows what comes after.

Go slow. Pace up and down if you need to. After this, the rest is easy, and a lot more personal.

This book addresses two main issues:

(1) What ought to exist? What would be the best possible state of existence?

(2) What evidence do you and I have, that what ought to exist does exist?

So far we have talked mostly about (2). In this chapter we talk mostly about (1).

We are ready to identify "the best possible world." We are ready to figure out *who decides* which world is best and what they decide.

EXECUTIVE SUMMARY

The best possible world is what *people* want. What machines want doesn't count.

In a significant sense, all the people agree on the best world.

They have an implicit but united opinion. All possible variations on people, existing or not existing, residents of the actual world or residents of any possible alternative to the actual world—all the people point to the same unique possible world as best.

DELUXE EXECUTIVE SUMMARY

The realm of logical possibility contains a great many alternatives to the actual world. And the alternate worlds contain a great many alternatives to actual agents.

Actual and possible agents include dogs, dolphins, spiders, bees, dinosaurs, fish, chess-playing computers, you and me, all the cats and humans who were ever born or ever will be born, all the cats and humans that might have existed but never will, little green aliens who might have existed but never will, intelligent centipedes a mile long who maybe exist somewhere and maybe don't—all the agents who populate this world or any other possible world. Those are the agents actual and possible. They are infinitely numerous.

Despite their numbers, all the agents actual and possible divide into just two kinds: subtle agents and spider-style agents.

The best possible world is what subtle agents want. *All* the subtle agents, actual and possible.

On the other hand, what spider-style agents want doesn't count.

Subtle agents mostly use comparisons to interpret their experience. You and I are subtle agents. We sometimes view certain people as short, by comparison to certain other people who are tall. Some people we might consider friendly, by comparison to other people less friendly. Some animals might be hairy, by comparison to animals less hairy. If you walk two miles to your job every day, while most people walk ten miles, then you might regard your commute as short. But if most people walk only one block to work, then you might see the same commute as long. If most people are starving, you might be happy to eat peanuts. If most people have a smorgasbord, you might be unhappy eating the same peanuts. You and I often use comparisons to interpret our experience and measure our satisfactions.

Chimps, cats, and dolphins are subtle agents also. They also use comparisons to interpret their experience. A cat might turn up his nose at kibble, if he usually gets herring or salmon. The cat regards the kibble as substandard, because the cat makes comparisons.

An agent is a subtle agent if he uses fluid comparisons to interpret his world.

Otherwise, the agent is mere machine, mere calculation, like a spider. What spiders want in a world, doesn't count.

(By "spider" I mean any agent who is not a subtle agent. For example, an ant is quite probably a spider. As it happens, I believe that the eight-legged, fly-catching critters on our planet are spider-style agents in that sense. Sometimes I will use such critters as a metaphor for all spiders.)

Spider-style agents are quite different from you and me. If a spider has an adequate web and an adequate number of flies to eat, then he's happy—even if all his neighbor spiders have larger webs and many more flies to eat.

If a spider has a nice big web, he doesn't pity another spider with a smaller web. Spiders make only limited use of comparisons to interpret their experience.

A subtle agent can be bored. If a subtle agent eats exactly the same food at every meal every day, he might get fed up with the monotony. A subtle agent might compare today's meal to yesterday's and the day before and the day before that. But if a spider eats exactly the same food at every meal every day, he will never get bored. For the spider, yesterday's meal and today's don't compare in that way.

A spider feels his satisfactions mostly independent of comparisons. He doesn't use fluid comparisons to interpret his world.

Any possible agent in any possible world, must be either subtle or spider. Either an agent interprets his experience by making fluid comparisons, or he doesn't. No third alternative obtains.

Spiders have no opinions about which of all possible worlds is the best. They don't make enough comparisons to have an opinion or imply an opinion.

By contrast, subtle agents do make enough comparison; they always have an *implicit* opinion that more subtle worlds are better than less subtle worlds. I'm not talking about opinions they articulate. I doubt we could persuade a dog to tell us which possible world betters all the others. But a subtle agent always has standards of good experience, those standards involve comparisons, and those standards always imply that some possible worlds compare favorably to others.

One way or another, a subtle agent makes fluid comparisons. How he makes comparisons, how he finds one experience better than another, always implies that some possible worlds *compare* favorably to others. The implication can be feeble or strong, depending on how subtle the agent is. But the implication is always there.

Subtle agents actual and possible, decide which world is best. The subtle agents decide what ought to exist. What spiders want doesn't count.

Subtle agents actual and possible, all of them, have a unanimous consensus as to which world is best. We will examine their consensus shortly. The consensus points to exactly one particular world. That's the world that ought to exist.

And what all the subtle agents want, they get. What ought to exist, does exist.

Those are my claims. That was the summary. Now let's travel over the same ground again, this time more slowly.

BEST IN WHOSE OPINION?

When I assert "Our world is the best possible," you might respond, "Best in whose opinion?"

That's a fair question. If you and I interviewed people on the street, and asked their *explicit* opinions about what the best possible world would be, they would surely disagree with each other.

Suppose you and I gave a particular description of our universe to various human beings of our acquaintance, and suppose they thought about that description and found it persuasive, and mostly they concurred that our own universe is the best possible world. Then maybe we could claim that our world is best in human opinion. But what about nonhuman opinion? Maybe the Andromeda Galaxy has nonhuman inhabitants who disagree with us, or don't even understand us.

Even worse, maybe *alternate possible worlds* have inhabitants who think *their* world is best. We like our world best, but they like their world best. Then how does our world have a better claim than theirs, to the title Best Possible?

In light of such questions, I need to establish these propositions: A unique possible world receives the *implicit* endorsement of *every* possible subtle agent in every possible world. The people agree, all of them, actual and possible.

Their *unanimous* opinion mandates a unique world as the best world.

TWO KINDS OF AGENT

When you and I figure out which world ought to exist, we need consult only the opinions of subtle agents. Only the subtle agents have relevant opinions.

All possible agents divide into two fundamental kinds, subtle and spider. Let's talk about the difference.

We humans are beings who make comparisons—lots of comparisons. We compare the comparisons, and compare those comparisons.

Alternatives to human agency, alternatives actual and possible, also make fluid comparisons—not in the idiosyncratic human style, but nonetheless mutable and fluid like our comparisons.

Another kind of agent fails to make comparisons as we do. Ants and spiders, for example. They have a hierarchy of satisfactions of different sizes and they pursue them in the order indicated. An ant considers fighting an intruder more important than finding food. But an ant does not feel the satisfaction, "I found more food than any other ant."

A spider has work to do and accordingly he performs. If a piece of his web gets destroyed, he does not feel unjustly persecuted in a cruel world. That feeling involves too many comparisons. Nor does he view his various options as vicious or virtuous. Again, too many comparisons required. The spider bypasses those complications. He just goes out and fixes the web, or defends it, or moves his operations elsewhere, as his programming indicates.

A spider feels the satisfaction of a full stomach. But a spider does *not* feel satisfactions like these: "My stomach is fuller today than yesterday. My stomach is fuller than my neighbor's stomach. As I grow older, I am getting more skillful at filling my stomach. Compared to me, my neighbor spiders are a disgrace to the race of spiders." Those satisfactions involve too many comparisons. A spider does not know or does not care that he could make those comparisons.

A spider makes too few comparisons to pity another spider. A spider makes too few comparisons to pity an alternate possible world. About the best of all possible worlds, a spider has no opinion.

We are beginning to sort out *in whose opinion* the best possible world is best.

SATISFACTIONS ABSOLUTE AND VARIABLE

For agents like us, who make lots of comparisons, almost all satisfactions have "variable size." The satisfaction of eating peanuts has "variable size." If most people eat a variety of tasty food every day, you might feel unfortunate to have only peanuts. If most people starve, you might feel fortunate to have exactly the same peanuts. In virtue of the comparisons you happen to make, in your own idiosyncratic style, your eating peanuts has "variable size," somewhere between enormous satisfaction and abject discontent. Indeed, you might feel satisfaction one moment and dis-content the next moment—with the same peanuts—as your com-parisons suddenly change.

By contrast, a spider mostly has satisfactions of "absolute size." A spider with a stomach completely full, feels a contentment of fixed size. He always feels pretty much the same degree of con-tentment, whenever his stomach is completely full. A spider does not modify that contentment, by caring how his stomach today compares to yesterday's stomach, or to another spider's stomach. Enjoying his full stomach, he does not suddenly feel regret for the starvation days of his youth. The satisfaction of a full stomach, or the dissatisfaction of an empty stomach, he does not modify by feeling envy, pity, pride, disappointment, gratitude to a deity, out-rage at the world's injustice, embarrassment that a fellow spider can't catch a fly, or some other comparison even more idiosyn-cratic. A spider does not link together the *three* different compar-isons in this satisfaction: "My skill at filling my stomach has increased with maturity." Spiders give size to their satisfactions in simple ways. They fail to use the perspective of comparative size that we humans use.

In that sense, spiders have simpler emotions than we have. Spider-style agents lack one of the dimensions of our agency. They make insufficient comparisons, to feel the "variable" emotions that we feel. For an agent like us, numerous comparisons he hap-pens to make, can radically alter the sizes of perceived goods and evils, even from moment to moment, and sometimes in highly idiosyncratic ways. Goods and evils, always and constantly sizing each other, become interrelated, complex, idiosyncratic, mutable, and fluid. But a spider feels simpler, "disassociated" goods and evils of more rigid size.

Consequently, spider-style standards of goodness also suffer from "disassociation." A spider who cannot pity another spider, also cannot pity an alternate possible world. He cannot make that comparison. A spider's manner of sizing goods and evils, does imply *his own* best possible experience: a big web, plenty of flies, lots of offspring, and so on. But many significant possible worlds have experience other than his own experience. For the spider, those worlds are mutually incommensurable. A spider's standards of goodness make no implications like this: a world containing only dolphins betters a world containing only mice.

A spider's standards, based insufficiently on comparisons, cannot point to one possible world as better than all the others. But agents like us have standards that do use sufficient comparisons: Our standards imply a commensurability among different agents' experience and among possible worlds. Where a spider mostly views his experience in "disassociated" ways, we view experience as having commensurabilities.

SPIDERS CAN GO TO HEAVEN

In the game of deciding which possible world is the best, spider-style agents have two disadvantages. They have no opinion about the best possible world. And agents like us, who do have opinions, assign no value to their satisfactions! In our opinion, spider-style satisfactions add no value to a possible world. Thus:

Suppose you overcome your personal computer at chess and it groans in despair. Or suppose an automobile says to you, "Please step away from the vehicle," and then expresses satisfaction by saying, "Thank you." An automobile can have that gratification over and over throughout eternity, and never tire of it. But the automobile and your personal computer and the Mars Rover are spider-style agents. They lack one of the dimensions of agency like ours. The lights are on but no one's home, as it were. The rigid absolute satisfactions they "feel" fail to count toward the value of any possible world.

A subtle agent may have her reasons for valuing, in a sense, the satisfactions of a spider. If you own a fine automobile, that asks intruders to "Please step away from the vehicle," you may want your machine to be happy. But you are really valuing your own satisfactions, not the machine's. Likewise, if you happen to like big, symmetrical spider webs, then you may want a spider to be happy. Again the value actually lies in *your* satisfaction, not the spider's. If not explicitly, then by implication, your standards of goodness actually assign zero value to a spider's satisfactions.

Spiders do have one advantage over agents like us. All spiders could have been happy all the time. They can go to heaven. Let a spider have for all eternity, a big symmetrical web, plenty of flies, no predators, lots of offspring—and he knows only happiness forever. His satisfactions having rigid size, endless repetition cannot diminish them. Indeed, an efficient spider does not care whether sunsets are alike or different. If every web he spins and every fly he catches and every spider offspring he produces, are the identical twins of all his other webs and all his other flies and all his other spider offspring, he can nonetheless continue supremely happy throughout eternity. A chess-playing spider might feel increasingly satisfied as he wins exactly the same game of chess again and again and again. Even if he views his experience as a single satisfying episode looping over and over into the past and the future, with endless repetition and absolutely no variation, a spider can still accumulate happiness throughout eternity. A spider is an agent, but very different from you and me. In our opinion, his satisfactions have no value. Not even the satisfactions of a very complicated and intelligent spider have value. They are mere calculation toward some efficiency. A spider can go to heaven precisely because he makes insufficient comparisons to recognize cardinal forms of hell.

By contrast, no possible agent like us, no matter what his circumstances, can avoid unhappiness. Agents like us can only have *comparative* satisfaction. For us, repetitive bliss gets old. As soon as we ascend to any heaven, it starts falling apart. Even the best possible world must have misery and evils. As discussed later in "The Measure of Good and Evil" (p. 156) and "Fiction" (p. 150), at least fifty percent of our collective experience must fall below average, and no more than fifty percent above—no matter what world we occupy.

"SUBTLE AGENTS" ARE DOOMED

Agents like us, who make so many comparisons that their satisfactions mostly have variable size, I will call "subtle agents." I give them that name, because their comparisons and variable satisfactions open the door to subtle experience. A skillful world can exploit their ability to make comparisons, and give them subtle experience.

Subtle agents are doomed. Because we make so many comparisons, our goods and evils size each other and balance. Everything we enjoy, must be erased. If we could enjoy eternal bliss as spiders do, we would no longer be us. We would no longer be subtle agents. We would descend to mere machine.

ANY POSSIBLE AGENT IS SUBTLE OR SPIDER

By the law of the excluded middle, agents must be either subtle or spider-style. For *any possible agent*, either the satisfactions he perceives are mostly absolute or mostly variable. Either they give size to each other by comparison, or they don't. Either that mutual sizing is sufficient to reach fluid balance, or it is not. If an agent perceives satisfactions in his world as having size by sufficient mutual comparison, then he has subtle agency. If not, he has spider-style agency. No third alternative can obtain.

THE BOUNDARY

Any possible agent must be either subtle or spider-style. But some agents seem difficult to classify.

Once I owned a fish who interested me strangely. This fish seemed to conduct his life with just a touch more subtle free will than a spider does. For several weeks he was the biggest fish in my fish tank. He coexisted peaceably with the smaller fish. Then, in my ignorance, I introduced a baby fish of the same species and the same sex. When the newcomer grew almost to the same size, he and the older fish began to fight. At times they locked jaws together for two or three seconds, as if kissing hard. After several encounters, the older fish seemed to avoid the newcomer. But now the older fish sometimes harassed various smaller fish, not of his own species. He became a bully. Was he simply satisfying a need for aggression triggered by a male of his own species? Or did he choose to create a comparison that might give him satisfaction?— "I'm still a big fish." Or both? To what extent did this fish have satisfactions of relative size? Did scaring the little fish gain importance for him because he compared his former status to his new status?

Perhaps so. After the two big fish stopped fighting, only the *former* top fish harassed other species. The new top fish—of the same species and the same sex—persecuted no one. Possible explanation: the two fish made different comparisons. The new top fish was satisfied with his status. He made a positive comparison to the past. The dethroned fish made a negative comparison to the past, and developed a personality disorder.

On the continuum, the fish who became a bully, seems to fall near the boundary between spiders and subtle agents. Whether his satisfactions mostly had size by comparison, or mostly had rigid size, was murky.

Perhaps the crucial test would be: Could the fish become bored with his experience? If he can, then his present satisfactions have fluid size by comparison to the past. His satisfactions move far enough away from rigid size, that he escapes being a spider. Just barely, he is one of us.

And if he can be bored, then he wants his experience to be sometimes new and different, under the comparisons he makes. Just barely, quite vaguely, the fish can perceive subtlety in experience, and he likes it. Although he cannot say so, he has a standard of goodness vaguely implying that subtle experience betters unsubtle experience.

The boundary between spiders and subtle agents, is also the boundary where standards of goodness start to imply a best among all possible worlds. Sufficient sizing of satisfactions by comparing them, (a) makes an agent subtle, (b) bars him from heaven, and (c) implies a commensurability among possible worlds. Thus, all and only subtle agents have implicit opinions about the best possible world.

"Sufficient sizing of satisfactions by comparing them," does not yet reveal the inner nature of any particular high quality subtle agency. The phrase "sufficient sizing" contains entire worlds. How do the satisfactions differ from each other? In what manner do they all remain commensurable for the agent? How are they actual and fictional, remembered and forgotten, expected and unexpected, imagined and not imagined? For any particular high quality subtle agency, we cannot list all the specifications. If we could, that agency would not be especially subtle.

But we do understand differences between all spider-style agents and all subtle agents. Spiders perceive goods and evils that mostly do not size each other. A spider cannot compare another spider's fortunes to his own. In the best-possible-world equation, a spider drops out at two points: He doesn't value anyone else's satisfactions, and no one else values his satisfactions. Not only do all the other possible spiders disvalue him, but all possible subtle beings also implicitly disvalue him.

THE UNITED OPINION OF ALL POSSIBLE SUBTLE AGENTS

All *subtle* agents, actual and possible, have an implicit but united opinion, that the most subtle possible world is the best possible world.

To show this unity among all the implicit opinions of subtle agents, we start with human opinion.

Humans have an addiction to subtle experience. One way or another, we are all addicted to finding out, What happens next?

Imagine a human playing an absorbing video game. Sometimes she shoots down the space pirates, and sometimes the space pirates shoot her down. Sometimes she gets a high score, sometimes a low score. Goods and evils are balanced for her within the game.

But she also feels another good. Sometimes she wins, sometimes she loses, but all the while *she wants to keep playing*. She feels a form of addiction to the game. She might say, "I like this video game. It's seldom boring, and often exciting." When playing the game, she feels an addiction to What happens next?

In a similar way, we humans feel addicted to What happens next? in our lives. Sometimes life is good, sometimes not so good, but all the while we mostly want to keep playing, to keep participating. We want to discover how events turn out. The subtle surprise and mystery of our experience intrigues us. Most humans would be justified in saying, "Being alive is good. My life seldom gets too boring for endurance, and sometimes it gets interesting."

(When negotiating with God in Joe's Bar, Satan overlooks the value of high subtlety in our lives.)

When a human feels an addiction to a particular video game, we say she likes the game. In this case, addiction is liking.

When a human feels an addiction to being alive, she likes being alive. Again in this case, addiction is liking.

Our addiction constitutes an *implicit* assignation of value to the subtlety of experience. Our addiction implies that for humans, subtle experience is valuable experience.

Moreover, the human addiction implies that high subtlety betters low. Our addiction makes us restless when our experience becomes boring, lacking in variety, lacking in subtlety. When subtlety is low, we start to lose interest in our lives. Human standards of good experience implicitly assign higher value to higher subtlety.

As addicts to the subtlety of experience, humans perceive a *large* difference between high subtlety and low, ranging from high value to low value. You and I can see where that graph points: the highest subtlety has the highest value.

But *any* possible subtle agent feels addicted to its subtle experience, one way or another, if only because the agent can be bored.

And any possible subtle agent assigns higher value to higher subtlety, if only because the agent sometimes finds its experience interesting.

Humans perceive a *large* difference in value, between higher and lower subtlety in our experience. A mouse perceives a *smaller* difference between high subtlety and low, ranging only a short distance between higher value and low. You and I can see that where the mouse's graph points, has less definition. In that sense, the mouse's standards more feebly imply that the most subtle world is the best world.

Each possible subtle agent has an addictive preference for higher subtlety over low. Later I will tell you why that's true. The agent, if it can use language to think and speak, might explicitly deny that it prefers higher subtlety. Nonetheless, the agent still has a contrary implicit opinion, based on the nature of its addiction.

We might visualize a central proposition—higher subtlety always betters low—reflected incompletely in each possible subtle agent's addiction, like the imperfect reflections of a flame in many little mirrors. *You and I are able to judge* that each individual subtle agent's implicit preference for higher subtlety over low, does reflect the more general proposition that higher subtlety always betters low. You and I can make that judgment; all the individual implicit opinions reflect the same general proposition, in our human judgment. And that's the sense in which the opinions are unanimous and united. Each possible subtle agent's standards of good experience, endorse feebly or strongly the principle that higher subtlety always betters low.

I'll say it another way. The *same* central proposition—higher subtlety always betters low—gets reflected in each possible subtle agent's addiction. Each individual's addiction differently instantiates the *same* proposition. You and I can judge that such is the case. And in that sense, the opinions are unanimous and united: higher subtlety always betters low. In our judgment, none of the addictions disagree. Each addiction agrees, feebly or strongly. We find an implicit but unanimous consensus, a united opinion, that higher subtlety always betters low.

If we discover that one possible state of existence would have higher subtlety than any of the others, then we find the state mandated by the united opinion, the state of existence that ought to obtain. The mandate will turn out to be just the most subtle world possible, alone and solitary. That's what ought to exist. That's the most subtle *and the best* possible state of existence.

Indeed, if one possible state of existence does in fact have higher subtlety than any of the others, then the united opinion points to *each and every specific detail* of that state. Even pigs and sheep point to all the details of that state, albeit feebly. Thus:

You and I know that the absolute highest subtlety—whatever that may be, *whatever the details*—is the most valuable subtlety, by human standards of good experience. Our addictions so inform us. In that manner, your addiction and mine shape the mandate in detail. The addictions of highly subtle agents shape the mandate; many or all of the higher addictions point to exactly the highest subtlety possible as the best state of existence. In particular, human addictions point to the most subtle world, whatever the details, as the best world.

Agents with lower subtlety, like mice and sheep, appear to have addictions less informative. Mouse and sheep addictions, being perhaps more limited, probably do not shape the consensus as ours do, but at least mice and sheep join the consensus. They concur with the consensus. Their addictions agree to some extent, feebly or strongly: Higher subtlety always betters low.

In consequence, the consensus is unanimous: The highest subtlety, in detail, is the best and most valuable. No one disagrees. Everyone agrees to some extent. And some of us agree all the way. The consensus is unanimous and specific.

(Indeed, consider the small minority of humans who wish to terminate their lives, on the grounds that their circumstances have become too dreary. Even they endorse the most subtle world as best. Such people no longer feel addicted to What happens next? They just want to check out. However, had their circumstances been more favorable, they would still want to be players in the world. Such people no longer feel addicted, but they were always addict*able*: they could be addicted under different circumstances. Their *potential* addiction to What happens next? already illuminates their implicit standards of good experience, which still point to the highest subtlety as best.

(For most humans, *actual* circumstances provoke and reveal our addictability. Actual circumstances, not hypothetical, reveal the human propensity toward addiction, and the human preference for high subtlety over low.)

In short, all the agents' standards, strongly or feebly, do imply that the most subtle world is best. In virtue of their respective addictions (or potential addictions) to the subtlety of their experience, all possible subtle agents agree or concur implicitly, that exactly the most subtle world possible is the best world. The agreement is implicit, and some agree more strongly than others, but to some extent they each agree. Hence their unanimous consensus, which I am calling "the united opinion."

That implicit but unanimous consensus among all possible subtle agents, determines what ought to exist: exactly the most subtle world possible.

The foregoing discussion of the united opinion, makes a number of assumptions, including these assumptions: (1) Subtlety is a coherent concept. (2) Subtle agents always prefer high subtlety to low. (3) As a subtle world with subtle inhabitants, one possible world actually does better all the others. And (4) the most subtle possible world alone, and not multiple worlds existing independently, constitutes the most subtle possible state of existence.

Those four assumptions and others, we will nail down toward book's end. "The United Opinion" chapter (p. 313) will talk about the united opinion again. Stay tuned.

Subtle agents have an implicit but unanimous opinion. Let's see what they do with it.

THE GHOSTLY CONVENTION

A spider assigns no value to another spider's satisfactions. He just does what his programming tells him to do. Nor do subtle agents assign value to spider satisfactions. A subtle agent's standards of good experience, imply that spider satisfactions have no value.

I'm still talking about *implicit* opinions. A human might think of her pet spider as a subtle agent when in fact it is not. She might say explicitly, "My spider gets lonely when I'm away." She may think of her spider as a little person. Nonetheless, she has an addiction to the subtlety of her experience, and the nature of her addiction implies that what her eight-legged pet actually does experience—the bare, straightforward imperatives of a machine, I believe—have in themselves no value for a world's subtle experience.

By their implicit opinions, subtle agents only value the satisfactions of other subtle agents having subtle experience. And that valuation implies a united opinion among subtle agents, that the most subtle world is best.

Now you and I know *in whose opinion* the "best" possible world is best. We might imagine a ghostly convention of all the possible agents who inhabit all possible worlds. They gather together to decide which world betters all the others. Each possible subtle agent, whether he knows it or not, has an opinion about which world is the best. His addictive preference for higher subtlety, implies an opinion. Accordingly, he has a pass to enter the convention auditorium, where the opinions confront each other. But none of the spider-style agents has an implicit opinion about higher or lower subtlety in a world. A spider's gratifications are too simple to imply even feebly that high subtlety in experience has value or does not have value. A black widow spider has standards of good experience implying the best state of existence for herself, but no standards implying the best state of existence for agents in general. Implicit human opinions do rank worlds. Spider opinions do not. Accordingly, none of the spiders can enter the auditorium. And inside that meeting chamber, none of the subtle agents value the satisfactions of spiders. They ignore what spiders want, and choose the best world for possible subtle agents.

The best world in the opinion of possible subtle agents, is just the world with the highest subtlety in its experience. All possible subtle agents have an implicit but united opinion, that said world ought to be the state of existence.

THE SOLE TOUCHSTONE OF GOODNESS

Why does the united opinion have so much importance? Exactly why do the implicit opinions of all the possible subtle inhabitants, constitute the sole touchstone of goodness for possible worlds and combinations of worlds?

Because the subtle inhabitants—and not the spider inhabitants—are the sole beneficiaries and victims of any possible state of existence.

Suppose a mysterious Supreme Being somehow supervises existence. Suppose this Being has sufficient efficacy to choose among possible worlds with people in them, and give existence to one or more such worlds. And suppose He operates upon some principle of selection different from the united opinion of all possible subtle agents. He omits to create *their* preferred state of existence, and enacts another instead.

Then He creates an inferior proportion between benefit and injury. He does a bad thing. He is officious.

No principle of goodness, preference, or selection can contravene the united opinion of all possible subtle agents, that the most subtle state of existence betters any other. The united opinion alone designates what ought to exist. It provides the sole and unique mandate for existence. No conflicting opinion has relevance, not even a mysterious Supreme Being's.

According to the united opinion, the "best" possible world can only be the most subtle possible: the world most felicitous to its inhabitants making fluid subtle comparisons.

We now understand the term, "the best possible world."

WHY THE MOST SUBTLE WORLD IS BEST

The unanimous opinion of all possible subtle agents—their united opinion—constitutes the sole touchstone of goodness for possible worlds. And by implicit but unanimous consensus, all possible subtle agents rank the most subtle world highest.

For subtle agents, only subtlety ranks worlds. The reason is simple: The quality of experience in a world improves if and only if the subtlety of experience improves. Therefore, the best world is just the world with the highest subtlety possible.

True, some subtle agents would like to rank the most beautiful world highest, or the world with the most justice, or the most satisfaction, or the most optimism, or the most virtuous inhabitants. But those subtle agents measure beauty, justice, satisfaction, optimism, and virtue, by comparing them to ugliness, injustice, dissatisfaction, pessimism, and viciousness—in the same world.

Within the *collection* of subtle agents in a world, beauty and virtue always have their counterparts, like shadows that follow them everywhere. If beauty increases, then the baseline references for sizing beauty, also increase. If virtue increases, then the baseline references for sizing virtue increase also. Beauty, virtue, satisfaction, and justice are always comparisons to ugliness, vice, dissatisfaction, and injustice in the same world. Beauty and virtue can never outrun their own shadows.

The relationship between valuable experience and *subtlety*, differs from the relationship between valuable experience and beauty, justice, satisfaction, grace, or virtue. When a subtle agent perceives beauty in a world, the agent perceives an element *within* a balance between good and bad. When the same agent has subtle experience, the subtlety is a property of the balance itself. Happiness and unhappiness must balance in a world, good and bad must balance in a world, but the balance itself can be less subtle or more subtle. If the balance is less subtle, the agent's experience has less value. If the balance is more subtle, the agent's experience has more value.

In a highly subtle world, a highly subtle *individual* has many, many ways to reach for higher quality in its experience. The subtle individual might try to win the lottery, or find love, or express its artistic nature, or solve the crossword puzzle, or go for a walk by the sea. Individuals have options.

But for the entire collection of agents in a world, experience can improve in only one way: it becomes more subtle. All the other improvements create their own balancing shadows. Consequently, in the implicit opinion of any subtle agent, subtlety alone ranks worlds.

Good reader, let's explore that conclusion. Let's get inside it and see what it looks like.

For the entire collection of subtle experience in a world, not all the experience can be happy. Half of it has to be unhappy. But all the experience can be subtle.

Suppose you and I pine for an alternate possible world, where *every* woman has physical beauty at least equal to Helen's of Troy. We find more beauty in that world than in our own. But if you and I lived out our entire lives in that alternate world, with beautiful women common as the air, we might not even notice Helen of Troy sitting right next to us in first period English. We would find her beauty neither unusual nor remarkable. Perhaps she would suffer the horrible disfigurement of one eyelash more than optimum. *As residents of the alternate world, we measure beauty by alternate comparisons.* Our baseline references shift to a new point of balance. Helen's beauty goes away. For us subtle agents, pining after a heaven and actually living in it, have that unfortunate difference.

Forty thousand years of human progress toward paradise, have raised our expectations about paradise. It recedes before us. But our strivings have fascinated us. Our lives today are at least very different than in Paleolithic times, and perhaps more subtle. We still have the same balance between goods and evils, but the goods and evils are new and different and perhaps more interesting. We have new comparisons to make. The tools and technologies and Life Lessons we build to grab happiness, affect our subtlety instead.

Indeed, precisely because our hopes and dreams are finally incoherent, and face defeat despite all our efforts, we can sometimes be exalted. The very incoherence of our struggle makes us receptive. And the best possible world takes advantage. Our most piercing satisfactions most completely surprise us. We cannot strive for them, nor expect them, nor hope for them, nor desire them, nor imagine in advance the forms they take. The best world does better than answer our pedestrian hopes and dreams. It gives us the surprising, and sometimes the ineffable. The best world gives us high subtlety.

Only subtlety ranks worlds. When a person improves our own world by adding virtue or laughter or beauty, the improvement does not appear in the perceived proportion of beauty to ugliness. Rather, the improvement appears in the subtlety of how beauty and ugliness are perceived. Thus, a world improves if and only if its subtlety improves, and only subtlety ranks worlds.

Suppose a sculptor in our world makes a beautiful, graceful statue. Now the plaster statuette in my kitchen seems a little less graceful by comparison. Grace and awkwardness still balance in my perception. But how they are perceived has changed. If the graceful statue improves the world, it does so by introducing new perceptions of beauty to its audience, thereby making their appreciations (and deprecations) more subtle.

If an artist in our world makes a beautiful statue, her creation subverts neither the perceived balance between good and bad nor the perceived balance between beauty and ugliness. However, her creation might very well change her particular audience, by causing them to perceive beauty (and ugliness) in a more subtle fashion. Moreover, her creation might inspire others to become artists, or to become art dealers, or art patrons, or to visit museums, or to make new friends, or to do something completely unexpected. A number of modern paintings, like Goya's series "The Disasters of War" and Picasso's "Guernica," have immense significance in politics and history. The artist's beautiful work does change the world's subtlety—but not its proportion of beauty to ugliness.

The subtle inhabitants of each possible world perceive in that world, balancing amounts of beauty and ugliness. By such perception within each world, a huge number of worlds all have the same and the highest possible proportion of perceived beauty—and of perceived virtue, justice, satisfaction, optimism, and so on. Those standards of goodness fail to rank worlds.

But the subtlety of experience has size independent of comparison to other subtlety. You and I do not give size to the subtlety of our lives by comparison to unsubtle lives. Yes, we do sometimes explicitly compare the subtlety of different experiences. And our standards of goodness imply that some experience has more subtlety than other experience, even when we do not or cannot actually make the comparison. But subtlety does not have size in virtue of those specific comparisons. Instead, our subtlety has its size in virtue of *all* the comparisons we make, whether or not the comparisons include comparisons to subtlety.

Some perceptions of beauty are more subtle than others, because some perceptions reverberate in subtle ways within the perceiver's interlocked matrix of comparisons. Beauty and ugliness still measure and give size to each other, but *how* they give size to each other can be more subtle or less subtle.

We often take the subtlety of our experience for granted, and neither strive for it, nor care explicitly what size it has, nor care explicitly that it obtains at all. In that respect, subtlety differs from happiness. We cannot be happy unless we know we are happy. We know by making comparisons. But our lives can be subtle whether or not we know they are subtle, and whether or not we actually compare that subtlety to alternatives. Even without comparison of one subtlety to another, all our other comparisons remain, and give size to our subtlety. A perception of beauty can be subtle, whether or not the perceiver knows it is subtle.

We don't understand subtlety well enough to strive for it in reliable ways. Will my life be more subtle if I travel, read books, meditate, run for political office, or take up mah-jongg? I don't know. Did my rough childhood drive me forward to some subtle perspective on good and evil? I don't know. The crucial details of my own subtlety, seem to dance both inside and outside my understanding. If they did not, my life could not be especially subtle.

We are fortunate that our lives have subtlety, however indistinctly we understand its particulars. Subtlety stands apart from the mutual measurement among all other goods and evils: Delight and despair must balance, but *the balance itself* can be simple or intricate, clumsy or subtle.

Thus, mice and humans have the same ratio of happiness to unhappiness. Both mice and humans struggle with their existence. For both species, the outcomes of their struggles are just as frequently unhappy as happy. But the elusive elements of human happiness, the diversity of our satisfactions, and the terms of our struggle for them, are far different than for mice. The outcome of struggle disappoints both mice and men, but the terms of human struggle are superior.

Indeed, a mouse's standards of goodness imply the superiority of human experience. Furthermore, as the human race might very well be less than the crown jewel of our universe, humans conceivably could meet an alien race whom we recognized as more subtle than ourselves.

The value of playing a video game is different from the good or bad fortune within the game. In a similar way, the value of human life we measure differently from good or bad fortune within our lives. A human life can go well or poorly, but our lives always have subtlety. The measure of subtlety stands outside the balances perceived by agents like us: agents who have opinions about the best world possible. Therefore, among the standards of goodness felt by nonspider agents, the standard of subtle experience does rank possible worlds, and picks out a best among them.

We can pine for a world more beautiful than ours. But the inhabitants of that world find *the same* proportion of beauty and ugliness, as we find in our world. The desire for beautiful experience, fails to rank worlds.

We can also pine for a world with subtlety different from our world. The inhabitants of that world would actually experience a *different* level of subtlety, than we do in our world. The implicit desire felt by all subtle agents, to have subtle experience, does rank possible worlds.

Only their subtlety ranks possible worlds. This fact raises the significance of *our* world's physical law, which well facilitates subtle experience.

The best possible world contains the collective experience with the highest collective subtlety. The best world is just the most subtle world. Not the most beautiful world, not the world with the most justice nor the most satisfaction nor the most optimism nor the most virtue—but the world with the highest subtlety. The proportion of beauty to ugliness, justice to injustice, delight to despair, virtue to viciousness—these are constant for subtle beings in any reasonably benign world. But the degree of subtlety does change from world to world. Therefore, the best world, the mandate of the united opinion, the world that ought to exist—is simply the most subtle world possible.

Now we know who decides which world ought to exist, and what they decide.

BLURRY VISION AND SHARP VISION

How do we know that our own universe is the most subtle world possible?

Human agents do have blurry vision about how individual experience is subtle. We understand the crucial details partway, but not all the way. In the actual world, subtlety consistently outclasses human understanding. It surprises us. It resists our manipulation. For each idiosyncratic human individual, for each idiosyncratic way each of us understands the world, experience has subtlety both inside and outside all expectation and all manipulation.

The Big Bang alone cannot account for this fine balance. The Big Bang is a blunt instrument.

If we each have blurry vision about subtlety, then what evidence do any of us have, that our universe is the most subtle possible world? What evidence shows that our world conforms to the united opinion?

We cannot inspect the details of all the lives in this universe, and recognize those lives as collectively the most subtle possible. For that kind of direct inspection, our information is incomplete and our vision blurry.

But we have other insights into subtle experience. First off, we can inspect how our universe systematically causes the *general* style of human subtlety. A long evolution, from the Big Bang to planets to people, pieces together human subtlety. We can watch the size and age of that evolution, its coherence, and its unified physical law, systematically constructing the *general* conditions of our own subtle lives—and dolphin subtle lives, and for all we know, subtle lives in the Andromeda Galaxy.

We do have blurry vision about how particular individual lives are subtle. But as you and I have already seen, we sometimes have sharp vision about the general properties of subtlety, and how our universe pieces together those properties.

Not the bare subtlety itself, but the *evolution* of subtlety, is the hard evidence for perfection in the world. You and I will examine direct and systematic causal connections between subtlety in human life, and ingenuity in the big evolution that fits our lives together. We have already done this, and we will do more.

Evolution from our Big Bang pieces together the general properties of agent subtlety, human and otherwise. Said evolution illuminates those general properties. Evolution reveals them as ingeniously felicitous to the making of fluid subtle comparisons. Hence the hard evidence for perfection in the world.

You and I will also look at a softer evidence for high subtlety in human life. Human subtlety transcends what evolution pieces together. Our best moments we cannot predict, strive to have, hope to have, nor even imagine in advance. Our best moments take us by surprise. The world around us tantalizes just at the edge of our understanding and control. Although our Big Bang evolution is a blunt instrument, our world walks a fine line.

THE ARGUMENT THAT OURS
IS THE BEST WORLD

Gentle reader, you and I have done most of the hard work. We have baked enough bricks to make a structure.

Now, in one short continuous narrative, I can tell you: who decides which world ought to exist, what they decide, whether they get their wish, and how we know they get their wish.

The argument that our universe is the best world possible, goes like this:

All possible agents divide into two kinds, subtle and spider.

Spiders are mere calculation. Their desires are the desires of a machine. Their satisfactions mostly have rigid size.

Subtle agents are people. Subtle agents make comparisons—lots of comparisons. We compare our comparisons and compare those comparisons. Our satisfactions mostly have variable size. Subtle agents use fluid, mutable comparisons to interpret experience.

From time to time we will talk again about subtle agents and spiders. That distinction has a lot of consequences.

All possible subtle agents—without help from the spiders—decide which possible world ought to exist.

All possible subtle agents have a *unanimous* opinion about what ought to exist. Our opinions are implicit but united.

Any subtle agent, actual or possible, implicitly prefers the most subtle possible world above all others. Not the most beautiful world, not the most just world, not the kindest nor gentlest nor safest nor most challenging nor most optimistic—but the most subtle world.

You and I will talk a second time about why the opinion is unanimous—after we talk about moral responsibility. Those issues are connected.

The most subtle possible world has a finite number of inhabitants, each with a life of finite extent. Rather like our own universe. Later I will tell you why.

The most subtle possible world is unique down to fine details, including the expression you have on your face at this moment. I will tell you why that's true.

The most subtle possible state of existence, is just the most subtle world single and alone. Not two or more independent worlds, just one big world. Again, more on this later.

The united opinion is a mandate, an authorization. The united opinion mandates what ought to exist: the most subtle world possible, alone and solitary.

Now we know who decides what ought to exist, and what they decide.

But do they get their wish? Apparently they do. Here's how we know:

On the evidence for high subtlety in our own universe, what ought to exist does exist. Our very own universe appears to follow the mandate of the united opinion. Our own world appears to have the highest possible collective subtlety.

The evidence that the actual world has high subtlety—and apparently the highest possible—comes in two forms:

The hard evidence appears in the general features of our Big Bang evolution. We do have an ingenious physical law. With reasonably high cunning, our physical law evolution promotes the general conditions of high subtlety, in our personalities and in our experience.

You and I have talked about the hard evidence, and we will talk about it further.

From time to time, we will talk also about the softer evidence. Big Bang evolution is a blunt instrument. It cannot account for fine tuning in our experience. Yet our lives exhibit an exceedingly fine tuning. Thus:

Our world walks a fine line. Our world is a tease. It saunters just outside our grasp. Rather consistently, our world transcends our pedestrian hopes and plodding ambitions. Our best moments take us by surprise. Our world gives us better than we strive to have, better than we can imagine having. Our subtle experience outguesses and outclasses our understanding. Our world tantalizes almost but not quite within our control. *It does that for everyone.* Our world expertly toys with our ambitions, plays off them, finally sweeps them away—and gives us better. The world knows what to do with us better than we do.

With reasonably high cunning, Big Bang evolution promotes our subtle experience. You and I would be hard pressed to find improvements to physical law. But what actually happens to each of us, exhibits a subtle fine tuning—beyond the blunt capacities of Big Bang evolution.

What ought to exist does exist. We occupy the most subtle world possible. The evidence for perfection is ingenious physical law, and our world transcending its ingenious physical law.

AMAZING GRACE

To me as an innocent bystander, something about all this is curious. What ought to happen, and what does happen, are the same.

In the realm of logical possibility, exactly one particular possible world is the best possible world. That fact is true *no matter what exists or does not exist*. It would be true even if nothing existed. All the details of the best possible world—the Big Bang, the composition of physical law, the assassination of Julius Caesar, the Moonlight Sonata, the battle of Midway, the death of Chairman Mao on September 8, 1976, the hour and minute of your birth, the color of your eyes, the number of hairs on your head at noon today—all these details obtain in the best world possible, no matter what actually does exist. The entire composition of the best world, everything that happens in it, all its details great and small, are a *necessary* truth.

A *necessary* truth is true no matter what exists or does not exist. "2 + 2 = 4" is a necessary truth. A *contingent* truth might have been false, depending on what does or does not exist, what does or does not actually happen. "You are reading this sentence" is a contingent truth.

Exactly one particular world, down to fine details including the color of your eyes, is the best among possible worlds. That's a necessary truth. It's true no matter what does or doesn't exist. The color of your eyes at this moment, always was a feature of the best possible world, and always will be.

That the best possible world actually does exist, is a contingent truth. In the realm of logical possibility, it didn't have to happen. But apparently it does happen. And apparently it happens exactly as it should, right down to the color of your eyes, the number of hairs on your head, the expression on your face at this particular moment.

What *ought* to happen is a necessary truth. What *does* happen is a contingent truth. Everything you and I do as free agents, each choice we make, is a necessary truth in the best possible world, and a contingent truth in the actual world. The necessary truth and the contingent truth coincide.

This curious coincidence, along with the logic of explanation itself, is enough to identify the spare reason why we exist.

Gentle reader, maybe you already know what the reason is. In the fullness of time, I will tell you about it anyway.

KIND READER, THANK YOU

If you have gotten this far, the rest is easy.

These ideas took me eight years to figure out. I started with an inarticulate insight, a rather prostrating vision, while under the influence of the strange whiskey.

Yours truly will never go anywhere near that village again. Once is enough.

Gentle and patient reader, you have worked hard for me. I appreciate your effort. I do trust that the pages following will reward you. I intend to make all these issues more vivid and more personal.

Stand beside me for a time, and look where I am looking.

We the Addicted

T he sublime must have a counterweight. Something that we want must be denied. And therefore, our world seduces us and crushes us.

After speaking in public, usually I want to end it all in the nearest pond. An audience of ten brings out my stammer, and one hundred give me lockjaw. In June of 1996, my unruly destiny, with one hour's notice, required me to orate in Mandarin to ten million people.

Yours truly is the foreign joint venture partner in a ceramic tile factory near Tangshan City, which dominates Fengrun County, about one hundred miles east of Beijing. Our factory held its dedication ceremony on Sunday, the Second of June, 1996. My Chinese partners insisted on making me the featured speaker. They wanted to show off their tame American. For months I had dreaded that day. I was expecting to stand at a podium and speak in Mandarin to about one thousand people: customers, suppliers, bank presidents, electric power officials, august civic and business leaders, officers of the city and county, and perhaps a few retired folks who like to mingle. That expectation was disappointed. Arriving at the factory and ceremony site at 9 a.m., I found the place crawling with TV cameras. Yours truly was the only foreigner around, the most obese person around, the chief investor, the only person wearing a necktie, and six inches taller than most everyone else. I was painfully conspicuous. The cameramen simply could not control their fascination with my person. My serenity-meter already pointed to the red zone, when Mr. Chen, one of the Chinese partners, reported his good news: radio and television would broadcast my speech live to ten million people. I began to have an out-of-body experience. Mr. Chen flickered and became both very small and very large. Reason abdicated her throne. The Automatic Pilot took over. "You are a VIP!" said my delighted mother-in-law, Mrs. Sun. The Automatic Pilot nodded and maintained a grave yet friendly demeanor. "I'd like to have a copy of the news broadcast," said the Automatic Pilot, from somewhere far away. "Certainly! Certainly!" said Mr. Chen, beaming at my enthusiasm. "No problem!" And he bustled off to make my happiness complete.

The Chinese partners were good businessmen. They built an efficient and handsome factory for about half the typical cost of comparable structures in China—and far less than the cost in America. They were ruthless at getting the most bang for the yuan. Their dedication ceremony was a masterpiece of excitement at low cost. Free of charge they borrowed the microphones, chairs, tables, tablecloths, and a sixty-piece marching band, from nearby middle schools. Each of the seventh-grade band members was ecstatic to receive a commemorative yellow cap for his or her efforts. Our "brother factories" donated the overpowering arrays of fireworks. Even the enormous festive banners were borrowed and then customized at negligible cost. But all the ceremony's events received meticulous planning from the four Chinese partners. Nominally second in command but in fact the prime mover, Mr. Gu did not sleep for several nights. Finally, on the last night before the ceremony, he sank into a coma for three hours, then rose and appeared at the factory at 4 a.m. to review his preparations. Only Mr. Gu's intimates could discern that he felt continually pressed for time on the big day. Unobtrusively he scurried about, and calmly he briefed everyone on what to do and what to expect, with only the faintest undertone of frenzy.

The day began as most days begin. My wife Lee Ming, her mother, and yours truly slept fitfully until 7 a.m., ate a modest breakfast at our hotel in Tangshan, took turns adjusting my necktie, met our driver at 8:15, and arrived outside the factory gate at 9. The seventh-grade band lay in wait, their eyes bright with excitement. They had arranged themselves in two columns facing the avenue of honor: a rather narrow passage leading to the safety of the factory gate. As we emerged from our vehicle, they greeted us without mercy at close range. They wielded twenty drums and forty trumpets. Feeling like General MacArthur reviewing the Munchkin Marching Band at ninety decibels, I led my "delegation" slowly and solemnly up to the factory entrance. The four partners were lined up to meet us. They pumped our hands until our teeth rattled.

During the next hour the Automatic Pilot maintained a grave yet friendly demeanor. Mrs. Sun disappeared on one of her mysterious errands. Lee Ming and I toured the factory, then sipped tea and chatted pleasantly with assorted potentates. From time to time we heard enthusiastic fanfares blasting the eardrums of new VIP arrivals. Reason gradually crept back to her throne, and made a dogged effort to sit up straight.

At 10 a.m., thirty-two of us notables took our ceremonial seats at four long tables placed on a big outdoor platform. The band moved inside the gate—to a distance comfortably away from us. Pretty hostesses served more tea to the notables. I congratulated myself on taking a whizz just minutes earlier. Each of us had a large name card propped up on the table. Mine read, "Approximately large body of water fearless incorruptible," which sounds roughly like "Yu-han We-lian-se." Close enough. At our backs stood the factory gate festooned with banners. Outside the gate—but still rather close—long strings of firecrackers, bombs, and skyrockets waited to make their statement. In front of us and facing us sat the audience, on stools trucked in from the various middle schools. As befits a People's Republic, uniformed factory workers occupied the first two rows. The vast sea of stools wasn't enough and people stood in back. Cameramen prowled here and there. At the ceremonial tables, Mr. Dong, the county leader, occupied the seat of honor on the right. He did not give a speech. Yours truly, the barbarian foreign investor and chief object of curiosity, occupied the seat of honor on the left. Outwardly I remained grave yet friendly, but inwardly I was trying to prop up Reason, still wobbling on her throne. As the news video clearly shows, I concentrated on breathing calmly, taking leisurely sips of tea, chatting unconcernedly with Lee Ming on my right, and generally behaving as if this were just another Sunday in the park. I would be the third speaker.

We kicked off the ceremony by enduring the "ten thousand explosions" outside the factory gate. Each firecracker was the size of a banana. Some of the bombs were bigger than coconuts. The explosions literally numbered ten thousand. They made me long for the marching band. Even with my fingers pressed to my ears, they were the loudest noise I have ever heard, by a wide margin. No evil spirit could possibly want to hang around that astounding sound. As it finally began to diminish, the band chipped in with another fanfare.

Mr. Gu, Master of Ceremonies, introduced the first speaker, Mr. Chen. Sitting right behind him as he spoke, I could see immediately that Mr. Chen was experiencing the biggest moment of his life. Desperately he gripped his notes with both hands, but notes and hands all trembled like a leaf. He was speaking on camera to a large audience and to all the people who would make or break his future career. Realizing that the persecution was general, Reason on her throne began to sit up a little straighter. Mr. Chen barked out his words like a drill sergeant and sat down.

Next up at bat was Mr. Li, our financial officer. His hands did not tremble, but his legs shook. Throughout his speech his pants were all aquiver. But he also managed to bark out his words like a modern-day Mussolini.

I heard Mr. Gu introduce the "approximately large body of water fearless incorruptible." This man and his wife, said Mr. Gu, had traveled all the way from America, just to be here today. Somewhere Madame Defarge was knitting my name. Slowly I rose and slowly walked to the microphones—positioned about four inches below my chin. The audience perked up noticeably. "Here comes the giant barbarian with the red necktie!" they were thinking. "I wonder what a barbarian sounds like when he talks." Milking the occasion—or stalling—I remained silent and gestured for my mother-in-law to join me. She came to my side, creating a dramatic stage wait. Now I leaned forward and down into the microphones to utter my first words. The audience was all agog. In the silence, I could almost hear the knitting needles clacking away.

An entire community had built our factory. Many of the vital contributors were neither employees nor direct beneficiaries. A number of banks, local utilities, and government officials helped us from no other motive than moral conviction. All these people were listening.

"Because I am a foreigner, aspects of China that may seem ordinary to you are amazing and wonderful to me. Watching this factory progress, I have been privileged to witness a side of Chinese life that is very poorly understood in America. What amazes me is how many different people worked together to make this factory possible. To me as a foreigner, the history of this factory is enormously positive, not because there were no problems, but because so many problems were overcome, and so many different people cooperated to overcome them. . . .

"To solve problems, the management team spent many days' hard travel on the road, bypassing all the sightseeing stops, sometimes becoming ill from overwork, transacting business at the lowest cost of time and money. They sacrificed themselves. They have no financial compensation beyond their salaries as county officials. They work hard, they are resourceful, they are thrifty, they are honest, they have high character. They exemplify the spirit of China's hardworking people. I am proud to be associated with this management team. . . .

"I have witnessed in Tangshan a highly ethical and idealistic side of Chinese business practice, a side which is largely invisible to people living on the other side of the Earth. . . .

"Right now this factory is young. It makes only simple tiles. But, I am confident that in the future, as the factory staff continues to gain experience and improve their expertise, and with continuing cooperation and support from many people in Tangshan, more and more wonderful tiles of high quality will be manufactured here. The crucial machinery in this factory is the best in the world. More machinery can be added to diversify and improve the tiles. I am confident that this factory will increasingly contribute to the City of Tangshan's reputation as a manufacturer of fine ceramic tiles. I am confident that not too long from today, the people who design and build beautiful buildings, both in China and in America, will prefer to use tiles bearing the stamp, 'Made in Tangshan.'"

Like a sleepwalker, I turned and sat down. The audience was applauding. Vaguely I realized that I had not stammered even once.

Three more speakers followed me. Each of them spoke with calm relaxation. Then the hostesses handed out pairs of scissors. The audience began to cheer with abandon. The thirty-two notables stood shoulder to shoulder and simultaneously cut a single long blue ribbon.

Later, at lunch, Mr. Dong sat next to me at a table of eight. China produces a variety of clear liqueurs that taste fabulous and pack the kick of a mule. Using thimble-sized goblets and one of these potent wines, the diners toasted each other from the beginning to the end of the meal. In this ritual, the toaster and the toastee clink goblets, rising from their seats if necessary, shout "Gan-bay!" (Bottoms up!), drain off the goblet at one delicious fiery gulp, and then produce the empty goblet upside down to demonstrate that indeed we are drinking ourselves stupid. Both abstention and dainty sipping are bad form. Yours truly was the most frequent toastee. People from other tables in the adjoining rooms kept bursting in to shout "Gan-bay!" with me. From time to time, when no one was looking, Mr. Dong filled up my little goblet with water, which made a good counterfeit for the clear wine. But when he toasted me himself, he first made sure the wine was real.

Late in the afternoon, the Chinese partners verified our safe arrival back at our hotel, then returned to their own homes to collapse. The three of us—Lee Ming, her mother, and I—strolled over to the Tangshan earthquake memorial in the center of town. On July 28, 1976, at 3:42 a.m., the City of Tangshan, population not quite 750,000, was struck by the most severe earthquake on record. The focus, eleven kilometers underground and directly beneath the city, registered more than eleven on the Richter scale.

The epicenter, within the city itself, measured 8.7. Only one corner of one building remained standing. Every other structure collapsed completely to rubble in seconds. In the dark of night, listening to the screams of their loved ones, 260,000 people died. 160,000 more were permanently crippled. The people of Tangshan refused nearly all outside help, and rebuilt their city with their own hands. On the day of our visit, young children played their young games around the memorial. Their laughter floated upward to the carved stone friezes, which depict a grieving people. The children delighted in climbing up the memorial's curved supports, and sliding down again. Their parents stood apart from them, and apart from each other, watching. The frolicking youngsters failed to notice that all of their parents stood absolutely still and silent, like so many lonely statues.

Later in the summer of 1996, the survivors commemorated the twentieth anniversary of their earthquake. As friends of the city, Lee Ming and I were welcomed to attend. The feasting and drinking continued for eight days, and finally ended from sheer exhaustion. Every day we consumed two banquets, and no banquet had less than ten courses of delicacies rare and exquisite. Equally exquisite were the fiery liqueurs. No one mentioned the earthquake. For eight days the people of Tangshan savored the fabulous food, laughed and shouted, celebrated their friendships, toasted each other in high spirits, and in their more reflective moments, spoke with anticipation of the sealed future.

The future will crush us again. But the future will be new and different and unflattened. In this cunning world, we the addicted go forward to our own destruction.

Part Five

THE BEST POSSIBLE WORLD

Flattening Evil

At times I have heard people say, "Why does the world need *so many* evils? Surely we don't need them all. If we carefully choose just one little bad thing and subtract it from the world, surely our lives could still be subtle. Suppose an elephant steps on the hand of a talented concert pianist. We lose the opportunity to hear her music. She loses what she loves most. If we delete that one little evil from the world, if the elephant steps six inches to the side and spares her hand, how is the human race worse off? We could still evolve from the Big Bang, live in a world that surprises us, have subtle experience inside and outside our understanding and our control, and so on."

Gentle reader, it's a sad fact, that this argument reduces to absurdity.

The present chapter attempts to refute certain arguments from evil against the best-world thesis. The above is an example of what I will try to refute. Here I want to show that such arguments don't qualify as accurate reasoning.

Many of us try to lessen evil in the world. We try to cure diseases, settle disputes among our friends, invent better mousetraps. We give money to homeless people. We encourage our children to be moral. We vote for the best candidate. And we try to be pleasant. Most of us want to be good people.

Our efforts to reduce evil, finally leave unchanged the world's collective balance between good and evil. That fact follows from how subtle agents perceive the world.

But our efforts to reduce evil, do make the world more subtle. They make the world new and different. We discharge our efforts against evil, against its variety and profusion, within a subtle causal structure. Sometimes, when we try to simplify the world, we make it more complicated. Our efforts have unpredictable consequences. And sometimes without trying to do so, we increase subtlety. The world's subtle causal structure receives our struggles to change it, like a spider web receiving new strands.

But suppose we change the world by omnipotent fiat, rather than by struggle. Suppose we ask ourselves, How would we change the world for the better, if we could enact any possible state of existence by executive command? What evils would we remove? What joys would we add?

The mental exercise of changing the world by omnipotent fiat, bypasses struggle. Omnipotent fiat can modify the world without struggle and without the causal consequences of struggle. Rather than add our endeavors to the world's causal web, we throw the web away and put another in its place.

However, the new web might be unsubtle. Changes in the world that are worthy goals of struggle, can be unfortunate when implemented without struggle, by omnipotent fiat. A case in point:

We humans struggle against nagging evils in variety and profusion. But suppose those evils don't obtain and never did obtain. They are just plain absent from the world. Suppose we lived in a world with no involuntary death, no decrepit aging, no disease, no natural calamites like floods, drought, tornadoes, or earthquakes, no repression, no exploitation, no famine, no war, no holocausts, no enmity, no selfish thoughts, no obnoxious neighbors; where everyone has a gracious spacious house, plenty of delicious food to eat, kindly neighbors who play bridge without gossiping and know when to go home, and a deeply devoted lusting spouse with great looks.

If those advantages were universal, then living with the sole husband who compulsively picks his nose, would be as the trials of Job. We would not view the house as particularly gracious, the food as delicious, the weather as mild, the neighbors as kindly, or the spouse as good looking. In *our* world we value those satisfactions. In *that* world they sink almost to nothing; their very abundance renders them tepid, banal, and vacuous. But the nose-picking would not be abundant. It stands unique and terrible—the worst evil in history, by a wide margin. In our world, one particular case of compulsive nose-picking has relatively small size, by comparison to famine and holocaust. But in that world, no comparison and no perspective reduces its awful size. On the contrary, all the comparisons intensify its size. Every hour of her life, the wretched wife dreads the next cruel moment, when her beloved's familiar finger ascends toward his nostril. She knows herself the most tortured individual who ever lived. Except for her unselfish devotion, she would throw herself from the nearest cliff. Except that she locks up her anguish inside, her beloved would leap from the nearest cliff. In that entire insipid world, she can find no counterpart to herself, no one who suffers as she does. She lives utterly alone in a hell we cannot imagine.

Removing a variety of evils by omnipotent fiat, leaves evil still quite large, but flattened into unsubtle shape.

The flattening happens merely because goods and evils have variable size—because they have size by comparison—*whether or not they have exact balance.*

"The Measure of Good and Evil" and "Fiction"—the next two chapters—talk about why goods and evils must balance exactly in human perception. Exploring this balance illuminates what we are. But the balance does not kill the arguments from evil against perfection. Those arguments are already dead! Let's take a look.

When we flattened the evils by omnipotent fiat, when we took out all the evils we could think of, except nose-picking, what else got flattened? How would that insipid world have epic poetry, tragic plays, profound novels? What pictures would its artists paint? How would different people have different kinds of friendship?

How well does that world exploit our ability to make comparisons? With what consummate skill does it addict us to being alive?

Flattening the evils, left the goods flattened also.

The actual world has high subtlety. Our struggles against the evils we hate, add to its subtlety. This elusive world has all the more subtlety, because sometimes we struggle to remove its nagging evils in variety and profusion. And sometimes we succeed. But flattening evil by omnipotent fiat, would only flatten the world itself.

Perhaps we were too ambitious. Perhaps we removed too many evils by omnipotent fiat. Let's try subtracting just one. Would the world be improved if—by omnipotent fiat—we removed stomach cancer? Or racial intolerance? Or child abuse? Or the injury to the pianist's hand?—just one evil.

If subtracting one evil does improve the world, then we can ask: Shall we subtract a second evil? A third? A fourth?

If we never say no in that sequence, if we keep subtracting evils one by one, then eventually we reach a world clearly flattened and clearly worse than our world.

Therefore, at some point in that sequence, subtracting further evils *degrades* the world. At some point in the sequence, the world benefits from keeping all its remaining evils.

When does that point arrive? When do we stop subtracting evil? After the tenth evil gets subtracted? After the fifth? After the first? After *none* are subtracted?

We don't know. We have blurry vision. For all we know, the actual world might already be the world that benefits from keeping all its evils. Some world in the sequence has that property, and it might be ours.

We are left with no evidence whatsoever, that the actual world has too much evil or too little evil. For all we know, the actual world might have evil in exactly the best possible pattern. The arguments from evil against perfection, reduce to the absurdity of a flattened world.

Starting next chapter, I will tell you how the goods and evils humans perceive, have an exact balance. But please notice: we have already killed off the arguments from evil, without mentioning an exact balance. All we needed to destroy those arguments, was the *variable* size of goods and evils, whether or not they happen to have equal size.

Good reader, I don't want you ferociously to resist my description of the balance, under the impression that you are bringing arguments from evil back to life. Those arguments are dead with or without the balance.

I have a different motive entirely, for describing human perception in terms of equilibrium. I'm going to tell you all about it, starting next chapter.

Our world betters the flattened world. Subtracting lots of evils was counterproductive. Somehow we need evils *in variety and profusion.* But why? What are their uses to us?

The short answer: Goods and evils in variety and profusion, help our Siren play on our facility to compare. For you and me, all those goods and evils change every day, sometimes a little bit, sometimes a lot. Partly in consequence of its many faces, our world does addict us and it does terminate us well.

This cunning world gives and it takes away. But *how* it gives and takes away, how it surprises us, how it substitutes the ineffable for our banal ambitions, we can only find out by going forward. And we do want to find out. That's our addiction.

Fiction

In this chapter and the next, I make this claim: each individual subtle agent perceives in his world, one way or another, an exact balance between goods and evils.

Prima facie, goods and evils do balance exactly for each human subtle agent, simply because they measure and give size to each other. That's how our perception works. And prima facie, balance implies equality.

But perhaps these balances can be skewed or subverted. Let's you and me think up some possible subversions and see if they pan out.

Maybe fiction skews the balances. Let's attack the prima facie balance, by considering the effect of fiction on how each human perceives the world.

Often we compare the world to fiction. We compare actual satisfactions to fictional satisfactions, and actual people to fictional people.

If you read lots of stories about the immortal Olympians and their quality lifestyle, you might compare actual earthly pleasures unfavorably to life on Olympus. If you have a weakness for Harlequin romances, the real world might seem a bit prosaic. If you read lots of fiction about the days of chivalry, you might view the actual people around you as comparatively base.

Under the influence of such fictions, the actual world changes for you. If you immerse yourself in certain stories, then fictional chivalry helps give size to selfishness in the world. Selfishness in the world helps measure the chivalry in the stories. Goods and evils balance, but some of the goods are fiction!

These changes in your perception would happen, whether you believe the stories to be true, or don't believe them, or believe them halfway.

Suppose you read about Sir Galahad and Sir Gawain, and shake your head sadly over the more sordid motivations of too many actual people. For you, viciousness predominates over virtue in the real world. About the actual world, you are a pessimist.

Nevertheless, actual goods and evils as you size them, remain in balance. Fictional stories describe people, things, and events that are not actual. But the fiction itself is actual. We really do have fictional stories in our world. This fact conserves the balance. Here is how:

Suppose you contemplate a beautiful statue, and in consequence, you see actual people as just a bit less graceful. Suppose the statue has that influence on your comparisons.

Now the world for you has people a bit more lumpish. But it also has a statue worth looking at. One balances the other: If now you must walk among clumsier people, you have as counterweight, the contemplation of a graceful object.

By sculpting her statue, by adding her statue to the world, an artist has raised your standards of grace and beauty. She has changed how you see the world. But the world also contains a new artifact, something new in your experience. The statue is graceful by comparison to ponderous people. Some of the people are lumpish by comparison to the statue. The artist has changed the balances you perceive, without subverting them.

The statue is not a real person. But it is a real statue. You can have experience of people and balancing experience of statues. What is real and actual in the world, still balances in your perception.

New experience causes you to change your previous views of the world. New experience alters your perception in idiosyncratic ways. Thus:

If some people cannot attend classes on art appreciation,

because they are too busy finding their next meal, then you may view some people as more fortunate, and other people as less fortunate. This feeling might be heightened after you contemplate the statue. After the statue, you might count yourself a bit more fortunate than previously. Not just your standards of grace and beauty, but also your standards of good fortune and bad, have changed. Moreover, after viewing the statue created by an artist, you might regret your career in house painting. You might regret that you can't afford to buy the statue. You might wonder why people work so hard to make worthy statues, but work so little to make themselves worthy. You might decide that unformed slabs of marble hold delicate secrets, or that making a statue is a lot of work, or that your cousin needn't brag about his artistic ability, or that you shouldn't have left your paintbrushes on the bus just because you didn't want to clean them. Your view of events, things, and people do change in idiosyncratic ways under the influence of new experience. But these changes cannot subvert your perception of the world in terms of balance.

Consider a man who likes to carve wood with a lathe and chisels. He sets up a woodworking studio in his basement. Whenever the world gets to be too much for him, he retreats to his basement sanctuary and makes snuff boxes until he feels better. He compares the serenity of woodworking to the turmoil in the world outside his basement. The outside world suffers by comparison. But the world entire, also includes his basement sanctuary and the comparative serenity he finds there. The world entire still has the same ratio of good to evil.

Because he has a sanctuary in his basement, which he finds serene, the woodworker might have higher standards of serenity than he would otherwise. If the woodworker has a neighbor who envies the peace of working with wood in the basement, the neighbor also has a higher standard of serenity. Owing to serenity in the basement, how they each view the world has changed. Yet their perceptions remain balanced.

Suppose in the evenings you read about Sir Galahad and Sir Gawain, about their idealism and pure motives. You lose yourself in a delightful fiction. But in the mornings, as you ride the elevator up to your office, you often encounter a boorish man who won't put out his cigar—a man nothing like Sir Galahad. You dread the mornings and the cigar. You look forward to the evenings, your book, and your comfortable armchair. Each experience helps give size to the other. And each experience resides in the actual world.

If you read in the evenings about fictional knights with wonderful personalities, real people in the cold morning light might seem obnoxious. The world has changed for you. Now it has nastier people—and a delightful fiction that you can contemplate. A writer has raised your standards of good behavior, by adding his work to the world.

The presence of a delightful fiction in the world, might cause events, things, and people in the world to pale under a higher standard of goodness. But the delight of the fiction balances this loss.

As the statue is a fake person but a real statue, so the fiction is fake events but real fiction. We really do have statues and stories in our world.

As an artist can create a statue, so an artist can create a fictional story. Both are a kind of artifact.

As we can find a marble artifact commensurable in grace with people, so we can find a fictional character—a fiction-artifact—commensurable in chivalry with people.

As immersion in woodworking can be a sanctuary, a welcome contrast to the world outside, so also can immersion in a fictional story. In each case, someone perceives a commensurability between the sanctuary and an outside environment less pleasant.

Statues and stories change you. Sometimes they transform you. Your balances change and your standards of goodness change, in highly idiosyncratic ways. The statue, the basement sanctuary, the fiction change your balances, by adding something commensurable to what you already know in the world. Stories and statues change your balances without subverting them. They only expand the domain of commensurabilities you perceive.

Spiders have limited use for fiction. To date in human history, our fictional narratives, these artifacts of our imagination, have generally enhanced our comparisons and our lives. They cause us to make comparisons in new ways, and therefore they affect our subtlety—generally for the better so far.

However, losing yourself in the experience of fiction, can also be perverse, a degradation of the balances you perceive.

Suppose you participate in a fiction technologically advanced. Having saved up a suitable nest egg, you decide to retire from the outside world. You buy some expensive equipment and set it up in your living room. You turn off the doorbell, enter the warm nutrient bath, insert the tubes, plug in the electrodes, close the lid, and turn on the reality simulator. You stay inside for one hundred years, until you expire. You have made-to-order fictional adventures. You have experience that caters to *your* happiness, as opposed to happiness in general.

Have you skewed the balance between good and evil? No. Moreover, you run the risk of unsubtle experience.

During the first few years, perhaps you find a wonderful bright new life, full of love and adventure. You never knew life could be this much fun. But now your former life, before the reality simulator, seems duller and more empty than you found it at the time. The balance remains.

After ninety years in the machine, with your former life receding ever further into the past, your new life seems more ordinary. On some days the simulated reality will be less wonderful and bright than on other days. New experience causes your baseline comparisons to change.

Even if the machine gives you more and more exciting experience, each year more wonderful than the year before, that game of something new would itself become old. You run the risk of finding your new life unsubtle—and your former life more subtle by comparison.

What simulation we devise can match the world's subtlety? *Truman's World* reveals the risk of heaviness in simulated experience. Surely we use fiction best as an adjunct to other experience, not as a replacement for the world's remarkable subtlety.

The actual world has us maturing from children into adults.

Just by growing into our majority, we usually experience our lives as more subtle from year to year. The world already plays the game of something new. But it does that for everyone. Our baseline expectations for the new and different, are already quite high; the game of something new, already happens to us quite well. Too much fiction, too much dependence on simulated experience, runs the risk of inferior subtlety.

Neither fiction nor any of the other artifacts we build, can change how we perceive goods and evils in terms of balance. But artifacts do affect the subtlety of the balance, for better or worse.

The Measure of Good and Evil

Good reader, I make these claims:

Subtle perception imposes balances on the world. A subtle agent organizes her world as opposites that balance each other. A subtle agent's perception causes good and bad to balance, by sizing them to balance.

Goods and evils can change in our perception, but they cannot go out of balance. If some of the evils fade away, then others must grow in size. If new goods appear, then others must shrink. For any non-spider agent, goods and evils have variable size.

In consequence, goods and evils balance *exactly* for any subtle agent, simply because they measure and give size to each other. No matter how perception varies, the exact balance persists. The balance persists in the perception of any subtle agent in any possible world.

Those are my claims about how perception works for subtle agents.

At first glance, observation does support those claims. When I look at the world entire and all the people in it, I see both good and evil. At first glance, the world's good and bad seem roughly in balance.

However, gentle reader, let's you and me play devil's advocate.

Goods and evils balance *exactly* for *any* subtle agent? Let's try to find holes in that statement every which way we can.

This chapter has ten major themes that weave together. I have roughly divided the chapter into ten parts, each dominated by one of the themes. On the balances you and I each perceive in the world, we will get down and dirty.

In part one, kind reader, we meditate on the balances we are trying to overturn. The more we know about them, the better we can look for subversions.

ONE—HAPPINESS AND UNHAPPINESS IN BALANCE

Human subtle agents make comparisons in a complex style. Compared to spiders, we have the extra dimension to our agency, that we can have fluid happiness and unhappiness.

Human happiness and unhappiness cannot be *reduced* to the formula of balance, but they do conform to it, I claim.

Whether or not you want it to, whether or not you pay attention, your mind automatically organizes your perceptions into many interrelated balances, I claim. These balances make sense of the world. They integrate and inform your perceptions. But they also impose a structure on the world. Fifty percent of human experience must fall below average. The good and the bad perceived by each human, conform to balances imposed on them by the very nature of human perception.

You and I each see good and evil in balance, one way or another. That's the master balance. And one way or another, we each see grace and awkwardness in balance, good fortune and bad in balance, delight and despair, optimism and pessimism, and many more. Those are sub-balances within the master balance, like substructures in a mobile.

Among humans as a collection, all over the world and throughout our history, happiness and unhappiness seem to balance. True, some humans are happier than others. And some individuals perceive happiness as predominant in the world, while others see a higher proportion of unhappiness. But somehow those differences even out. In my perception, and perhaps in yours, human optimism and human pessimism appear to balance.

(Some of the balances appear to hold within certain periods of history. In my perception, human optimism and pessimism seem balanced in the twentieth century, the eighteenth century, and the first century.)

Looking for subversions, we will explore the balances from different perspectives: How they might have been otherwise. How they might have failed, and left us spiders. How the balances we perceive might have been less complicated. What goods and evils really are. How for humans the master balance between good and bad has an ambitious style: plastic, labyrinthine, sinuous, and fluent.

A reminder: The arguments from evil against perfection are already dead. They do not get any deader, because good and evil turn out to be equal companions. In this chapter, the arguments from evil are not at stake. Instead, we are exploring subtle agency, and especially subtle agency in the human style.

Happiness and unhappiness being quite complex for humans, you and I will look at a simpler proxy: optimism and pessimism. Some people feel optimistic about their own future lives and generally optimistic about the future for everyone they care about. They feel optimistic about the proportion of happiness to unhappiness in the world. Others feel pessimistic.

Each person perceives optimism and pessimism in other people. Prima facie, optimism and pessimism among people generally, balance in the perception of each observer. In that sense, happiness and unhappiness at large in the human race, are balanced. Such is the structure imposed by the nature of human perception.

Of course no one can understand all the optimism and all the pessimism felt by all the people in the world. Each individual views a limited collection, with greater or lesser accuracy. His collection may include the neighbor he met last week, who talked about starvation in Africa, and his dour boss at the burger hut, who rarely sees anything good anywhere, and his sunny pet dog, whom he regards as a little person, although no one else does, and his science teacher, who discusses human progress and the resulting comforts, and his grandmother from the second generation previous, who told him that his wishes will come true if he wishes hard enough, and an evaluation of human endeavor as futile and unsatisfying, by Marcus Aurelius nearly two thousand years ago. He may be completely unaware that last week a certain Li Zhi Bai was successful in love and now hears the birds chirping everywhere. Each human being has a different perspective and different information. Paleolithic people, Roman societies, the 101st Airborne in Korea, and my landlord all view the world under different circumstances. Each person makes different observations—but each person's observations conform to the same weighting mechanism.

The human mind imposes a structure on the world. Optimisms and pessimisms as viewed by each person, measure each other. Prima facie they balance exactly for each person. Less information or more information cannot upset their balance. If somehow a person had exhaustive information about the world's optimism and pessimism, their exact balance would persist. In the absence of complete information, the balance persists anyway. No matter the strange idiosyncrasies in how the individual views the balance, it persists nonetheless.

By that prima facie argument, each human observer sees in human society generally, a balance between optimism and pessimism. But each observer sees his own private version of that balance.

In what sense, then, does "the world as it really is" have balanced goods and evils? The world as it really is doesn't have good and evil. It only has data. Good and evil is our interpretation of the data, our interpretation has rules, and prima facie the rules entail that goods and evils balance.

But human beings are not that simple. The structure our minds project onto the world, has high complexity and idiosyncrasy. You and I will put considerable pressure on the prima facie argument.

For us humans, goods and evils do appear to have their sizes almost entirely by comparison to each other. They appear to have variable sizes, not absolute sizes. For example, in the world's richer countries, a mud cottage would be a hovel. In the poorer countries, the *same* mud cottage would be a stately residence.

I have personally witnessed such opinions, in rich and poor countries. The difference lies in the observer, and in the comparisons she makes.

Sometimes we make the usual, expected comparisons. Sometimes we can be more idiosyncratic. If five people stand together and gaze upon the same mud cottage, their respective appraisals might be: "Dirty wretched shanty" . . . "Simple to build" . . . "Romantic" . . . "Lonely" . . . "Lays bare the insufferable pretension of modern society." Each of the five observers has a different mental landscape. For each, the same mud cottage inspires different comparisons.

Different people have different mental landscapes of comparison. Each of us has his idiosyncrasies. And each of us has different experience. Residents of the Lao jungle have different mental landscapes than residents of Cleveland, Ohio.

Suppose an inhabitant of ancient Rome came forward in time and visited us in Cleveland, just long enough to notice our automobiles, airplanes, electric lights, central heating, cable television, cell phones, and personal computers. He might very well go back to his own civilization with the unhappy sense of something missing. But we who readily obtain those conveniences—are we happier than the population of ancient Rome? They measured their delight and despair by different comparisons. None of their friends and neighbors traveled on airplanes. None of them had telephones. They were content with the Roman mail. Their letters express satisfaction and dissatisfaction in roughly the same proportion as our own correspondence. Likewise, Stone Age cultures still visited today have celebration and laughter just like Information Age cultures. On the evidence of observation, goods and evils have the same balance in the Roman State, Han Dynasty

China, and the Pleistocene epoch—as predicted by the prima facie argument.

We humans measure each satisfaction or dissatisfaction by comparing it to others. But our comparisons have a lot of idiosyncrasy. We are better off or worse off than our neighbors, our ancestors, our previous selves, our potential selves, the characters we see in movies, even historical figures who died long ago. If you have struggled out of poverty, possession of ten million dollars might be enormously satisfying. If you have struggled out of poverty determined to become wealthier than any other human being, ten million dollars might make you feel worthless.

Other people try to influence your landscape of comparisons. If your parents told you, "Children in China are starving," they may have wanted you to look more favorably on the cold, flaccid broccoli slowly decomposing before you.

Humans sometimes compete with each other, when trying to influence landscapes of comparison. If someone says, "At my age, Mozart had written forty-one symphonies," his companion might reply, "At *my* age, Beethoven had been dead for three years."

Prima facie, humans make complicated and shifting comparisons, all within the purview of mutual sizing and mutual balance.

Now let's look for subversions, all kinds of subversions. Let's see if they pan out.

TWO—INJUSTICE

Suppose we use omnipotent fiat to eliminate injustices. Perhaps a world with more justice could also have a better balance between good and evil.

Regrettably, the balance only gets flattened, not overturned. Let's take a look.

We humans spend a lot of energy crusading for justice. We get rather exercised about man's inhumanity to man. And rightly so. But suppose you and I did have omnipotent fiat to change the world. Suppose we could discard the world's causal web, and substitute another. Shall we right all wrongs? Shall we give complete justice to everyone always? What alternate world with justice shall we make?

Suppose our alternate world *manifestly* has no injustice ever. In that world, everyone knows that bad fortune follows bad behavior, and good fortune follows good behavior. Everyone knows that each unpleasant experience has inevitable and exact compensation. Stifling! Justice is expected, unremarkable, taken for granted. No one would ever face a genuine choice between altruism and selfishness. No one could take risk, because risk involves injustice. No one would wonder very hard how to conduct his life: Just find the most virtuous way to behave, and *everything else* in his life gets optimized. Existence reduces to the selfish exercise of being virtuous. Indeed, viciousness and virtue lose their meanings. We would evaluate our options by mere calculation. We would resemble spiders—or more precisely, a society of ants.

Existence reduced to finding the most virtuous way to behave, would resemble a hunt for Easter eggs. A spider, or a colony of ants, can be programmed to cover the territory and find the eggs— find the virtue—in the most efficient manner. With no manifest injustice in the world, with the rewards of good behavior visible and reliable, then how to behave reduces to calculation.

Suppose a possible world *secretly* has no injustice ever. If a man seduces his neighbor's beautiful wife, has a long passionate affair with her while consistently lying about it, then dumps her and marries another beautiful woman who loves him unselfishly, and meanwhile his stock portfolio goes to the moon, and he dies loved by all at age ninety-six—then surely some *enormous* but invisible sorrow has crept in somewhere.

Because this omnipresent justice somehow remains imperceptible, we get to keep all the benefits of injustice: wondering whether life will reward us, taking risk, improving the world's justice, choosing between selfishness and altruism, and so on. Could that arrangement somehow be coherent *and* subtle? I don't see how. But if it could be, then maybe it already obtains in the actual world!

Shall we make the world a bit less unjust, but not all the way? Incoherent. If fewer high school students have acne, the remaining victims attract more notice and suffer more cruelly. Equal justice demands that every seventeen-year-old have precisely the same number of undeserved pimples on prom night. The pimples are distributed either justly or unjustly. No middle ground.

A possible world can be just or unjust, but not halfway in between. Either it does have mountains and valleys, or it does not. If it does, the mountains are great or small only by comparison to other mountains in the same world—not by comparison to the mountains in our world. Either we are spiders or we are doomed to suffer injustice. If the latter, then justice and injustice give size to each other. That's how our minds work.

When a spider knows his web damaged, he does not feel himself unjustly persecuted in a cruel world. Nor does he view his various options as vicious or virtuous. He just fixes the web, or defends it, or moves his operations elsewhere, as his programming indicates. His existence reduces to mere calculation.

A world completely devoid of any injustice, works against a subtle agent's ability to make comparisons. Such a world would be horribly symmetrical and predictable, with agents so straightforward that they are spiders.

In a world where injustice has few details, justice and injustice still size each other. Injustice remains quite large, but flattened into unsubtle shape.

For highly subtle beings, circumstances must be unjust and subtly unjust. The actual world has a subtle, detailed injustice that persistently roils us. The actual world's injustice gives us elusive experience, continual moral conflict, problems with self-deception, the desire for revenge, the desire not to desire revenge, labyrinthine stresses between selfishness and altruism, higher purpose, the problem of becoming better, the ability to love others for their goodness. Without these, we are spiders who merely calculate.

THREE—WORLDS WITHIN WORLDS

Let's look for still another perspective on our subtle agency. Let's try another potential counterexample to the prima facie balance between good and evil. Let's try to escape the balance—find a loophole somewhere—while remaining subtle beings.

The murder I read about in the newspaper, upsets me less than my wife breaking her finger. I care more about what happens to the people I know well. Even if the human race as a whole, exhibits a positive for every negative, what is that fact to me? Most of the human race I never met.

Humans often do care more about some goods and evils than others. But this true fact doesn't overturn the balances we perceive. It only modifies them.

For satisfactions and dissatisfactions, we humans have many "almost independent" reference systems, smaller than the experience of the entire human race in the entire actual world. For example, a circle of friends might compare many of their satisfactions and dissatisfactions within their circle. Popularity, wealth, serenity, romantic success, childhood traumas, career satisfaction, and many other components of happiness, sometimes do get measured within a group of friends, as opposed to the entire human race. The experience uniquely known and shared within that group, constitutes an "almost independent" reference system. We measure many of our satisfactions and dissatisfactions within the uniquely shared experience of our family, our friends, our colleagues, our social peers, our cultural group, our contemporaries, and our epoch. Sometimes, more idiosyncratic collections of experience have special influence, as when a statesman considers his place in history, or General Patton compares himself to Hannibal.

But that phenomenon doesn't change the balance for any observer, whether inside or outside an "almost independent" reference system. It does strongly affect the identity and sizes of the different elements in balance. But it leaves intact the balance itself. Here is why:

Suppose a close group of friends live in a privileged country, in circumstances typical for their country. They feel fortunate or unfortunate, in money and love and career satisfaction and life satisfaction, by comparison to each other. These friends have lots of shared experience. They have strong feelings of mutual comparison. Within the world at large, they have their own world.

Yet they have also a "background awareness" that they live in a relatively privileged country. They have little shared experience with the inhabitants of less privileged countries. They don't think about that experience very often. The comparisons among themselves have far more importance for them. But their satisfactions do have a somewhat higher level of equipoise, caused by indistinct awareness of their privileges. They have an "almost independent" reference collection of experience, with a *higher than normal* level of happiness. Within their group, happiness outweighs unhappiness.

Has the balance been overturned? Do the friends perceive more good than bad in the world entire? No.

For each member of that group, the vague awareness of distress elsewhere in the world, constitutes the exact counterpart to his sense of privilege. The more vague his sense of privilege, the less awareness he has of suffering elsewhere. In the perception of each observer, *the world's* goods and evils still balance exactly.

But they do balance in very different ways for different observers. We each of us care about some people more than others. We each have our own personal fortunes and misfortunes. We each assess the world around us with high idiosyncrasy.

Twentieth-century humans and first-century humans constituted "almost independent" systems of reference, for most of their respective inhabitants. Hence their similar ratios of optimism to pessimism, as predicted by the prima facie argument. However, now and then, twentieth-century humans made comparisons to other ages. Our world wars made us feel unfortunate. Our technological progress and longer life spans made us feel fortunate.

Without disturbing their balance, different humans measure goods and evils by completely different references. Denizens of the Roman State or Han China or the Pleistocene, perceive goods and evils balanced exactly—sometimes within their own epochs, or within their own circle, or in the world entire, or in ways more idiosyncratic—but one way or another, always balanced. The references change; how we organize them stays the same.

The human mind does something versatile yet organized.

FOUR—BALANCES WITHIN BALANCES

Including fiction, you and I have looked at three potential counterexamples to the prima facie balance. How they fail gives us perspective on human agency, on how the world balances for each human observer.

But now let's explore a different kind of counterexample, that gives us perspective on goods and evils themselves.

The balances perceived by subtle agents, have this implication: Every good becomes an evil somewhere else, and almost every evil becomes a good. Gratuitous, senseless mayhem can be a virtuous act—in an extremely bizarre but possible alternate world. That's the implication. But is it true?

Every good or evil takes size and shape from its surroundings. Every good or evil has slippery mutability, as it migrates among possible worlds. Each has relative size and relative identity. Every good becomes an evil somewhere else, and almost every evil becomes a good. We will watch those transformations happen.

We saw the human mind being versatile yet organized. Goods and evils balance for us in Han China, in the Roman State, and in the Pleistocene epoch. They balance, even though the balance entails injustice in the world. We perceive a balance among real goods and evils, even though the balance involves comparison to fiction. How the human mind constructs the balance, transcends all those difficulties.

But our minds do something even more organized. For us, goods and evils come in myriad flavors. Thus:

Many *subcategories* of goods and evils, give size to each other and balance exactly. The mobile-in-progress has a master balance, and numerous sub-balances. Human cognition has that organization. Virtue and vice, grace and awkwardness, beauty and ugliness, optimism and pessimism, and many more, balance exactly for every human observer. *We humans* perform the comparisons that determine their sizes; human mental processes automatically perform those comparisons, often without our conscious intent or awareness. Virtue and vice, beauty and ugliness, and so on, have the same balance for any subtle human observer in any possible world.

Humans have an ambitious style of subtlety. We have reasonably high subtlety. Let's examine the mechanics of all those subbalances. Understanding the subcategories will help us watch goods becoming evils, and vice verse.

Good and bad fortune measure each other and balance. Human beings living in any possible world have exactly the same proportions of good and bad fortune, because their fortunes have exactly the same proportions above and below average. The good fortune in the actual world of living in good health to age 120, would face different comparisons in an alternate world where average human life expectancy is 400 years. The size of that good fortune would change in the alternate world. The size might even go negative: the circumstance of living in good health to 120 might be good fortune in one possible world, and bad fortune in a different possible world. Good transforms to bad.

Good and bad health measure each other and balance. In the actual world and in the present epoch, full of obnoxious and sometimes deadly diseases in great variety, I normally do not feel sorry for myself when I catch cold. I consider the symptoms minor. But if the world had few diseases and almost no discomfort from disease, then, other factors being equal, I would view the "common cold" as a major calamity, and feel sorry that I must suffer its horrible, relentless symptoms. My friends might send me flowers when I catch cold. That particular dissatisfaction has *variable size* in alternate possible worlds.

Notice the reason why the size varies. In the alternate world, largely free of disease compared to our world, the occupants make no comparisons to our world. They make all of their comparisons within their experience of the alternate world. Their experience has the same proportion of satisfaction and dissatisfaction for them, as ours does for us. They have different circumstances than we do, but they have mental processes of organization in common with us. They proportion their satisfactions and dissatisfactions with the same equipoise we use. The common cold, along with other dissatisfactions, must have larger size in their world, and smaller size in ours, to satisfy the homologous perception of balance.

In the actual world, you may catch cold from time to time and feel annoyed by the symptoms. If you had a nagging cold that never quite went away, you might feel a bit unfortunate. But suppose you lived in a world where everyone except you contracts a deadly virus around age twenty, gradually wastes away in agony, and finally kills himself or expires before the age of thirty. You alone have permanently escaped that disease—but you have a nagging cold that never quite goes away. Someone asks you how you feel. You have your usual sore throat. None of your friends or acquaintances has a cold, but they all suffer the agony of the deadly virus. You might very well say, "I feel wonderful."

Grace and awkwardness measure each other and balance. If everyone in the world moved with *exactly* equal grace, why would we attend the ballet? We would not find the dancers particularly graceful. For the category of grace and awkwardness, distance from the level of equipoise would fall to zero—as a consequence of the human mental process of organizing comparisons. In that world, everyone and no one would be graceful. With no awkwardness to balance grace, the size or degree of grace shrinks to nothing.

If everyone in the world moved *almost* as gracefully as ballet dancers, but not quite, then the same human mental process would elaborate the variations—tiny by the standards of our world—into a detailed domain of awkwardness and grace. In the actual world, devotees of the ballet actually do make that elaboration, within various reference collections of professional ballet dancers and their performances. Thus, two performances that look about the same to me, would be different as night and day to an expert. What I regard as graceful, the expert would regard as clumsy.

Beauty and ugliness measure each other. If you say about a

stranger, "Isn't she beautiful!" I may conclude that you find many women not as physically beautiful. But if every woman in the world were just as beautiful as Helen of Troy to every observer, you might never say about any woman, "Isn't she beautiful!" No woman would be beautiful in that way—again as a consequence of the human mental process of organizing comparisons.

Completely symmetrical beauty would negate our ability to make comparisons. But even an unsubtle break in the symmetry gives us an opening. In a world where—by our standards—every woman looked *almost* the same as Helen of Troy, one extra eyelash might be a hideous disfigurement. Helen with one extra eyelash, would be repulsive.

In that world, we do perceive beauty and ugliness, but perhaps ugliness gets flattened into unsubtle shape. Variety in our circumstances can be overdone or underdone. The chapter on "The Upper Limit to the Quality of Subtlety" (p. 334) elaborates.

Virtue and viciousness measure each other. In the actual world, Pol Pot's Cambodian victims numbered in the millions. He and his lieutenants directly executed many people, and killed many others by deprivation, overwork, forced marches, and the imposition of combat. But imagine an alternate possible world where almost everyone lives out his short life in Buchenwald or Auschwitz, perhaps because that world has more viciousness by comparison to our world. In that world, a man who farms the land with no guards or barbed wire or beatings until age thirty, and only then gets executed for bourgeois tendencies, might be quite pleased with his long and fortunate life. The camp inmates might envy him. They might consider him well treated. But in the actual world, that man's same circumstances horrify us. By comparison to life in Pol Pot's Cambodia or the concentration camp at Buchenwald, many of us live in comfort and safety, and for that reason we find ourselves horrified more easily by circumstances so different from our own. Our comfort and safety, and perhaps our relative ability to curb human viciousness by comparison to Cambodia's, raises the levels demarcating equipoise, and increases the distance of Pol Pot's victims from those levels. Hence our horror, and our perception of the viciousness that causes it.

A good life in the alternate world, transforms to a bad life in our world.

Of course many denizens of that alternate world would want to improve their circumstances. But many of us here in the actual world also want improvement. Forty thousand years ago, when humans had an average life expectancy of maybe twenty-two years, did we have stronger desires than now for better circumstances? Many of our distant ancestors surely hoped to live in good health to age fifty. How many of us in the present, aspire to death at fifty? Continually we adjust our comparisons to new references. Now we want to live with good health and sound mind to age ninety. At fifty we start paying closer attention to developments in medicine. With each step we take toward heaven, it recedes before us.

Justice and injustice measure each other. If an alternate world had complete justice for everyone always, then justice would be expected, unremarkable, taken for granted. It would have zero size as a good. No one could be a moral player or a subtle being. Existence would reduce to a single fatuous exercise: find the most efficient way to satisfy the demands of virtue. We would be spiders, or more exactly, a colony of ants.

If an alternate world had *almost* complete justice, then injustice only gets flattened, not reduced. A single catty remark might scandalize all of society. Insinuating unjustly that the stew could use a little more salt, would be the most vicious remark in living memory. Men would go into the woods at dawn and shoot each other with pistols. Almost complete justice leaves injustice still quite large, but flattened into unsubtle shape.

The catty remark is minor in our world, but a mortal offence in certain alternate worlds.

The human mind organizes its perception of the world. How our minds organize our perception, imposes on the world a great many balances. We see good fortune and bad, advantage and disadvantage, the expected and the unexpected, friend and enemy, a fair wage and an unfair wage, justice and injustice, virtue and vice, beauty and ugliness, grace and awkwardness, clarity and confusion, health and sickness, youth and old age, triumph and defeat, delight and despair. All these give mutable size to each other.

The balances form fluid hierarchies within a master balance of good and bad. Each sub-balance describes a different way of being good or bad—but not in a rigid way. The unexpected can sometimes be good and sometimes bad. Sometimes old age is good and sometimes it's bad. Sometimes awkwardness is endearing and grace threatening. Sickness and frailty can be qualities we desire in an enemy. A person can be known favorably by who his enemies are. Defeat measures us and reveals our dimensions. Death causes us to value life.

The balances we impose on the world—the master balance and its sub-balances—are highly fluid. Humans have an ambitious style of subtlety.

But at least one feature of the balances does have rigidity. When the mind perceives a balance, when it perceives opposites in the world, the opposites have size by comparison to each other. That's a rigid fact about our comparisons. Whether the opposites have detailed differences or few differences, they still have size by mutual comparison. Because our perception imposes balances on the world, we cannot reduce the world's proportion of bad to good. As our world changes, bad and good writhe and wriggle to remain in balance.

That fact helps dictate how our world ought to be. What's important about the world is its subtlety, not its ratio of happiness to unhappiness, nor its ratio of good to bad.

Good and evil balance, but the balance is less subtle or more subtle. You and I can perform good deeds that help other people's potential to have subtle lives. We cannot improve the actual world's balance between good and bad, nor any of the myriad sub-balances. But in myriad ways, we can improve the world's subtlety. We have prodigious scope for our good deeds. More on this later.

FIVE—ABSOLUTE DEFINITIONS

Gentle reader, I've been telling you that good and bad reside not in the world but in our perception of the world. Every good and every evil takes size and shape from its surroundings. Each has slippery mutability as it migrates among possible worlds. Each has relative size and relative identity. Every good becomes an evil somewhere else, and *almost* every evil becomes a good. That's what I've been telling you.

In particular, virtues and vices grow, shrink, even change polarity, as they migrate among possible worlds. Virtue and vice reside in our perception. Any virtue can be a vice in another world, and vice verse.

But let's resist that assertion. After all, it does appear to have peculiar consequences. Could the gratuitous intent to harm others be a virtue? Could a mass murderer full of hate, be a virtuous person in another world?

Prima facie, virtues and vices balance and measure each other. Our perception assigns each of them an identity and a size, such that they balance.

But let's play devil's advocate. Let's resist.

Perhaps at least some virtues and vices can be defined in absolute terms, such as "intentionally causing harm to others," without making overt comparisons. Would an absolute definition circumvent the mutual measurement argument? Would it subvert the balance?

No. The absolute definition contains hidden comparisons. It's not absolute. The comparisons sneak in everywhere. Usually the definition *identifies* a virtue or vice, without fixing its size. Even worse, the definition itself relies on comparative terms.

For now, let's assume that "intentionally causing harm to others" contains no hidden comparisons in the definition, that at least some virtues and vices have absolute definitions independent of comparisons. Nevertheless, their *sizes* are comparative. Identifying a vice is different from sizing it. For example:

I do not give money to support starving African children. As a result of that intentional omission, certain children in Africa have insufficient food or education. I cause harm to others. My associates regard my omission as a minor vice. But suppose I lived in a society where people generally behaved differently than in our society, and everyone gave money to support destitute African children—everyone except me. That society might regard my omission as monstrous. People in that society might accuse me of blighting the potential of another race, of slowly torturing and killing other humans, by selfishly withholding support for their food and education. They might say, "Everyone else gives money to African children. Why do you have to be so mean and stingy? You're the worst person we know." In my actual society, my vice is minor. But in a different society, with different norms of behavior, it might be major. The definition of the vice remains the same, *but the size varies*, depending on our "landscape of comparisons" with other people's virtues and vices. In the actual world I am a good person, but in another possible world, I might be the most evil creature who ever existed, and fully deserving of execution. Thus, virtues and vices have mutually dependent sizes, not absolute sizes. If we change the *amount* of vice in the world, we change some of the references by which the inhabitants size virtue and vice.

For us humans, the balance between satisfactions and dissatisfactions works mechanically like this: We have a pond full of water. All the water on the left represents satisfaction. All the water on the right represents dissatisfaction. We can add or take water out of either side of the pond, but we cannot change the balance.

Changing the water in the pond is a metaphor for constructing an alternate possible world. In all possible worlds containing humans like us, those humans always find that various categories of goods and evils have the same proportion above and below average. As a metaphor, the pond always has the same proportion of water on the satisfied left and on the dissatisfied right, no matter to which side of the pond we add or subtract water.

Some people would like dissatisfactions subtracted from the world by omnipotent fiat. They want water taken out of the pond, but they expect the cavity to remain and the rest of the pond's surface to stay at the same level.

In fact, *much of the pond must adjust and move after the removal of just one drop.*

In human perception, good and bad are mutable.

SIX—GOOD CHANGES TO EVIL AND EVIL
CHANGES TO GOOD

Now let's push the envelope. Let's put pressure on the details of how we humans compare goods and evils.

Suppose we remove a large amount of dissatisfaction from the right side of the pond. Suppose we remove all deadly diseases. As a result, average life expectancy in Midville, USA, increases from 60 years to 120 years. At first glance, *two* kinds of adjustment appear to follow: Lesser diseases, like the common cold, seem worse. And some circumstances that previously were satisfactions, like living to age 90, now become dissatisfactions. Metaphorically, balance in the pond appears to get readjusted in two different ways: Some of the drops of water on the dissatisfied right get bigger. And some of the drops on the satisfied left move over to the right.

Likewise, the vice of intentionally omitting to support starving children might grow or shrink in different landscapes. But Joe's serving peanuts to his customers is a *virtue* if all the other bartenders serve no condiments with the beer, and a *vice* if they all serve a buffet. Again, it seems that the drops of water can grow, shrink, or change sides of the pond, as the circumstances of the world change.

We can watch this process at work. Suppose life expectancy in Midville jumps from 60 to 120 years. Then the dissatisfaction of dying at age 30 remains a dissatisfaction in both landscapes, but with different sizes. The satisfaction of living in good health to age 150 remains a satisfaction in both landscapes, but with different sizes. The middle condition of living to 90 *changes polarity* from satisfaction to dissatisfaction. Good transforms to bad.

Suppose we consider a series of sixty-one Midvilles, with life expectancy 60 years in the first, 61 in the second, 62 in the third, and so on to 120 in the last. As we place the circumstance of living to age 90 into each Midville in turn, it begins as a sizable satisfaction, gradually shrinks, passes through the zero point, and continues to shrink into *negative* size as a satisfaction—equivalent to growing as a dissatisfaction.

The drop of water passing from one side of the pond to the other is really just another form of shrinking. The drop shrinks down to zero, then reappears as a growing drop on the other side of the pond. Alternatively, we could envision a stationary drop shrinking in size, passing through zero, and then growing as a *negative* volume.

This pond has some strange water! Or perhaps we should say, humans have some remarkable mental processes. The pond's search for equilibrium under our gaze, causes the water drops to grow and shrink, and sometimes to pass through zero and reverse polarity. Bad turns into good. Good can transform into bad.

All the goods and evils are still mutually dependent for size, and they still balance in equilibrium. They even have sub-balances also in equilibrium. No matter how we alter the pond's water—no matter which possible world with humans we consider—the balance between good and evil still remains exactly at the same place in the middle of the pond. Our mental processes organize different ponds to have the same balance.

For us, the world could have been much different, but it could not have had a better balance between good and evil.

Now let's revisit the contention that at least some virtues and vices have absolute definitions independent of comparisons. The vice of intentionally omitting to support starving children for no good reason, might grow or shrink in different landscapes, but *apparently* it can never shrink down to zero size, much less pass through the zero point and reverse polarity. Apparently, intentionally omitting to support starving children for no good reason, cannot be a virtue in any possible world.

But it can.

Consider a world where everyone intentionally causes harm to others, and no one ever intentionally causes benefit to others. Do we still have a world in which virtue and vice balance in equilibrium? Does that world have any virtue at all? Have we found a loophole?

Conversely, consider a world where everyone intentionally causes benefit to others, and no one intentionally causes harm. Wouldn't that world be better than the actual world?

If everyone in the "virtuous" example world has *equally* strong intention to cause benefit, then the world has no virtue and no vice—analogous to a world where everyone and no one is beautiful or graceful.

If everyone in the "virtuous" example world has *varying* strength of intention to cause benefit, then, by *their* standards, some of them will be vicious—by reason of insufficient enthusiasm to cause benefit.

The "absolute" definition of virtue contains a hidden comparison.

The analogous observations can be made about the other asymmetrical world, where all intentions toward others are harmful. Imagine a world where everyone continually plots ways and means to commit torture and murder, and does so whenever opportunity presents—except for one guy. This fellow likes to make gratuitous ironic remarks intended to annoy. He has absolutely no redeeming virtues, by our standards. However, his intention to annoy is so feeble and halfhearted, that usually he gets distracted by his hobbies of watching his ant farm and collecting matchbooks. The other inhabitants of that world would consider him virtuous: an individual of beatific forbearance. Because of his comparative virtue in that world, his society might be much prized.

In the actual world, he would just be annoying.

We see that virtues and vices defined "independent of comparisons" *can* shrink to zero size. They can even pass through zero and reverse polarity—within extremely flattened worlds. The definitions "intentionally causing benefit to others" and "intentionally causing harm to others" do involve comparisons. The magnitudes of intentions to cause benefit or harm have various comparative measurements. Moreover, the nature of the benefit intended also has comparative measurements. The comparisons sneak in everywhere.

Intentions have comparative size. But *that form* of comparison gets obscured by the normal composition of the alternate possible worlds we consider. Most of those alternate worlds contain a mixture of intentions to cause harm and benefit—with the mixture not thoroughly unbalanced. In such "mixed" worlds, intention to cause harm cannot become virtuously small. Only in extremely flattened alternate worlds, with all intention to cause benefit subtracted, can the intention to cause harm fall through zero, reverse polarity, and become a virtue.

Gratuitous intent to cause harm can be a virtue, in some possible worlds. Those worlds would be flattened, grotesque, and unsubtle, but they are logically possible.

We still have a pond with all the goods and evils mutually dependent for size, and still balanced in equilibrium—still implying that any possible world we humans inhabit has exactly the same proportions of good and evil as the actual world. We humans have highly organized cognition of mutable shadows.

Indeed, all the goods and evils we have considered so far can reverse polarity. Even the rapacious intent to inflict grievous harm on everyone within reach, can become a virtue—in a sufficiently bizarre alternate world, where most people have the *extremely* rapacious intent to inflict *extremely* grievous harm.

Good and evil are strange critters. They are not facts about the world. They are facts about our perception of the world. To make them balance, we sometimes transform one into the other.

SEVEN—WHEN THE DENTIST DRILLS YOUR TOOTH

Let's consider another attempt to find an evil of absolute size, independent of comparisons.

When your dentist's drill hits a nerve and you cry out to all the powers in heaven, to what extent are you comparing that experience to a relaxing day at the beach, or to any other satisfactions or dissatisfactions in your life?

The pain you feel gets transmitted directly into your brain's distress center. It bypasses the mind's perception of balance. No matter what other experiences the human race has had, that pain appears to have at least a component of absolute size.

True, it may also have a component of relative size. You might be thinking, "The last dentist was better than this." or "I'd rather be at the beach." By those comparisons, your dissatisfaction has a *component* of relative size. Nevertheless, your body and brain have a direct reaction of physical pain. Your dissatisfaction has a large component of absolute size, unfiltered by comparisons.

Your perception of good and bad in the world might very well be unbalanced while the drill is actually drilling. Even if the dentist is your best friend, you might shove him away in mindless agony.

However, as soon as the pain stops and loses its immediate urgency, your higher brain functions reemerge, and your normal balanced perception returns. After the drilling has mercifully stopped, you can rationally compare it to having bad teeth, decide that the drilling is the lesser evil, and elect to go forward with the suffering as best you can. The balances in your perception have returned.

I believe that many of our physical dissatisfactions have smaller components of absolute size, but with the dentist's drill, the absolute component suddenly rivets complete attention to the primordial brain. I have difficulty believing that such pain could drop to zero, much less become pleasant, in any possible world.

We find an exception to the variable size of goods and evils. For humans, physical pain has an absolute size. When I stub my toe, or when the dentist drills and hits my nerve, the pain has a component of absolute size independent of comparisons.

That arrangement appears to have advantages. Humans do have ambitious subtlety. For us, goods and evils have an intricate balance with intricate sub-balances. Some of those balances appear to benefit from an anchor. Some of the balances we each perceive, seem to benefit from a check on their mutability. Thus:

For us, the system of balances at times can almost be unstable. From one moment to the next, a human can view defeat as victory, victory as defeat, an unfriendly act as a friendly act, a fair wage as an unfair wage, sympathy as deception, an exciting game as monotony, a long journey as short, a sunny day as stifling, grace as awkwardness, beauty as ugliness, and so on. For us, many of the balances can sometimes be kaleidoscopic.

However, causing gratuitous physical harm to another person, changes somewhat less readily into benefiting that person. Physical harm to another has a component of absolute size.

Some of the comparisons we each make, have a check on their mutability. The kaleidoscope sometimes gets slowed down by an anchor.

For a person under extreme torture, physical pain has an urgency that renders other goods and evils tiny by comparison. Immediate pain dominates perception and obscures the intricate balances. Good and bad become *un*balanced.

We are each vulnerable in that way. We cannot always hide inside our relative comparisons.

Under more typical circumstances for humans, pain has smaller size—too small to overthrow the balances between good and evil. Pain in small doses gets absorbed into the general balance between good and bad—absorbed as anchor.

If human subtle agents perceive the world in terms of balancing opposites, then physical pain is the exception. But all the other goods and evils have their size by mutual comparison, including comparison to physical pain.

The consequence is this: The world's goods and evils balance exactly, in the perception of each human subtle observer, whenever he is not under extreme physical torture.

I can't think of any absolute *satisfactions* enjoyed by us humans. Consider heroin, for example. Like the dentist's drill, heroin does bypass our sophisticated comparisons, and it does directly affect a primitive part of the brain. But we humans react differently to primitive bliss than to primitive pain. Our universe did not make a mistake.

Suppose we could have the intoxicating heroin high, at the level of the first initial rush, as long as we wanted, with no inconvenient side effects and no obligations neglected. The bliss doesn't wear off or diminish. We never feel withdrawal symptoms. We never have that desperate feeling: where can I get more heroin *now*. We simply enjoy the bliss unbroken and unrelieved, and other people are universally supportive.

However, we are true subtle beings, not spiders. We size our satisfactions by comparison—*all* our satisfactions. We compare today to yesterday and the day before. Just as grace, justice, virtue, and beauty have zero size when they become absolutely universal, so also does narcotic bliss. For us, positive comparisons dilute each other. The first day's heroin high would be quite nice: better than shlepping to work and pretending to respect the boss. The *nineteenth* day of the *same* bliss—just a tad less nice. One year of completely unrelieved heroin bliss, would definitely suffer from dilution. The bliss, though still intense, would move toward zero size as a satisfaction. One *billion* years might demote the bliss all the way to torture.

If the dentist drills right into the nerve, and continues drilling a live nerve through all eternity, I believe the tooth would hurt like hell even after a billion years. Not much diluting comparison there. Apparently, *human* subtle agents have this asymmetry: physical pain has a component of irreducible absolute size, but all our satisfactions have relative size. That fact denies us refuge from a skillful Siren. Our universe did not make a mistake.

We need to modify the pond analogy.

Let's add some rocks to the pond. The rocks cannot grow or shrink. They cannot move to the other side of the pond (reverse polarity). They just sit on the bottom. They represent dissatisfactions of absolute size.

If the pond has a lot more water than rocks, the balance between good and evil still works exactly as before. The rocks participate in the pond's equilibrium, and as anchor they slow down the water's turbulence. But the rocks don't pile up above the water's surface and subvert its balance. Whether we add or remove water or rocks from the pond, the whole still balances—so long as the pond has a lot more water than rocks.

Subtle agency requires a *sufficiency* of comparisons. Our satisfactions and dissatisfactions don't need to be entirely comparative, just mostly. With *sufficient* comparative goods and evils—with sufficient water in the pond—the absolute evils don't overturn the natural balance.

Collectively, we humans do have the sufficiency of comparative goods and evils. Even our absolute dissatisfactions figure into the comparisons. If today you screamed in agony at the dentist, most of your pain has absolute size. No comparison can diminish that agony. But tomorrow at the beach, you might say, "What a lovely day. This sure beats going to the dentist." And some of your friends, after hearing about your hour under the drill, might think to themselves, "That poor bastard. Thank God *I* have sound teeth." And when your obnoxious, gloating neighbor says, "I'm going to buy a Lamborghini and make you turn green," you can look concerned and say, "Your teeth look a little green right now. I know a dentist who can fix you right up." After he visits your dentist, he won't dare buy a Lamborghini, for fear of your sardonic smile.

We cannot improve the actual world's proportions of good and evil by adding more and more direct physical agonies—more and more absolute dissatisfactions. Nor can we improve the actual world by subtracting some of the existing direct physical agonies: The actual world already has too little absolute dissatisfaction to disturb natural equilibrium between satisfaction and dissatisfaction. The pond corresponding to the actual world already has *a lot* more water than rocks. The rocks don't pile up above the surface. Hydraulically, the pond reaches equilibrium with or without its rocks. Removing rocks neither brings nor overturns equilibrium. If no one had teeth susceptible to pain from the dentist, our dissatisfactions would still balance our satisfactions.

And finally, we have no refuge in satisfactions of absolute size. None are available. Not even the bliss of heroin can protect us. We cannot put that wax in our ears. From the Siren that devours us, we cannot take refuge as worthless spiders.

Why do we humans feel physical pain of absolute size, while every other good and evil has relative size? Does the world box our ears to keep us awake? Does it compel us to care what happens? Does the world insist that we be vulnerable? Does our intricate system of relativities need an anchor somewhere, an element of absolute size, to slow down the kaleidoscope? And does that anchor itself have an optimum size and position within the system of relativities?

Yes all around. That does seem to be what happens.

Even with absolute dissatisfactions added to it, we *still* have a pond whose point of balance, between goods and evils, cannot be improved in any alternate world. We perceive balances and sub-balances, we compare comparisons, we can organize an enormous variety of circumstances, we each use idiosyncratic references, we even use fictional references—but the balances remain. Such is the human mind. Such is our vulnerability to a skillful Siren. We are subtle beings indeed.

EIGHT—ALTERNATIVES TO HUMAN AGENCY

Shall we try another line of attack? Let's look at alternatives to human agency. Let's swap out humans from the world. Let's replace them with agents almost human, but not quite. Can we subvert their balance between good and evil?

What if we *change human agency,* so that *satisfactions* have absolute size? What if heroin bliss never dilutes itself, even after a billion years? The bliss has absolute size forever. Have we found an escape from the balance between delight and despair?

Of course we just mentioned that particular wax-in-the-ears. An almost-human having eternal bliss of absolute size, with no downside whatsoever, doesn't come close to escaping. As a *subtle* being, he would be incoherent: After a billion years, a subtle being would say, "Great Jupiter and all the gods! Not *another* perfect day." Absolute satisfaction forever is incoherent for a subtle being. His experience contradicts itself. Therefore, he must be a spider, enjoying non-comparative spider bliss.

But a spider can blissfully spin webs for all eternity, and still we do not envy him.

However, let's refurbish that counterargument. Let's make it as strong as we can. Could the almost-humans somehow be given a bias toward positive comparisons, that does not dilute itself? If our agency were a little different, could we emphasize positive comparisons without shrinking them? Could *subtle* agents in an alternate world be similar to us, and balance their goods and evils, but balance them differently than we do, such that their happiness improves?

No matter what the circumstances compared, every positive comparison has a corresponding negative comparison. If you have more teeth than I, then I have fewer teeth than you. Any bias toward positive or negative comparisons, that does not dilute itself, must reside in the agent himself, as a structural component independent of circumstances. What could that structural component be like? Let's make the strongest case we can.

I might have biases to notice and emphasize certain kinds of comparisons. You might have different biases. For me, having sound teeth might be a large component of my happiness. For you, understanding the nuances of Abbott and Costello might be a large component. However, if my teeth get hit by a hockey puck, my rapture over my teeth might turn to despair. My negative comparisons seem to have equal importance to my positive comparisons. If you enjoy Abbott and Costello too continuously, you might become disenchanted with the sameness of their humor. So far, neither of us appears to have a true bias toward noticing positive comparisons.

Accordingly, let's consider an alternate world with two people resembling you and me. In that world, when I lose my teeth to a hockey puck, I forget about teeth. I don't mourn the loss of my teeth, nor sadly remember the pride I once felt in my pearly whites. For you, continuous Abbott and Costello never palls, because their want of variety never intrudes very sharply on your awareness. In that alternate world, people in general have a systematic bias to notice the positive comparisons and downplay the negative or diluting comparisons. They have lots and lots of sunshine, but they enjoy each sunny day just as much as if sunshine were often absent. They enjoy their friends while they are alive and present, but do not mourn them when they go away. Do the *alternate people* in that alternate world have more happiness?

Those alternate people have taken a large step toward spider-style agency. A spider's satisfactions all have absolute size. Spiders have only rocks in their pond, not water. The rocks might come and go, but they never change each other's size. A spider does not know or does not care that certain comparisons obtain among his experiences. His agency lacks that dimension. We do not envy the most elaborate and successful spider. For those alternate people we are considering, negative comparisons have lost importance. Many of their positive comparisons are freed from the measurement of negative comparisons and diluting comparisons. Consequently, the remaining positive comparisons have more rigid size. They become less like comparisons, and more like satisfactions of absolute size. For example, Abbott and Costello and continuous sunshine never dilute themselves very far. Those satisfactions have components of size immune to comparisons. Friends and teeth can be present or absent as satisfactions, but those satisfactions have lost the relativity in their size, measured by the possibility they might someday go away, and the pain their absence would bring. Without those relativities, the satisfactions have large components of size ungoverned by comparisons.

Happiness becomes too straightforward. Satisfactions have rigid sizes. Finding them becomes mere calculation, like an Easter egg hunt. A spider can be programmed to cover the territory and search for the eggs—the satisfactions—in the most efficient manner. We do not envy the satisfactions of a spider.

Because those alternate people have lost so many negative and diluting comparisons, their "comparative" satisfactions have large components of absolute size. They have rocks that pile up on the positive side of their pond, break the water's surface, and destroy the fluid equilibrium *we* find among relative goods and evils. The high proportion of rocks to water, pushes them so close to spider-style agency, that we cannot envy them. They have satisfactions similar to straightforward, programmed machine satisfactions. Better a man dissatisfied.

Spiders can go to heaven. Circumstances that maximize their absolute satisfactions, constitute their heaven. Simply pile on all the happy rocks available to a spider—plenty of flies, a big web, and lots of little offspring, day after day after day throughout all eternity—and that spider reaches his peak of contentment. His satisfactions remain undiminished even if he lives among other spiders that also have *their* satisfactions maximized. His satisfactions remain undiminished even if they arise from exactly the same experience looping over and over for all eternity. He does not measure his happiness by comparisons to other spiders, or by comparison to his own happiness yesterday and the day before. He feels "disassociated" satisfactions of rigid size. He has satisfactions immune to comparisons. He never gets tired of exactly the same perfect day repeated to infinity.

But we humans are subtle beings. We have an extra dimension to our agency. Subtle beings make comparisons—lots of comparisons. We must have comparative satisfactions. We cannot go to heaven. We become inured to the charms of any heaven. Alternate worlds do not help us. We are designed—rather carefully—to feel both positive and negative comparisons in any world. And any world has a negative comparison for every positive comparison.

Let's make a more subtle attempt to design alternate agents similar to humans, but happier. Imagine agents similar to humans, but they measure and balance their goods and evils differently from the ways we balance them. Unlike spiders, all their satisfactions have relative size. They do notice and care about negative comparisons. But the positive comparisons make them happier than the negative comparisons make them unhappy. They mourn when their friends leave them, but not so much as we mourn. Continuous sunshine or continuous narcotic bliss dilutes itself for them, but not so rapidly as for us. Their satisfactions have size by comparison to dissatisfactions and to other satisfactions, but something in their agency makes the satisfactions larger than the dissatisfactions.

By substituting these agents for humans, have we found a way to improve subtle experience?

Those alternate people as described, are incoherent. They cannot be aware that their satisfactions have larger size than their dissatisfactions. Except for their balancing sizes, what other measurement do *comparative* goods and evils have? By what references could an agent discern that one side of the balance is larger than the other? He can only discern the balance itself.

If the alternate people are unaware that their satisfactions are larger than their dissatisfactions, in what sense *are* they larger?

The water on one side of the pond, cannot be higher than on the other side. That's how subtle perception works.

Goods and evils remain obstinately balanced. But attempting to dislodge that balance, illuminates the structure of goods and evils.

And now we have reached a key insight into the human style of cognition.

NINE—BIASES TO BE HAPPY OR UNHAPPY

The actual world does have people for whom satisfactions are larger than dissatisfactions. The actual world has optimists. Such people take pride in their teeth, but serenely forget about teeth soon after the hockey puck has removed theirs. They enjoy Abbott and Costello even after they recognize tedious repetition. The pleasure of continuous sunshine diminishes slowly for them. They thoroughly enjoy their friends, and remember them, but only for a little while mourn their passing. Such people do have something in their agency that emphasizes positive comparisons.

But we recognize such people, and they recognize themselves, only by comparison to their counterparts in the same world. And now we have another glimpse into the comparison of comparisons. Without making a mistake that turns us into spiders, our universe gives us biased comparisons. Each of us views the world through his own idiosyncratic bias.

The actual world also has people for whom dissatisfactions are larger. Some people are just plain determined to be miserable.

In the actual world, optimists and pessimists each make comparisons that measure their emphases on satisfactions. An optimist knows that his satisfaction-emphases are larger, because he compares himself to pessimists. Each observer of an optimist, observes an emphasis on positive comparisons, only because each observer has the human race, as he perceives it, for baseline reference. No subtle observer can perceive only optimism wherever he looks. Optimism and pessimism themselves are relative terms. They constitute comparisons, and they themselves have size by mutual comparison.

Consider a person *we* would view as an optimist, a child growing up in the mountains all by himself, completely isolated from contact with any other human being, without even the knowledge that other humans exist. This child spends most of his time gathering nuts and berries, and whistling or singing. When he skins his knee and feels pain, the experience doesn't overly trouble him. When he can't find enough to eat, he doesn't worry or feel depressed. Sometimes the darkness scares him, but his fright quickly evaporates in the morning sunshine. In our eyes, by comparison to the human race at large, he emphasizes the positive. But *he* would consider himself neither an optimist nor a pessimist. Because of his isolation, he has different references than we have. Both his experiences and his reactions are normal to him; he compares his reactions to his own level of equipoise, not to ours. On the days when *we* would view him as less optimistic than usual, but still quite optimistic, he would view himself as having a pessimistic episode. Only when he comes down from the mountains and witnesses other people dwelling to various degrees on their misfortunes, does he understand his own emphasis on positive comparisons.

Optimism and pessimism in the world, thus balance exactly for each observer. If the world—any world—is wonderful for some people, it must be horrible for others.

Spiders also have biases in their perceptions. Upon encountering a rather large female who might devour him, some male spiders decide to take the chance of mating. Others wait for a smaller opportunity. In their perception of the large female, male spiders can be viewed as optimistic and pessimistic. Spiders have that idiosyncrasy. But it is only an idiosyncrasy in a mechanical calculation. Spiders are not all the same, they calculate differently, but they are all spiders who only calculate.

Humans have idiosyncrasies that propagate and reverberate throughout a fluid system of perception. We rise far above mere calculation.

The cold wind blowing from the future, has a different feel to children barely aware of it, to vigorous young adults, to mid-life-crisis adults, and to the elderly. Unknown to any spider, the cold wind rattles and echoes throughout all mature human comparison. It changes us again and again. It sounds us to our limits. It gives size to the ineffable and the sublime. It makes our future selves mysterious. Perhaps it makes each of us finally unknowable to anyone else or to ourselves. Our idiosyncrasies and our biases do rise far above mere differences in calculation.

Biases to emphasize positive and negative comparisons, can be different for different humans. Those differences make us more idiosyncratic and the world more subtle. But the biases themselves have their sizes by comparison to other biases. Goods and evils still balance and sub-balance within their shifting hierarchies, like a mobile-in-progress. Goods and evils still have mutable size, not absolute size, despite all their complications. We are complicated without freezing up and descending toward spiders. Sometimes we seek after brilliant sunlit pleasures, sometimes shadows enticing in the moonlight, and sometimes intermittent hypnotic images invoked by lightning. We have a nonspider dimension to our agency. Such is the human mind.

Our biases are all different. We are highly idiosyncratic. Our idiosyncrasies reverberate throughout our comparisons. But the balances we each perceive, endure.

TEN—THE MOVING FINGER WRITES

Let's make one last attempt to disrupt the prima facie balance between goods and evils, and find one more insight.

At the *beginning* of the plague years in Europe and Asia, people were generally more distressed than previously. Then, as the plague continued year after year, new norms of satisfaction gradually replaced the previous norms. People grew a bit more accustomed to the plague.

Similarly, when scientists announced a cure for leprosy, surely, for many observers, that day was a bit brighter than the day before. Only with time did we grow accustomed to having one less deadly disease.

When human or natural activity, within the world's causal structure, introduces a new satisfaction or dissatisfaction, the transformation of the satisfactions and dissatisfactions already existing will not be instantaneous. Temporary imbalances seem to occur. Does the proportion of satisfaction to dissatisfaction, wobble up and down from its baseline balance? Does the mobile shudder and oscillate?

No. The mobile evolves sinuously and fluently.

When bin Laden's terrorists destroyed the World Trade Center, life suddenly became darker for many in Manhattan. To some degree, life became darker for many in the world. But that darkness has a balance. The past suddenly became the good old days. For many in Manhattan, life before the terrorist attack seems better now than it did at the time.

The human perception of balance has a dimension in time. The inalterable past can change.

At the beginning of the plague years, observers viewed the recent past more favorably than once they did. On the day when the cure for leprosy was announced, the past sufferings of lepers seemed a bit more gratuitous. An observer always perceives an exact balance between satisfactions and dissatisfaction—at their various points in time. Indeed, a balance independent of changes over time, would be unsubtle.

The inalterable past can change in highly subtle ways. After several decades of the feminist movement, many Westerners have new perceptions of Cleopatra and Catherine the Great. Today many Americans view their Civil War differently than we did in 1920. The interim saw a great number of relevant events, including *Brown v. Board of Education* in 1954. The moving finger writes and moves on, but continually the words written have new meaning.

We know and we do not know what we are. Human agency may not be the best possible form of subtle agency. Present human society may not be the most subtle possible form of human society. Neither of those observations constitutes evidence against our universe, as the most subtle possible world. If the actual universe is the best possible apple tree, it does not follow that contemporary human society is the tree's most exquisite apple. It does not follow, gentle reader, that you or I have taken the measure of subtlety in our own existence. Your life and mine can be different and new, whenever the world wishes. This world will outguess us whenever it wishes. All the complicated balances that circumscribe your life, fail to reduce its dimension of unpredictability.

Quite the contrary. Precisely the intricate balances that enclose us, cause the inalterable past to change, and point to mysterious shapes in the future.

Of the Siren's mortal allure, spiders know nothing. For them, the inalterable past remains inalterable, and the future confines itself to brute facts from nowhere. For them, heaven is coherent. But we are not spiders. Good and evil continually reverberate throughout our comparisons. We can be sounded. Then give us our Siren sublime, and let our footprints disappear.

The Guangzhou
Train Station

China has too many people and not enough capital. Capacity on the Chinese railways can accommodate about seventy or eighty percent of the people who want to travel.

Another problem in China, worse than poverty and overcrowding, is the national lack of self esteem. Among Chinese living in China, friends respect friends, but strangers often have contempt for strangers.

Beginning in the early eighteen hundreds, China passed through a period of abuse from some Western nations and from Japan. Perhaps during this period, Chinese learned to think poorly of themselves. As recently as 1947, foreign gunboats still ranged the rivers of China with impunity. Then the Chinese people reclaimed their sovereignty in a long paroxysm of rage, insanity, and worship of one individual almost as a god. As the German humiliation and economic distress brought forth Hitler and his brownshirts as savior of the nation, so the deeper humiliation and more profound economic distress in China produced Mao and his Cultural Revolution. In their frenzy to obliterate every vestige of Western influence, real or imagined, the Chinese people turned on each other and tore themselves to pieces. As the Chinese curse puts it, "May you live in interesting times."

Lee Ming and I have several times visited Guangzhou, near the mouth of the Pearl River. Her family has friends in that city. In

1994 we stayed for three weeks in a university dormitory on the rural outskirts of the city. We took our meals with the students in their cafeteria, watched their movies with them on Saturday night, played ping pong and Chinese chess with them, and went hiking with them in the hills. The word "Mao" was never mentioned. The new generation in China impressed us.

From Guangzhou we traveled by train to Guilin, and then by bus to Yangshuo, a tiny tourist backpacker Mecca close to Guilin, and situated among some of the world's most unique and most sublime scenery. Even the old peasant farmers, lifelong residents near Yangshuo, sometimes stop and stare at the unearthly round mountains floating atop their reflections in the flooded fields. People watching these apparitions do not speak, and disturbing them is considered bad manners.

But travel from Guangzhou to Guilin by train requires a ticket, and the tickets are sold at the Guangzhou train station.

Generally, Lee Ming and I travel on the train third class. The third-class railway cars have narrow hard beds stacked three deep, all on the same side of the car, in steerage style without compartments or privacy. Also provided, just across the narrow aisle against the opposite windows, are tiny tables with attached stools that fold out. During the day, smaller travelers can sit on a lower berth and look out the window on that side, while taller people sit on the stools and look out the window on the other side. The experience can be quite cozy and convivial. With nothing much to do for thirty or forty hours at a stretch, except eat and sleep and perform ablutions, strangers fall easily into conversation with strange foreigners. Sometimes the food toted aboard by various passengers gets shared communally, to vary the culinary experience. Onion sandwiches are my favorite. The hepatitis vaccine is recommended. The manifold scenic delights include the occasional band of small boys perched on a hilltop, trying to break your window by throwing rocks from high above. They often hit the roof of the train but hardly ever the windows. Difficult angle. Raucous music blasts everyone awake at 5:45 a.m., to make sure we take full advantage of life on the railway.

The first-class cars operate a little differently. Here the passen-

gers are just a touch more snooty and aloof. The beds are wide and soft and stacked two deep, with four to a compartment. The compartment has a wood-paneled door with a fancy handle. The door can be shut and locked. The tables and stools against the opposite windows are larger and more comfortable, and the stools don't fold away when you get up. Visitors from third class are frowned upon. Within the first-class compartment, the occupants have the option of turning off the loud speaker and sleeping past 5:45. But usually the staff becomes anxious for your safety if 6:30 rolls around and you have yet to show signs of life.

In fifth class, you sit on a hard wooden bench. If you have luggage, you don't close your eyes. Fifth class is just fine for day trips, but many Chinese travel long distances sitting upright in a crowd on that hard bench.

For completeness I should mention that the toilet situation, in all classes, can be a bit messy. You must aim for a small hole in the floor, while the car sways and lurches down the track. The bathrooms are locked whenever the train comes to rest at a station, out of consideration for the city masses. And I recommend not relying on the dining car, except for alcohol. China has a variety of exotic and tasty alcoholic beverages. However, getting drunk does increase and complicate your visits to the bathroom. For me, the worst sensation on a Chinese train was having the desperate urge to pee while the train sat placidly with locked bathrooms at some obscure city station. Drinking and visits to the bathroom must be carefully managed. Never let your tank get too full.

First-class tickets are difficult to obtain. All of them are sold "through the back door." Only if you are good friends with a ranking railroad employee can you travel first class. Lee Ming has a cousin in Qingtao who works for the railway police. He packs heat and people respect him. Sometimes, in the course of his duties, he draws his weapon in anger. He has an unhappy marriage and he works hard to advance his career. We can travel first class on any journey that begins in Qingtao. Otherwise, we have to squash in with the middle classes. And we must get hold of the tickets ourselves.

Guangzhou has a small industry devoted to helping the well-heeled traveler avoid the train station. In 1994 the third-class ticket to Guilin cost 103 yuan (about fifteen dollars). For a surcharge of three to four hundred yuan, a volunteer would go to the station and buy a pair of tickets for you. In China, many factory workers don't get three hundred yuan in a month. And yet, no matter how many different people we asked, the surcharge required was never less than three hundred yuan, and often more. This phenomenon aroused our curiosity about the Guangzhou train station. We decided to buy the tickets ourselves.

Lee Ming and I took a bus to the station, on a chilly March morning. We arrived about ten o'clock. A uniformed railway policeman intercepted the big-nosed foreigner and his "translator" just outside the station. He spoke briefly with Lee Ming, then escorted us through one of the many parallel doors. Outside, the temperature was just below freezing, about thirty degrees Fahrenheit. But inside the vast unheated station lobby, perhaps eight thousand crowded bodies raised the temperature to at least ninety degrees. From each of thirty ticket windows stretched a long, long line of hopeful ticket buyers, hundreds of people in each line. They waited for hours, sometimes all day, often without assurance they would ever reach the front of the line before closing time. Almost all of the would-be ticket buyers were men, and none of them were old or feeble. The few women in line were young and vigorous. Each person in line always, always kept both of his arms wrapped tightly around the person in front, to avoid losing his place. Even the young women had to cling tightly to the man in front. The lines of people clinging to one another stretched across the station lobby like enormous human snakes. Chaos was not far away. People tended to press forward toward the ticket windows. Railway police kept constant vigil. We saw two other uniformed men wade out into the lobby, slapping faces hard and fast in all directions. But none of the ticket buyers let go of the man in front. To let go was to lose one's place in line. The long snakes writhed away from the uniforms, but no man raised an arm to defend himself. The men's faces were red from the heat and from the slaps they received.

The uniformed police carried nightsticks, but we saw no evidence they were used. Our escort led us toward the front of the lobby. All around him, the men's eyes grew big and remained fixed upon him. The snakes twisted and undulated to move away from him, creating a path for us. We followed him right up to the ticket windows. Then another man appeared above us, standing on the narrow counter ledge running the length of the building just under the ticket windows. This man, not wearing a uniform, wielded a big roll of heavy paper. From his perch above he knelt down and began to clear a space for us in front of one of the windows. His arm rose and fell in rapid cadence, whacking away at the ears and faces of the men still clinging to each other, or clinging to the counter. But the men, so close to their goal, gave ground reluctantly. The man with the rolled-up paper needed twenty seconds to produce a small clearing around him. The ticket buyers backed away and stared up at him, again with big eyes, just out of his reach. A tense standoff ensued. For five seconds no one moved. Then Lee Ming stepped forward to the point of sale. A heavy wooden barrier separated the clerks selling tickets from the people buying them. Each "window" was a hole in the barrier not much larger than a credit card. Lee Ming stepped to the window in the clearing and bought two third-class tickets for Guilin, paying the same price as everyone else. Then I made my own path to the nearest door, with Lee Ming following.

The next day we took the convivial overnight journey to Guilin, followed by an hour's bus ride to Yangshuo and its scenery sublime. You and I perceive balances in the world.

Subtlety and Physical Law

As discussed in "Opinions and Spiders" (p. 125), only their subtlety ranks possible worlds. Only the subtle experience in a world, gives it a value rank among other worlds.

That fact casts new light on actual physical law, which does ingeniously support subtle experience. Let's look now at our world's skillful and felicitous engineering.

Modern times have witnessed a kind of existential funk or angst based on our "insignificance" in the enormous universe. This evaluation is unjustified. It derives from a misunderstanding of how subtle experience must be constructed.

As a *single tree*, in virtue of its complicated organic systems, reflects a biological evolution covering an entire planet for more than a billion years, so a *single person's* complicated mixture of structure and randomness in her experience, reflects a physical evolution of two hundred fifty billion galaxies for almost fourteen billion years.

Physical evolution from the Big Bang, does more than impart quality structure and lightness to experience. Evolution achieves that result using methods intelligible to the inhabitants. Evolution is transparent: Physical evolution produces subtle agents able to understand physical evolution.

In the physical principles underlying our universe, we humans find potency and simplicity combined. Our physical evolution does much with just a few, simple, transparent principles.

Our world manages to give us multiple descriptions of ourselves. We gain perspective on us, by contemplating Roman history, medieval art, Confucius, politics, the dinosaurs, the solar system, human psychology, the Big Bang, the dawn of the human species, last night's date, and Grandfather's construction business during the Great Depression. All of those happenings help show us what we are. All of them figure into the evolution of us today.

We gain a more coherent insight into ourselves, and greater power to act, by understanding all those happenings as elements of a coherent evolution; by understanding how they all relate to the same underlying physical principle. Humanity is perhaps just beginning to do this.

Physical law does many things. It operates coherently on a scale both infinitesimal and colossal. Physical law enables our everyday world of perception and interaction. It permits a process of discovery. It gives increasing scope to our agency. Physical law generates the high quality randomness in our everyday lives. It spins out our idiosyncrasies. It weaves the mixture of the expected and the unexpected. And most crucial, all these faces of physical law can be understood coherently.

Order, surprise, complicated yet coherent agents, wide scope for our will, multiple perspectives on ourselves, lightness, idiosyncrasy, mystery, transparency—to achieve all this in one evolution, all these demands pulling in different directions, physical law must be very potent yet very simple. And that's just what it is. Our universe uses ingenious methods to resolve the conflicting demands on its structure.

Let's talk about those methods. Let's talk about the resolution of conflicting constraints on structure; how the universe manages to do everything with the same intelligible evolution.

You and I will focus on three techniques for combining potency with simplicity.

First, physical evolution uses the same specific structures over and over again in many different roles. If we understand how one phenomenon works, then we understand how many phenomena work. This is a coherent universe.

Second, evolution uses its giant size and age to advantage. This is a patient universe.

The third technique is the masterstroke. Physical principle produces irreversible events. Starting with the Big Bang, the same phenomena are both a falling down and a building up. We will talk about that.

In virtue of irreversible events that build up while they fall down, our universe generates randomness and order in tandem. We will see how.

In virtue of irreversible events, our universe will someday run down and stop, we are told. Our universe has a natural progression in time, from beginning to end.

In virtue of irreversible events that build up while they fall down, the passage of time has significance: the inhabitants are mortal and their experience fleeting, yet they have goals, expectations, and dreams for a future growing naturally out of their past. Throughout all phenomena, physical principle infuses a coherent progression in time. It does that in a simple and clever way. This is an ingenious universe.

In fact, all three techniques feed on each other. Dividing them up is artificial. After looking at them separately, you and I will watch them operating together.

We live inside a physical evolution both simple and potent. Only subtlety ranks worlds, and our physical law ingeniously supports subtle experience.

REUSING THE SAME STRUCTURES

Gentle reader, consider how many different causal roles the *stars* play in your subtle, idiosyncratic experience on Planet Earth— experience with coherent structure and high quality randomness.

Stars, proto-stars, and dead star ashes help constitute galaxies. Stars create heavier elements from hydrogen. By exploding, stars randomize the distribution of those elements. Subsequent stars, as they are born from gas clouds containing those heavy elements, trigger and randomize the condensation of planets. Both of those randomizing functions are known to be influenced by the shapes, sizes, and interactions of galaxies; therefore, the stars *transmit* these forms of galaxy-randomness to planets, including biologically viable planets. Stars of different sizes have radically different life cycles, again randomizing the composition of planets and transmitting galaxy-randomness to them. On our particular planet, the same stars appear in the night sky and push us to imagine, wonder, and investigate. And one particular star enables photosynthesis in our planet's biological evolution, evaporates water from the oceans, pushes clouds around the sky, gives us tides and eclipses, gives us our seasons, turns on the illumination each day, regulates the warmth of our surroundings, shines on our faces, marks the passage of time, and gives us beautiful dawns and dusks. One physical feature—a blob of simple gas fallen in upon itself—performs all of those causal roles in your subtle experience on planet Earth.

If humans understand how stars work, we already understand much about ourselves. We can see physical principle staying simple and producing a limited range of structures, but giving the same structures many different causal functions in our experience.

Another example of physical principle being potent yet simple: The same atomic structure—the same periodic table—plays different causal roles under different temperatures and pressures. The same periodic table supports both stellar fusion and DNA chemistry. Atomic structure supports both the evolution of planets and evolutions on planets.

Moreover, the very same atomic structure gives potent scope to our technologies.

Again we have one physical structure with many functions in your experience and mine.

Still another example of physical principle being potent yet simple: Biological evolution uses cell-chemistry and DNA chemistry over and over again. The same relatively simple small-scale chemical principles of self-replication and mutation, pass through gazillions of iterations for more than a billion years. Slowly those simple principles elaborate into entire fluctuating ecosystems. The random idiosyncrasies infused into the host planet, plus random mutating cosmic particles and the occasional random extinction event from without, gradually shape and build the fantastic pottery turning so many times on the wheel, elaborating for eons both the idiosyncratic structure and the high quality randomness within the structure.

If we understand DNA chemistry, we gain unifying insight into a sprawling biological evolution. We can relate the dinosaurs to ourselves. And we can embark upon dangerous and radical technologies. Physical principle is simple enough for us to understand, yet very potent.

Another example: The laws of gravity and momentum have multiple causal functions in our experience. Gravity causes the rain to fall, the wind to howl, the tides to rise, and the clouds to scud. Gravity causes the formation of galaxies, stars, and planets. Gravity enables the galaxies to turn and the stars to burn. It gives us meteors and the occasional comet. Gravity causes the phases of the moon. It causes the planets and the moon to journey through starry fields. It produces the Milky Way. Gravity and momentum account for Planet Earth's revolution, rotation, precession, and nutation, and thereby gives us hours, seasons, and epochs. Momentum and gravity allow us to play billiards and baseball. And gravity causes a river to search for the sea. The same simple principle does all that.

When Sir Isaac Newton understood gravity, he understood the apple falling on his head and the planets moving through the sky. By using the same principle in many different settings, our complicated universe makes itself intelligible.

And another example of structures repeated: electromagnetic radiation. That structure elaborates into myriad phenomena, from X-rays to radio waves to the rainbow and the Aurora Borealis, simply by varying the wavelength.

Today's physicists could tell you much more. But you get the idea. Physical law manages to be simple, by supporting a limited range of structures. It also manages to be potent, because the structures have multiple causal roles in our experience. Physical law is both simple and potent. In consequence, we can understand the giant evolution that assembles all the elements of our subtle experience. We have that description of ourselves.

ENORMOUS SIZE AND AGE

The picture of our evolution has a foreground and a background. In the foreground, a biological evolution on Planet Earth assembles us humans. Perhaps other subtle beings get assembled on other planets. In the background, planets able to support biological evolution, themselves evolve from the Big Bang.

The foreground evolution elaborates a simple, primitive DNA molecule into a complicated ecosystem, with species in the trillions and creatures in the trillion trillions, by passing the molecule through many iterations. Many, many iterations. Our planet's biological evolution has simple principle, but plenty of room and enormous age. Simple but potent.

The background evolution also uses size and age to advantage. Our universe does in fact create a very large number of planets or near-planets orbiting stars. Only a tiny fraction (some people believe only one) of all these planets are "biologically viable": conducive to a *sustained* biological evolution that assembles highly subtle beings. In our own solar system, we have eight "failures." Planet Mars may have had life, but surely not people. Other nearby planets and moons seem to be outright barren, or able to sustain only a limited evolution of living forms. Throughout the universe, probably the overwhelming majority of planets and moons fail to be biologically viable: they cannot produce people with high subtlety.

If we think of planets as dice, then the universe throws enough dice to get lucky and create biological evolutions of creatures highly subtle.

When it throws the dice and creates planets that grow people, the universe becomes a random procedure for choosing a planetary environment in great detail. By throwing the dice, our universe chooses at random the distance of the planet from its star, the strength of its gravity, the amount of oxygen and nitrogen and carbon present, the thickness of the atmosphere. And if the planet be viable, the dice-throwing also chooses weather patterns and ocean currents for billions of years. It chooses the mutable shapes of rivers, lakes, mountains, glaciers, oceans, and continents for billions of years. It chooses earthquakes, volcanoes, and the composition of the soil. The background evolution chooses the patterns of the clouds and the colors of the sunset for billions of years. It chooses at random an entire complex and idiosyncratic structure—that shapes the people grown.

Planet Earth is biologically viable. On Planet Earth, a mixture of structure and idiosyncrasy forms a matrix for our long biological evolution. That mixture governs the daily lives of the species evolving. It produces varied and changing habitats. It produces unique but coherent survival strategies with wide variation among species—and considerable variation among individuals of the same species. Our planet's structure-with-idiosyncrasy gets reflected in biological evolution. It gets reflected in our own human personalities. It relates to a certain balance in our experience, where we know what will happen each day and we do not know.

Viable planets are rare for good reason. Rarity corresponds to lightness. Rather than make elementary pancakes and have them succeed often, our universe makes ambitious soufflés that succeed almost never.

In other words: The high proportion of dud planets in this universe, causally corresponds to complex detail with high quality randomness, in the viable planets. The high percentage of dud planets, causally corresponds to quality idiosyncrasy in the planets that do successfully grow and shape people.

Therefore, gentle reader, the giant dimensions of our universe, correspond to high quality idiosyncrasy in your personality and in your daily life. Our universe uses its size to advantage.

In the foreground of our evolution is biological assembly on a suitable planet. In the background is the infusion into that planet of complex detail with high quality randomness. Both processes rely on vast dimension, to be simple yet potent.

FALLING DOWN AND BUILDING UP: IRREVERSIBLE EVENTS

Randomness and order are conflicting constraints on physical principle. Our daily lives exhibit *high* idiosyncrasy and quality randomness, within a *complicated* coherence. These are strongly conflicting constraints.

Yet that conflict gets resolved, and it gets resolved in a way we can understand.

Our universe resembles a giant pachinko game (a Japanese gambling game, in which small steel balls fall vertically, from top to bottom, through an array of horizontal nails, off which they bounce as they fall, creating a random distribution of balls at the bottom). Imagine a huge number of identical steel balls, starting together in a row at the top of the game. They begin to fall straight down. But now and then one of the balls hits a pachinko nail and hiccups a bit. The falling balls start to jostle each other. All the pachinko balls have little pieces of glue on them. As they fall and jostle, sometimes they glue themselves together. The balls start at the top all single and alike. But as they fall, and hiccup on the pachinko nails, and jostle together at random, they start forming complicated conglomerates different from each other. Idiosyncratic constructs begin to build. The falling and the jostling cause both randomness and order.

The pachinko game combines "falling down" and "building up." And so it is with our universe. Result: Our experience has order, infused with high quality randomness.

The pieces of our universe "fall down" in this sense: A raw egg can be scrambled far more easily than a scrambled egg can be made raw again. Hydrogen changes into helium far more easily than the reverse. Gas clouds readily condense into galaxies, but a galaxy changing back into an homogeneous cloud of gas would be a spectacular miracle. Wood burns to ashes and hot gas, but ashes and hot gas do not readily turn back into wood. And so on. Our world has many, many forms of "irreversible" combustion. Our universe has a statistical tendency to "fall" from less stable states toward more stable states, like a pachinko game.

But the more stable states toward which the universe falls, tend to have more structure. Sometimes, as they fall, the pieces of our universe also "build up" like this: When stars burn, masses of only-hydrogen "fall" toward larger, more stable atoms. Helium has more structure and more stability than hydrogen. Iron has still more structure and stability. Hydrogen glued together to form helium, does not readily come unglued again.

Likewise, when a large gas cloud condenses, the rather amorphous cloud "falls" toward shaped and articulated galaxies. The galaxies have more structure and more stability. They do not readily turn back into an amorphous cloud of gas.

And a more intricate example: Biological organizations of molecules have tendencies to evolve into more and more complicated structures, that more and more effectively replicate themselves. The jostling molecules gradually glue together into intelligent and capable structures. But that process uses up a lot of solar power. An evolved intelligent creature cannot be turned back into a younger star.

Combustion is a form of "falling down." Combustion is an "irreversible" process. In the foreground evolution, biological structures burn their way to more complexity. Through photosynthesis and oxygenation, they burn solar power. For fuel they eat each other and they eat sunlight. Biological structures are complicated fires that "fall" toward intelligence and emotion and idiosyncrasy.

And in the background evolution, the inanimate pieces of the universe—gas clouds and stars and hydrogen—also "fall down" and "build up" at the same time, like the pachinko game. Falling down produces randomness. Building up produces order.

Randomness and order are conflicting constraints on physical principle. By falling down as it builds up, like a pachinko game with sticky balls, our universe produces both in tandem.

Our universe resolves conflicting constraints so ingeniously, that we can understand the resolution. And the benefits of this transparency are legion.

Because it falls down, our universe has a natural progression from beginning to end. It has irreversible events. From an undifferentiated beginning, our universe falls naturally toward randomness and order. It progresses toward complicated beings with quality randomness. But it also progresses toward a natural ending. Any story can go on too long, and any story can be too complicated. The finite pachinko game and all its finite parts must at last come to rest. You and I are mortal.

THREE METHODS COMBINED

Physical evolution makes complicated, idiosyncratic, yet coherent people. Evolution infuses their complicated experience with lightness. And evolution remains simple enough for its people to understand how it works.

In short, physical evolution combines complicated order, quality randomness, and simplicity of execution.

To be all that, evolution uses three methods. It reuses the same structures in different settings. It uses giant size and age to get the most from those structures. And it combines falling down with building up.

Let's watch those three techniques operating together.

The stars have multiple causal roles in our lives. They help physical law to be potent yet simple. And the same stars push the pachinko game forward toward order and randomness: They release randomized energy in all directions. They cause hydrogen atoms to fall down into more complicated elements. And sometimes the stars explode. They hurl their complicated elements into space, in all directions at random—a spectacular pachinko hiccup.

The periodic table has multiple causal roles in our lives. And the same periodic table collapses irreversibly from simple atoms to complicated atoms, while releasing randomized energy.

DNA chemistry and cellular chemistry achieve much with just a few processes. And they burn fuel in the pachinko game: They build up complexity at random, by a falling down process of combustion.

Gravity is a simple principle with diverse influence on our lives. And gravity often causes irreversible collapse toward complex structures, while releasing randomized energy.

Electromagnetic radiation elaborates a simple principle into myriad phenomena. And the same electromagnetic radiation constitutes much of the randomized energy released by gravity and by combustion—by the collapse of our universe toward complex structure. Thus, as the pachinko universe falls down, it builds up structure, randomizes structure, elaborates structure into myriad forms, and keeps the whole process intelligible.

The early history of our universe also shows the three techniques combined for potency and simplicity. Early on during the evolution of viable planets, our universe falls down, from large homogeneous gas clouds, to shaped and articulated galaxies. Before stars and planets can be crafted inside galaxies, the galaxies themselves must condense from discrete clumps of gas. To make *clumps* of gas, our universe begins with *two* explosions three hundred thousand years apart. First we have the Big Bang, and then a kind of echo of the Big Bang. According to the current story, the second explosion goes like this:

For three hundred thousand years, super hot plasma from the Big Bang gets agitated, expanded, thrown in all directions, randomized. Finally, the plasma cools to a tipping point and explodes—a big pachinko hiccup. This explosion marks the advent of hydrogen atoms, and even a few helium atoms. This massive explosion is an irreversible falling down, from a less stable plasma toward more stable hydrogen. The explosion roils and randomizes the universe, while building up the structure of hydrogen. And it does something more. Because the plasma pulses and agitates before it explodes, the explosion produces some two hundred fifty billion discrete clumps of matter: the proto-galaxies.

The clumps have idiosyncratic sizes, shapes, and momentums. Thus the second randomizing explosion falls irreversibly toward *two* structures needed in our evolution: the hydrogen atom, and idiosyncratic proto-galaxies. Simple yet potent.

We understand these events from the distant past, because plasma-matter and hydrogen-matter have a common structure accessible to our understanding. Evolution is potent yet transparent. Indeed, as new generations continue to think and experiment, we may find evolution still more potent and still more transparent.

And the last example of three techniques combined: The Big Bang itself is a process consummately simple, considering what it achieves. That phenomenon gives us crucial insight into the structure of physical principle, including the structure of time and space. The universe assembles our lives, and the Big Bang is a big clue to how the universe fits together. The Big Bang is intelligible organization of a complicated universe. It functions well as a giant pachinko hiccup toward order and randomness both.

The Big Bang is sufficiently simple that we can understand it, yet sufficiently potent to organize all of physical principle. The very same Big Bang initiates the pachinko game: It helps roil and randomize the universe, even as it propels the universe down the pathways to complex structure.

Thus the size and age of our universe, and its profound cunning, focus ruthlessly on the task of making subtle experience. Each day we know what will happen and we do not know. For agents like us who make fluid comparisons, conditions are ideal.

AMAZING GRACE REVISITED

For convenience I have been speaking as if the Big Bang causes us to exist. It does not and cannot. Here is why.

In modern times we look at the universe as part structure and part blind randomness within the structure. That picture gives us insight into how our lives have idiosyncrasy and surprise. And it has many other uses. But it's incomplete. "*Blind* randomness" is a misdiagnosis.

The world's overt physical evolution of idiosyncratic people with idiosyncratic lives, would account only for blind randomness in our experience. Evolution as we see it proceeds in a good direction, but it remains a blunt instrument. It cannot account for a fine tuning that raises experience to adventure.

Our daily lives do exhibit fine tuning. Human lives have more than surprise. Our lives have consistent surprise. Our world *shapes itself* to our idiosyncratic desires, by always remaining just elusive enough. It does that consistently for everyone in a different way. We can almost but never quite grasp our perfect happiness. Our world is a skillful Siren. Thus:

The more control we exert over the world, the more control it exerts over us. No matter how well we understand the world, it moves outside that understanding. With predictable regularity it transcends our strivings. These persistent facts do not follow from the Big Bang and blind randomness.

We humans are actually rather simple-minded and clumsy about the circumstances of happiness. We fumble toward happiness as best we can. When we do achieve what we set out to achieve, we often find it empty. We have plodding ambitions, banal wishes, incoherent dreams. But the world plays on our strivings. Consistently it tantalizes and torments just outside our reach. It surprises us just enough. The world sounds us. It changes us. Sometimes it gives us better than we can imagine for ourselves. In its own way, the world knows what to do with us better than we do. By its own mysterious and alien agenda, the world refines our lives.

Wandering blind randomness fails to account for a transcendence so proficient, personal, and persistent. The world's overt physical evolution of idiosyncratic people with idiosyncratic lives, remains finally an unfocused instrument. The Big Bang proceeds in a good direction, but unaided it cannot fine tune human experience. Yet our lives exhibit an exceedingly fine tuning, albeit mysterious and alien. Effective as they are, the universe's size, evolution, and physical law remain insufficient to produce the inhabitant's subtle lives. They illuminate our subtlety, but do not account for it. They give us understanding, but not full understanding.

The Big Bang has many uses. The benefits of a *transparent* physical law, of a physics both potent and simple, are legion. Since the dawn of the human species, this transparency has favored us. Evolution overtly generates a curiosity that investigates evolution. In "The World's Peculiar Structure" (p. 271) you and I will look at the benefits.

Yet the Big Bang and physical evolution fail to account for what exists. They account for neither consciousness, nor free will, nor the elusive nature of all human experience, nor the world's consistent ability to give us different and better than we could wish to have.

Our best moments take us by surprise. We cannot understand them or even imagine them in advance. Our best moments lie outside the purview of the Big Bang and outside the purview of our own hopes and dreams. We don't get the steak we strive to have, we are disappointed often, but as compensation we do receive an amazing linguini.

Good reader, perhaps you already know the reason why we exist. In the fullness of time, I will tell you about it anyway.

She Walks in Beauty
on the Night

Gentle reader, you and I live in a world that destroys us. Our perfect Siren always outguesses us and always defeats us, at its subtle discretion. For that reason, the triumphs we do enjoy have the greatest possible value. Some of our triumphs transcend our own desires. This world gives its subtle agents—all of us together as a collection—the most tantalizing, absorbing, and rewarding lives we can have. But it gives elusively and subtly, at a price. This world astonishes us with its grace and its malignance both. Our Siren beckons and we follow.

How far do our lives resolve into the single moment? Our single moments cannot protect each other. Everything we care about flickers into nothing. As hope diminishes, as that tenacious part of us begins to yield, something that was always in the background, something attractive and fearful, comes forward.

I am telling you the same story twice, in two different ways: from the bottom up and from the top down. We cannot be us unless we are defeated. Our world chooses to defeat us without remorse and without justice. Only a lethal world can hold our attention. We journey into intoxicating kingdoms unknown and we journey into ruthless new forms of darkness. The world beckons and we follow. Each day we encounter a palpable indifference to our desires and to our ideals, each day we encounter an alien power, but ours is the most subtle of all possible worlds. Every thought is the perfect cast of many dice.

And how seductive the casting. On the lonely hush of night she smiles. Look upon the heavens! Look upon them from the darkest mountain, moonless and cloudless, in all their splendor, bisected by our own white galaxy, flowing outward from the glowing white river at their center. Do you see them? Do you feel the unearthly affinity? The strange unease? Observe, then, the sharp teeth no longer concealed. They devour the ages. Behold this silent jeweled ocean, this lofty cathedral unmoved by our brief prayers, this alien part of ourselves. We drink from it! We never exhaust it. It destroys us. Behold our terrible doom in her splendor! She walks in beauty on the night.

Part Six

THE IMPORTANCE
OF BEING DOOMED

The Necessary Failure
of Immortality

Spiders can go to heaven. A spider in heaven spins beautifully symmetrical webs every day, catches all the flies he wants, produces multitudes of offspring, and for all eternity never tires of these repetitions. But a spider has no value as a subtle being. It makes insufficient comparisons.

For a subtle being, comparisons underlie almost every conscious thought. The hallways of heaven, however resplendent, might begin to bore him, after he walks them a billion times. Subtle beings, making comparisons, eventually tire of repetition, even the repetition of bliss.

Pigs qualify as subtle beings. Can a pig benefit from immortality? He cannot. No matter how happy a pig may be, or how long he lives, the value of his life falls below the finite value of your mortal life or mine—because he lives out his life at a level of subtlety substantially lower than the human level. Therefore, even a happy, immortal pig has a life of finite value, below the finite value of your life. Toward the beginning of the pig's life, each new day adds to its value. But eventually this value plateaus. Although each of the pig's days may differ from all his other days, unlimited repetition of new days nevertheless reaches a point of diminishing returns. At best, each day adds value, but the successive added values decline and approach zero, as in the series

$$1/2 + 1/4 + 1/8 + 1/16 + \ldots = 1$$

At some point, after a finite time, the value of the pig's life becomes indistinguishable from the value of immortal life. Because his subtlety has an upper limit, immortality fails to add value to his life. Two million years of life are no better than one million years—and perhaps worse.

Does the value of continuing life plateau when limited to a pig's level of subtlety, but accumulate beyond any finite plateau when limited by some other level of subtlety? Does subtlety at different levels somehow change from nonlinear to linear accumulation? Highly implausible.

Beyond reasonable doubt, we may conclude: No possible subtle being, with experience capped by any particular level of subtlety, benefits from immortality. Unless you and I can become more and more subtle beyond any finite limit, we would find immortality worthless—or worse.

In "The Upper Limit to the Quality of Subtlety" (p. 334) I will give the evidential argument that the quality or level of subtlety does have an upper limit, for any possible subtle being, even an angel or a god.

Humans have short lives and lots of problems. Rather infrequently has our chief dissatisfaction been too much success and bliss and new adventure. Most of us would rather be *more* immortal, not less. But some humans, at times, do feel unexpected negatives from continued good living. What happens to us, that at last takes all worth from our existence, if we live long enough?

Whiskey Lao

Good reader, I will not deceive you with the truth, as the whiskey deceived me.

On the return journey down the Mekong River, the whiskey took advantage. It sank the inconspicuous harpoon. On the first intoxicating blissful afternoon, in my altered state of consciousness, as I seemed to be thinking pleasantly about nothing in particular, the whiskey strangely centered my attention. It took advantage. It rotated my head and pointed my nose in a new direction. I forgot humanity's misery, injustice, despair, and deliberate cruelty. I forgot my own death. I centered on the subtlety of human experience. The whiskey brought forward these questions:

Does the periodic table of elements facilitate subtle experience in the actual world? Does the organization of molecules from atoms facilitate subtle experience? Stellar fusion of heavier elements from hydrogen? Stars and planetary systems? The revolution, rotation, and precession of planets? The phases of the moon? Eyes and electromagnetic radiation? The metamorphosis of matter under various temperatures and pressures? The condensation of planets? Mountains and oceans and rivers? The distribution of moisture on a partly cloudy planet? The progression of shape and color in the sky? DNA chemistry? The organization of living cells? The complementary processes of photosynthesis and respiration? The oxidation of living tissue as food? The resulting interdependence of living forms? Biological evolution? The growth of trees from seeds? The growth of adult humans from

babies? The process of discovery? The idiosyncratic formation
and distribution of stars, atomic elements, and planets within
interacting galaxies? The underlying coherence of a potent yet
comprehensible physical law?

Why does *our* world have so many coherent and ingenious
physical features related to subtlety?

The whiskey gave me a curious insight. Perhaps I have passed
it on to you. But will this knowledge make you happy? Is this mes-
sage upbeat and positive?

For the space of that first glorious afternoon, I believed it
was. That afternoon, the whiskey showed me the radiance of perfection in the world. The whiskey seized and enslaved my rapt
attention. Then, with masterful timing, it slowly drew aside the
glowing veil, to reveal the vast edges drear and naked shingles
even in the perfect universe. If we already occupy the best possible world, then we already come as close to heaven as we can
get. We cannot go on to a better world. An afterlife becomes
incongruous and pointless. Surely our death extinguishes us.
Surely our sufferings have no compensation in another life. The
world we are stuck with has a dark side—organized, deliberate,
unjust—that none of us can escape. In the perfect world, in the
best of all possible worlds, we must suffer and die. If we are
lucky, we will *gradually* shrivel up and die. If we are very lucky,
everyone and everything we care about will *gradually* shrivel up
and die. Many of us will be less fortunate. All of us who reside
in the best possible world must be its victims. The malignant and
the sublime are two faces of one perfection.

Following that first blissful glittering afternoon, the whiskey
showed me my victimization and then explained it to me in
remorseless detail. I had already accepted perfection and I could
not turn away from the consequences. I was unhappy to get the
bad news. Good reader, I will not deceive you, with a guileful
sequence of presentation, as the whiskey deceived me. Here you
will find the dark side of perfection wearing no Siren mask of
serenity or bliss or hope. You and I are lost in every way, lost so
completely that we must abandon hope—and cling instead to that
which hope may obscure.

Among its first acts, the whiskey dismantled my former reasons for believing in God, my former reasons for disbelieving in God, my bitterness toward God if He does exist, and my bitterness if God abandons us and stubbornly chooses not to exist. Every theory I had ever had about the existence of God, and every complaint about the world, the mischievous whiskey exposed as flawed. According to the whiskey, the world's perfection admits no outside help, just as it admits no reproach. According to the whiskey, I complained about the world and believed in an incoherent God, because I have incoherent hopes and dreams.

I could no longer believe that God intervenes in the world, that somehow He makes everything right for those who accept Him. I could no longer understand myself as His image. Neither could I understand my existence as haphazard and unrelated to a larger context. Then what am I? I turned to our modern scientific scheme of the universe: a physical evolution produced me and accounts for me, tells me why I exist. But again the whiskey threw my comfortable beliefs into confusion. Slyly it whispered to me, "If our world is the most subtle possible, if its virtue lies in the subtlety of our *experience*, then science and evolution mechanically describe our lives, without explaining why we have them."

I was confused. My question had been, Is there a God? But as I learned, that question divides into two questions with opposite answers: Does a higher context give meaning to my life? and Can I be rescued?

Said the whiskey, "Do you want God to rescue you from the context that gives meaning to your life? Do you want God to rescue you from God?"

Yes, we mortals inhabit the best possible world. Out of the myriad possible agents of our form, only we fit the perfect universe and only we gain existence. We are the Chosen Ones. But we are chosen for addiction and annihilation. We have a tenacity which the world both encourages and defeats. Before I drank the whiskey, I was already addicted, because already I needed to search for it on that soothing and exciting river.

We are addicts to a subtle delight and a subtle hell. We are addicts and demons possess us. But we inhabit our highest heaven.

The whiskey deceived me with the truth. Its first insight was pleasant. But the first insight had something attached.

Against that attachment I struggled and rebelled. I confronted the whiskey:

"You can't make me believe that perfection destroys *all* of us. Some people change the world forever. Their lives have eternal meaning."

"Yes," came the whiskey's sedate reply, "every now and then a unique individual comes along. Humanity might spend ten thousand years, or a hundred thousand, or a million years, gradually forgetting he ever existed."

"Those seem like lengthy periods to me."

"And why do they seem lengthy? Because the rest of us fade away so much more quickly?"

For a long moment we were silent. Then I said, "Even so, a few of us fade away a lot less quickly."

The whiskey shrugged. "We can't all decay at the same rate. That pattern would be unsubtle. It doesn't follow that some of us have eternal meaning."

"Maybe we can't live forever. Nevertheless, we can make contributions that endure. We can have that satisfaction."

The whiskey spoke softly. "Yes, we can have that satisfaction. Even comparative immortality can be a major triumph. But the size of the triumph measures our discomfort that we ebb away."

For another moment we were silent. But the whiskey was nowhere near exhausting my defiance. "All right. We ebb away and we don't like it. All of us. So what? My life has meaning anyway. It has meaning whether or not the meaning is eternal."

The whiskey still spoke softly. "Yes, of course your life is well worth living. I have told you that it is. But you pay a price. You must have predicament intractable. To have its meaning, your life must be hopeless. Everything dear to you, without exception, must be swept away."

"I'm not a child. I don't expect a life in Lollipop Land. I will hold dear what is dear. As to the price, I will resign myself and prepare myself."

"Prepare yourself for what? Most of your annihilations come like a thief in the night. They come as masked changelings you have never imagined. Out of all possible worlds, you inhabit the most cunning and the most ruthless. Resign yourself to what? Some of its weapons, no one but you will ever face. However skillfully you prepare yourself or resign yourself, the world around you has far greater skill. Whenever appropriate, it turns your preparations against you!"

I made no response. I bided my time.

The whiskey paused exactly long enough to underscore my silence. Then it took up afresh the same soft voice. "Sometimes the giants among us have the sharpest predicament. Sometimes they have sharp insight, triumphs, sorrows, and defeats, that you perceive more dimly. No one escapes predicament. Sometimes our very impermanence, our consciousness of it, impels us to seek immortality, to stand up and make a difference, to push back oblivion for a time. But in this elusive, cunning world, none of us comprehends the dimension of his own predicament. Each of us is doomed in his own way." And the whiskey looked at me directly.

I looked back directly. "Maybe I'm doomed in some ways. But certain things I care about will last forever. I care about the truth, and the truth is eternal."

"Still grasping at the eternal, are you? Understandable. And futile. The truth may be eternal, but your experience of it passes away."

"All the same, I have experience of something eternal. And I care about the truth. Because I care about it, I can have the satisfaction of sharing it. I can even publish it for posterity."

Now the whiskey had a quizzical smile. "Interesting. 'The truth is eternal! May it never be forgotten!' Sounds a bit dissonant. Strange how hard you work to preserve the eternal."

I maintained another tactical silence.

"You *care* about the truth," continued the whiskey. "Exactly what do you care about? Human beings have a peculiarity. For humans, the truth has only one *emotional* value: it might affect a person. You tell me, 'I care about the truth.' You really mean, 'I care about finding and knowing the truth' or 'I care that the truth be respected ahead of self-interest' or 'I care that the truth be shared and preserved.' Yes, you care—but only when the truth has some relationship with a person, either yourself or someone else. You have *feelings* about the truth because a person gets involved with it, has some connection to it. Your feelings might be, 'How exciting! I see the truth! I experience it. My knowledge of it affects me thus and so. I want to share this experience with others. I want to teach this knowledge and publish it. I want it remembered for all time.' You have emotions, but not about the truth bare and alone. The cause of your emotion is people having relations with the truth. You care about *knowing* the truth, your own knowledge or someone else's, searching for the truth, your discovery of it, their discovery, your attitude toward it, their attitude, the truth governing our lives, someone knowing the truth thousands of years ago, someone knowing it thousands of years from now, contemplating the truth, a human being having a relation to the truth, maybe even an alien being having a relation to the truth—these you care about. A person must somewhere be tangled up with the truth, before you have emotions about it. The truth may be eternal, but people are not. Knowledge and memory waver and finally pass away. All relations between the truth and people pass away. What you care about passes away. You want posterity to know the truth, to keep this knowledge alive for you, as you keep it alive for them. But every part of you dies, or little by little fades to nothing. No one escapes predicament. Each of us has his own particular doom."

I still resisted the whiskey's savage, bleak view. I took several deep breaths. Each of us has his own particular doom? I thought about my own life, and opened a new line of attack. "My situation isn't so bad. I have options. I don't let life get me down."

"Sure, we have lots of ways to deal with our dilemmas," said the whiskey in soothing tones. "Getting lucky can do wonders for predicament. Achieving resignation often helps. Belief in an incoherent afterlife can give us equanimity. Getting drunk sometimes softens predicament. Growing older and wiser may put predicament into perspective. The best possible world has refinement and restraint whenever it wishes. It destroys us at its subtle discretion. It destroys us at the right moments. It doesn't knock us to pieces at every opportunity. Our lives *are* worth living. But the value lies in our addiction—which makes us vulnerable. All of us have an addiction to subtle predicament. All of us want more perfection than we can get. Living in subtle predicament must always be identical to impermanence and dying. No exceptions. All of us suffer the fate of the hopeless addict."

"Hopeless? Why must addiction be hopeless?" I saw my chance. "If I'm addicted to Whiskey Lao, then I can withdraw from addiction, as many Buddhists do. I can seek Zen enlightenment and escape predicament entirely."

"Yes, I can see you as quite the executive," replied the whiskey. "There you sit, in your high-backed leather chair, behind a big desk, completely in command: 'It has come to my attention that the world puts me into predicament. After reviewing my options, I have chosen Zen enlightenment as my most effective response. Accordingly, I will now enter a Zen monastery and remain there until I reach enlightenment.'"

"Why not?" said I.

"Take a look at the people who make that decision. What happens to them? Most of them get bored in the monastery and miss their former predicament, or struggle for years without reaching enlightenment, or fall in love with another disciple, or get bilked out of their life savings, or reach some completely unpredictable outcome."

"And some of them reach enlightenment."

"And what do they reach, when they reach enlightenment? Escape from predicament? Freedom from duality? Your expectations may be oversimplified and too rosy. Precisely the world's darkness motivates the Zen disciple to seek enlightenment. Would enlightenment be unattainable unless we first suffer in confusion? Does serenity get measured by the comparison to confusion and despair? Is serenity in fact founded on duality? Some Zen masters, believed to be enlightened, have talked about a contrast between enlightenment and nonenlightenment. What might that contrast be, if not duality?"

"It might be a new and improved duality. Enlightenment might be a better way to have experience."

"Perhaps it is. The enlightened masters seem to prefer that state. However, it appears that some have expressed dissatisfaction even while in the state of enlightenment. Some have expressed anger at the stupidity or duplicity of their fellow beings. Would enlightenment reliably subdue all suffering and all emotion? Is our subtle world really so simple after all? Yes, it's plausible that the unenlightened individual inflicts significant misery on himself. Perhaps he struggles uselessly, or leaves his thoughts in disarray. Nevertheless, clouded mental perspective cannot account for all of our predicament. The enlightened one still feels hungry, cold, wet, and sick. He may experience causation in a new way, but he does not escape the world's causation. He still has dissatisfactions that no enlightenment can overcome. If pierced by a poisoned arrow and sent into convulsions, he feels his serenity compromised. Other people can disturb him or anger him or disappoint him. He remains serene at the world's forbearance. Whenever it wishes to do so, the world's cunning randomness can take his serenity away, or take his life away, just as it can take away your own happiness and your own life. Don't confuse enlightenment with invulnerability. At the right moment, the world destroys each of us."

"If I were enlightened, maybe I wouldn't care that my life ends."

"If you get drunk enough, maybe you won't care that your life ends."

"Then why must I care?"

"You have the privilege to care. You care because you have much to lose. And you have much to lose because you care. It's a predicament. Enlightenment cannot be indifference or numbness to predicament, or escape from it. Those are the strategies of struggle."

"And yet, for many people, Zen enlightenment has been effective with predicament."

"But *how* has it been effective? Does enlightenment make predicament go away?"

"Maybe it does. Maybe enlightenment is escape from predicament."

"But what if enlightenment is cessation of struggle? What if enlightenment is escape from the desire to escape predicament?"

Suddenly I could not speak. The whiskey calmly pressed home its advantage. "Imagine yourself driving a car around a hairpin turn. It skids off the road. You are falling a thousand feet to your death. But you are enlightened. How does your enlightenment help you? Does it put the car back on the road? Or does it simply remove from your last moments the distraction of frantically seeking some way out? Surely the enlightened one knows, that he never did have a way out."

The whiskey understood my weakness. I *had* wanted enlightenment to be my shield. Indeed, I would grasp at almost anything that might shield me.

But I was still standing and still defiant. "Does the world really have such absolute power? Yes, I have to die, but right now I have my life. Yes, the world has randomness, and yes, a massive amount. But the randomness doesn't control my life. I have the power to act. How can randomness deliberately set out to frustrate me? How can randomness be 'cunning' as you say? It's only accident and unpredictability. I can study it, compensate for it, work with it. Often I can protect myself from it. I don't have to be tossed around like a cork on the ocean."

I was recycling the same arguments. The whiskey began to watch me steadily. But it merely said, "Events in our perfect world surprise or mystify us in just the right ways for our subtle experience. In that sense, we are embedded by 'cunning randomness.' And yes, the world can overpower anyone whenever it wishes."

"All right, but even if the random world does overpower me, I can go sit in a Buddhist monastery and learn to tune it out. If randomness inhabits my initiatives in the world, I can withdraw from the world. If randomness touches my passions, I can quiet my passions. If I have a landscape of comparisons in my mind, I can sit in contemplation and disavow the landscape. If I don't like the world's dilemma, I can always practice Zen. I don't have to be tossed around like a cork on the ocean. I have options."

Such was my last protest. But I had already accepted perfection in the world. The inconspicuous harpoon was delivered on the first afternoon. My defiance was mortally pierced. Almost gently the whiskey put it to rest:

"To various extents we are happy and unhappy, successful and unsuccessful, fine and base, wise and foolish, all as part of our subtle experience. Our world is the most subtle possible. Therefore it doles out happiness, unhappiness, success, failure, enlightenment, mystification, and so on, according to the most subtle possible pattern of experience. Whatever makes the most subtle experience, that's what happens. Our subtle world appears to like diversity. It makes us all different. In the most subtle possible world, some people sell insurance, some find peace, some practice Zen, some reach a state of enlightenment, and some don't. If we set out to transform ourselves in some way, to find peace, to experience enlightenment, to reach our sales quota, to do whatever, the requirements of the best possible subtlety decide whether and how we are transformed. We achieve enlightenment or peace or a sales goal if and only if those conditions fit the most subtle possible world. In fact we do not always achieve what we set out to achieve. Sometimes we do, sometimes we don't, and sometimes we get a completely unexpected result. When we examine the pattern of subtle experience for all of us, we find that some of us fail at selling insurance, seek peace but do not find it, or practice Zen with varying results. If the practice of Zen always worked well as an antidote to dilemma, for anyone who tried it faithfully, our world would be less subtle. If regular visits to the doctor always guaranteed good health, our world would be less subtle. In many respects, the most subtle possible world doesn't like guaranteed, complete, final answers. It likes dilemma. It promotes duality. When viewed as a device to put us into subtle predicament and keep us there, the whole universe suddenly fits together. In many respects, partial, maybe answers correlate with experience more subtle. Our world creates exceptions and unexpected outcomes. We make a lot of decisions, but *we* don't decide which developments and which outcomes make the best possible subtlety. The world makes that decision for us. When any individual practices Zen, the world decides the outcome; the requirements of the best possible subtlety decide the outcome. The world's decision may go counter to what the practitioner wants. Even the enlightened Zen master remains at the world's mercy, just as the most robustly healthy creature remains subject to sudden expiration. Among the myriad possible agents of our form, the relatively few agents who actually come to exist are those who fit the pattern of the best possible subtlety. Whenever we achieve what we set out to achieve, whenever we achieve anything, whenever we have anything desirable, we have our triumph only at the world's mysterious sufferance. Even in the best possible world, our subtle experience must be transitory and founded on passionate duality. We have momentary fragments of triumph, measured by our despair, on the road to defeat."

In that patient manner, the whiskey overran all my defenses except the last. For six weeks following the first afternoon, I resisted the consequences of perfection. I argued and refused to argue, consented and withheld consent, resigned myself and still clung to my hopes and dreams.

Self-pity was my last fortification, and here the whiskey left me alone inside. The nadir lasted several days. At that time, Lee Ming and I lived in Chiangmai, Thailand. I walked the foreign city, or just stared at it, feeling disoriented and sorry for myself.

Fortunately, that reaction slowly gave way to another. Intimate knowledge of my doom became a stimulant, a bracing sense of seductive dread. Finally and at last, I began to yield. Fear and desire began to shadow one another. Each gave shape to the other, like the mingled reflections of dark and light on a rippled surface.

Some issues were resolved for me. I began to think about my death in a way that shifted my perception of living. But still I had questions for the whiskey. "Do we try to change this hopeless world for the better, or do we give up? Did Thomas Edison waste his life? Did Martin Luther King, Jr., waste his life? Or should many of us follow his example?"

The whiskey, usually so direct with me, pirouetted around

these new questions with dazzling dexterity. "Martin Luther King, Jr.," said the whiskey, "left behind a humanity still disfigured by racism and violence. Even when those iniquities disappear, worse will take their place. In one sense, MLK Jr. was doomed from the start.

"In another sense," said the whiskey, "the impossible odds against him only highlight his greatness. He had the courage and vision to take arms against an *endless* sea of troubles. The size of the problem measures his nobility, and makes his dream beautiful.

"Suppose we lived in a world where all the difficulties are comfortably manageable, if only we can get ourselves sufficiently organized to deal with them. Then MLK Jr. could rise no higher than being an excellent manager. We could not aspire to a dream, only to efficiency. But in the actual world, precisely because the problems are finally hopeless, a singular individual can be a Knight of Faith."

"You have not answered me," I said. "I already know he was a great man. I want to know who should follow his example, and under what circumstances. I want to know how far our tenacity has useful function. Just when I abandon my incoherent hopes and dreams, you start talking about the value of hopeless dreams. Do I dream or not? Do I take arms against the sea of troubles? Or do I give up and cultivate my own garden?"

But the whiskey only smiled and said, "Those questions you must answer yourself. The world is too subtle and elusive to answer them for you. The most hopeless world permits the best achievements and the most beautiful dreams. You have unlimited scope for your tenacity, but sooner or later your tenacity must be defeated. Will you dream anyway? Dreams have their own seductive beauty. In our subtly diverse world, people are great and barbarous with and without faith. You have no obligation to recognize your addiction. By your own preference and decision, you recognized it. But no strategy in this world, and no knowledge, and no faith, and no resignation, makes you less vulnerable. No matter how conscientiously you see only what is, whether or not you have the faith to dream, whether or not you work to change the world, whether you act selfishly or unselfishly, no matter where you turn for help or offer help, the world leaves the future concealed. Such decisions come from you, with no stage whisper from the subtle world outside."

Sometimes, when I seem to need it most, the whiskey fails me.

High Class Prostitute

Said I to the whiskey, "If the actual world is the best possible, then why do I want to live in a different world? I'd like to escape all this perfection, and live in a world of peace and plenty."

With its slender smile, the whiskey answered. "In a different world, you make different comparisons. Incessant peace and plenty have shrunken value. They are tedious. You still see evil and good balanced, but flattened to unsubtle shape."

"Are you telling me I shouldn't want peace and plenty for all humanity?"

"Better to struggle for them in subtle ways, than have them always everywhere by omnipotent fiat. To be valuable, your dreams must be fragile and elusive, difficult to make happen. But don't be too surprised if the world gives you different from what you struggle to have."

"Maybe I don't want the world to give me different. Maybe I don't like that."

The whiskey's faint smile seemed to migrate from its lips to its eyes. "This is a ruthless world. Recognizing it as the best possible, and actually wanting to live in it, are different. One does not follow from the other."

"If I don't want to live in it, then it can't be the best possible."

"Not so," said the whiskey. "As a subtle being, you have warring desires. Impossible to satisfy them all."

This was new. I waited. The whiskey sat down in my armchair and made itself comfortable. Then it continued. "Suppose you have spent sixty years in prison. You believe the outside world to be more interesting and satisfying than prison. You recognize the free life as superior to confinement. But given the chance to leave the familiar prison you have known for sixty years, and enter a strange new world, you might decline. You want freedom but you also fear it. You know you will be fine in the outside world, everyone says so, but you fear it anyway, and you prefer to live in prison.

"Here's another example. You might like popular music better than classical. But you also believe that people who like classical have better taste in music. If you listened to classical, your taste and your listening experience might change for the better. But maybe you don't want to change for the better. You prefer the music you believe to be inferior and you resist change. People can be that way. Your standard of good experience has warring elements."

The whiskey crossed its legs. "Some men pine for the days when any man rich enough could assemble a compliant harem, with little fuss and no feminist picketers outside his door. The same wistful men might also concede that more equal relationships with women have more fascination, more satisfaction, more love. They recognize equality as better, but they want the harem anyway. Some men, given the choice between a compliant harem and marriage to an equal, would deliberately choose the alternative they believe is second best. Such men happen to have a weakness for harems. They have an unfortunate addiction to easy sex. They may recognize that other men who prefer equality have superior taste in relationships, but they want the harem anyway. Such men can be different and better, but they don't want to be."

The whiskey paused for a moment, while it leaned back in my chair. "Do you remember the fate of the concubine Yang Guei Fei?"

I remembered. Among all the Chinese emperors, only one chose to put away his harem and be fascinated by a solitary woman. She was forty-plus years old and exceedingly fat. This particular emperor, in the brilliant T'ang Dynasty, finally got fed up with the endless parade of beautiful youth. Finally, he developed a superior taste in relationships. He never got fed up with

Yang Guei Fei. Her name translates as "High Class Prostitute." She was so-called all her adult life, and history knows her by that name. But this professional courtesan had an inner beauty. She shared with him her sensitivity to the wonder of being alive. "When the flowers blossomed, they went to see the flowers. When the moon shone, they went to see the moon." She understood him and she changed him. He took no further interest in his plans for military conquest. Their unique love has surely inspired more poetry than any other couple's in history.

"Not all men would emulate that emperor," said the whiskey. "Not all men choose to be wise."

Indeed not. His best friend betrayed him as a weakling. His own army commanders strangled Yang Guei Fei with a silken cord. And many of the same poets who rhapsodized over the emperor's excellent taste, themselves indulged in a succession of young women.

"Recognizing a world as the best possible, and wanting that world, are different." said the whiskey. "You want to live in a world of peace and plenty, not in the actual world. Even if you believe the peace-and-plenty world to be tepid, unsubtle, and no happier than the actual world—even if you believe it to be inferior to the actual world—you might want to live there anyway.

"As a subtle being, your desires mutually contradict. The best possible world uses that fact to advantage. It *tantalizes* your desires. It provokes their inherent contradictions. The best possible world just about drives you crazy. You ask for steak and get linguini.

"Spiders benefit from peace and plenty. They benefit from immortality. You benefit from something entirely different: subtle comparisons. Your comparisons become far more subtle, when you don't always get what you want, when the world stays just outside your grasp. Your desire for change becomes complicated, poignant, and subtle."

I was still skeptical. "I live in the best possible world, and I want to change it? A paradox."

"A subtle paradox. If you don't want to change the world, how can it engage your strongest passions? How can it put you into the sharpest predicaments? Without strong disapproval, you have no strong approval. A world you do not wish to change has nothing very valuable in it."

Sympathy for Genghis Khan

JOHN WILLIAMS, SANTA FE, APRIL 23, 1999

Lately my life subverts itself. Former pleasures become unendurable. The person I was, contained his own hidden termination, waiting to be discovered. Yesterday my wife departed for Beijing. Lee Ming has only brief business there, but she lengthens her stay to five weeks, at my request. Not long ago, I would have gone with her to China, and stayed a year. I very much enjoyed that brave new world. I wanted to visit and revisit every exotic corner of this planet, and every society where people look at the world in startling ways. But that deceptive fervor reveals itself as its own opposite. Lee Ming still has energy and enthusiasm. She has enough to animate the life we share. For ten years my wife almost never abandoned me, and never for more than a few days. Her presence comforts me. She insists that I follow orderly routines. I must wear clean clothes, shave, get my hair cut, exercise, eat healthy food. She scolds me when I sleep by day rather than by night. Both of us are headstrong. Sometimes we quarrel. At forty-three, nine years my junior, Lee Ming grows more beautiful. She denies it, but she believes in romance. We quarrel, not so often as before. Neither of us can bear a long estrangement. We have no children, despite all the doctors and all the medicines. My regret is mostly for her. Sometimes at night she has a recurring dream: she brings home a baby someone left behind at the supermarket. Yet she doesn't want to adopt. And she still has enthusiasm. I like to think of her remarried after I'm gone. I've lost interest in traveling. With fondness I remember our former life in strange lands: nine months in Chiangmai, Thailand; five months in Singapore; five months in Portuguese Macau; Hong Kong; Tahiti; Australia; Mexico; several years in China—wonderful memories. I am grateful. And yet, I would be horrified to return again to any of those places, even for one day. Easier to shut out the plain vanilla USA. I no longer seek friendships with new people. Discreetly I keep old friends at a distance. I fear death more than ever, yet I could not bear to be young and falling in love again. Such an effort, being young. So many briars and brambles. But in my detachment, some distractions remain, not many. Writing distracts me. A soft rainfall, a glowing veil slowly drawn across the moon, a heaven that speaks with color—these remain. And my shining memories remain. Wherever we traveled, the moon was the same, and the clouds different. Most everything was different. Lee Ming and I rent by the month, as usual, but she has filled our small apartment with furniture that belongs to us outright. Curious to own impassive tables and couches. My life has been very fine. I wish to go nowhere and see no one. Lee Ming and I still have some good fun. We connive and scheme together, and pursue our clever strategies. We go to the movies. We dine out. We have company and practice the art of conversation. Lee Ming stands between me and my sadness. Her presence comforts me. Today I will emerge from her comfort. I intend to draw the curtains and sit alone in this shrunken apartment for five weeks. Yes, I miss her, but I want to feel what prickles and thorns remain. Did I mention my dysfunctional family? They will distract me for awhile. Often I feel a bittersweet fortune to have brothers and sisters so rapacious. As a child I stammered badly, to their pleasure.

I still stammer under pressure from my siblings. In this world I must not be too comfortable. I have returned to the bosom of my family, who would gladly devour me. I may yet devour them instead. My adoptive father has reached age seventy-eight. Every day he takes more than a pound of assorted vitamins. Of course he will die anyway. His seven children, natural and otherwise, struggle over his will. He knows. Sometimes he approves, sometimes he deplores. In vicious earnest we struggle. But almost we pretend not to notice our competition, like African hyenas subtly shouldering each other aside, when the kill cannot satisfy all the hunger. I want to feel their hunger, and share it. My life has been fortunate, and perhaps I could thank my family. For years I enjoyed putting the entire planet solidly between them and me. Now I have submitted again to our private painful universe—willingly and unwillingly. Their enmity moves me forward. Underneath my rational thoughts, I try to write a masterpiece, to compel my family to love me, to combat their power to give pain. They will never love me. I will never love them. But I need this perverse motivation. Writing is such an effort. I cannot write without the strongest motivation. This business about our inheritance happens to be timely. I think of their long disapprobation, and sit down to my inoffensive word processor with a vengeance. And perhaps I will confound the other hyenas. I have returned to the bosom of my family. I borrow their hunger. Already my brothers and sisters begin to fear me, for the first time in their lives. But this game cannot last long. Unwonted victory over my siblings, would rather postpone dissatisfaction, than bring satisfaction. I watch myself from a distance. When I finish writing, I will be finished also with my family's bosom, win or lose. Once again, and more successfully than before, I will cultivate an indifference to their affections. My childhood only seemed unfortunate. It was not. Wanting to be valued, I fled, and found a rich world. When I was twenty-one, an exquisite young woman took me into her arms a hundred times, and loved me. I seem to remember every moment.

No loneliness, no tormented childhood, no self-pity past or future, could survive her solace. I felt it all the more sweetly, for having been unhappy. I have known happiness in the interval. And now Lee Ming daily shows her care for me. Today, at fifty-two, with absolutely no reproach against the world, I feel a disconnection. Where it originates, I do not know. I felt its vague beginnings eighteen months ago. My family is not the cause. With them or apart from them, I watch myself from a distance. My approaching death is not the cause, much as I fear it. The dread specter of death began as the dread nuisance of death, when I was seventeen. Sometimes I like being haunted. But neither of those dread specters, my family nor my death, has lengthened noticeably in eighteen months. My wife, far from causing detachment, would somehow bring me to myself. As to sturdy little offspring all about me, comical and endearing, little mixtures of Lee Ming and me, lots of trouble and anxiety, such an effort: my desire has long faded. I feel a sharp appetite, but scant interest in any particular food. I cannot understand why. Where I recoiled from pain, now I seek vitality. Where I found vitality, now I recoil from pain. Shadows of a former life begin their own life. I can be distracted, but I cannot understand, or find my way to understand. About this bitter, wonderful world, I no longer know what to think.

Within Western cultures, some of us have the notion we might go to heaven and enjoy eternal bliss. Others have given up eternal bliss as wishful thinking: as a treat that might have been arranged for us, had our indifferent universe given our satisfaction a higher priority. Western views of heaven derive from ancient Greek cosmology, where the Olympians sip ambrosia and stay young forever. These immortals never get tired of ambrosia, no matter how many billions of times they swallow the stuff. The actual stingy world gives us nothing like eternal bliss in the Greek style. Mostly it gives us fleeting triumph, vanishing delight, and scattered glimpses of wonder. We make our way as best we can, and then we die. However, the actual world does avoid a transience too monotonous. Occasionally we discover more durable triumph, more persistent delight, and rather perennial vistas of wonder. Under these more heavenly circumstances, our happiness leaks away in a different direction. Persistent satisfaction changes us, and uses up the ways we can be satisfied. Where the world remains elusive, we run after it as best we can, our lust intact. Where the world holds steady and lets us feast on it, we fill up and become shadows.

My life is hardly the first to subvert itself, nor does it have the most pronounced inversion. Alexander the Great, as you may remember, would not leave his tent, to look at the world he had mastered. His advantages and unprecedented triumphs led to despair. During childhood, Alexander had Ptolemy as hired older brother, and Aristotle as personal tutor. His father's military successes left Macedonia invigorated. The well educated Alexander, after ascending his father's throne, quickly subdued all the Greek states to the south. Alexander embodied learning, youth, and triumph. He asked his defeated opponents, Would they like to spread Greek culture and win some booty? They took pride in their culture. They said yes. Having long warred among themselves, they were good fighters. Alexander conquered wherever he went. He was a good problem solver. Consistently he prevailed against vastly greater numbers. After a decade filled with success, he arrived at the fringes of India. At that time in India, a hundred flowers bloomed, including the recent school of Gotama Buddha. Those flowers, however, were invisible from a distance. Like other Indian philosophies that found language slippery, Buddhism was still a completely oral tradition, carefully bestowed from one person to another unique person, perhaps like faith or hope. More apparent than India as garden of discourse, was India as booty. But Alexander's army already had booty. They were tired of conquering the world. They wanted to go home. Alexander was still in his early thirties. For him, the prospect of returning home was horrible. And yet, in some sense, he too was tired. On this occasion he did not summon the will to motivate his army. Instead, he took to brooding, spent long hours alone in his tent, sickened, and died. His lieutenants divided up his empire, which lasted about four hundred years. The spread of Greek culture lasted longer. Even today, in the Western world, familiarity with the Greek classics is a mark of education and refined sensibilities.

Genghis Khan had a more unsettled childhood. He had no tutor and no education. He could not read or write. His father died a defeated man. The son at one point had approximately three warriors and four horses. Nevertheless, he subdued and united the nomadic tribes of central Asia. These tribes had also long warred among themselves. They were illiterate and had little culture to spread, but their new Khan motivated them expertly. Except for modern armies with rifles and cannon, his military machine became the most formidable in history. All of his warriors were mounted on fast, rugged little ponies. Until they chose to give battle, they remained widely dispersed, as a swarm of small scouting parties. They had eyes everywhere. Their enemies could not catch up to them, and mostly had no clear target to chase. The small dispersed groups communicated with great skill, using smoke by day and lanterns by night. Scouting reports flowed accurately to the commander, and orders flowed smoothly back to the scattered army. At the chosen time and place, they converged. Their enemies struggled against an invisible army that could suddenly materialize, all ferocious and barbaric, at precisely the worst moment. Sooner or later, each lumbering opponent made a mistake and perished. Genghis Khan led illiterate men, but they were good fighters. The armies of World War II, using radio, radar, and air reconnaissance, turned their intelligence reports to less account in battle, and coordinated their movements with substantially less skill, I do believe, than the Khan's armies of the thirteenth century. Genghis Khan created his fighting machine through the effort of his will. He was a motivator and a tactician. Without too much difficulty, his creation conquered most of the known world worth conquering. For more than a hundred years they were never bested in a single skirmish. Their empire had greater extent than any other before or since. Eventually they ruled over populations some two or three thousand times more numerous than all of central Asia's tiny nations together. Imagine Wichita conquering North and South America. The nomad fighters who bestrode Asia, at all times aggregated fewer than a hundred thousand men. Near Budapest, one of their lesser regional commanders engaged a sizable European army, and annihilated it more easily than most of the victims. Much of Europe lay exposed, but the commander elected not to overrun a continent, at that time, rather backward and dirty. In the fourteenth century, they finally lost a battle—in the jungles of Vietnam. Despite their ephemeral numbers, their empire proved more durable, by some measures, than the British empire. Genghis Khan created this fighting machine through the effort of his will. He thoroughly avenged every affront to his family and every disrespect from his enemies. He enjoyed riches and discovered wonders. He was feared, hated, and loved. From desperate beginnings, he achieved the most complete military success known to any individual human. He lived to about age sixty-eight. With all significant opposition destroyed, yet his followers and admirers still eager for more adventure, he lost interest, took to brooding, spent long hours alone in his tent, sickened, and died.

⚜

We believe we will die, and we don't believe it. We don't want to believe it. If he truly knows he will die, all his children will die, and their children; by the omnipotent erosion of time all memory of him will die, and though he shouts his existence down the long eons ever so shrewdly, all echo shall at last be silent: why does anyone bother to conquer the world?

Perhaps he wants to assuage his feelings. We have all manner of feelings, some of them quite noble. We are not rocks or fence posts. But no longings are so acute, or feelings so bruised, or sensibilities so generous, they can be assuaged forever.

Perhaps he wants to distract himself, to cast his eye on the outcome of his wiles and strategies, to indulge his curiosity. Our world lives for curiosity. We can pursue the world and explore it and test it as far as we wish. With astounding skill it surprises us. We never know what might happen next. We find out only by staying alive.

Wherever we look, the world surprises us. But how long does that game fascinate?

⁂

Genghis Khan knew the human character. Historians have been reluctant to admit how much was seen and felt by an illiterate nomad. They emphasize his cruelty and his limited perspective on the possibilities of being human. Against the indigenous peoples of the new world, similar charges were leveled, with similar justice. They reflect a form of civilized snobbery. In fact, the Khans started wars and also prevented them. They inflicted a rather low ratio of people killed to people conquered—far lower than the Europeans inflicted. After conquest, the nomads governed well, over men and women very different from themselves, and allowed them considerable dignity. No European power gave better government to native peoples, not even the British in Hong Kong, and Europeans typically gave far worse. The nomads supported education, tolerated religions, permitted scholars to publish, encouraged farmers and merchants to prosper, and stimulated commercial and cultural exchange throughout the length and breadth of the known world. Genghis Khan's grandson, Kublai Khan, and *his* grandson, Temur Khan, governed China for just over one hundred years. During this period, the Chinese people enjoyed: the lowest levels of crime, the best roads and mails, the most grain stored against famine, the lowest taxes, the least corruption in government, the most efficient government responses to natural disasters, the highest and most reliable levels of inter-regional economic intercourse, the highest levels of prosperity throughout the country, and the most universal access to prosperity—all of these by substantial margins—than at any other time in China's long history. This was the government given to China by a foreign invader. By contrast, our own highly successful democracy in the United States, was founded on genocide. Moreover, our own United States, dynamic as it is, wonderfully creative as it is, nevertheless has certain areas of shabbiness and decay, a venality tolerated, and a long sad list of problems postponed, quite out of character for the China so energetically goaded by primeval horsemen. Indeed, these nomads often embarrassed civilized people in debate. They observed in us an hypocrisy that we ourselves have observed more slowly. We civilized folk read Aristophanes, write poetry, and design gas chambers. These particular barbarians did not confuse education with virtue. They could be exploitive and murderous, but without hesitation they found the darkest causes in themselves, not in their victims. They well knew barbarity when they saw it. But we take pride in our culture. We can be exploitive and murderous, and say we are not. Perhaps for this reason, our management of the world compares unfavorably to the barbarians'. They did not always value us as we value ourselves, but they had sound management techniques, intelligent leaders, open minds, and a less convoluted conception of integrity. We are disquieted, that the nomads brought a dark side of human nature into the open. They displayed and expressed savage feelings. They encouraged others to believe them savage, and used that belief to their advantage. But when they governed, they governed their savagery. About ourselves, we cannot say as much. Historians overlook the subtleties of the nomad mind. Only their subtlety can explain their peerless military success and their peerless administration of conquered peoples. Genghis Khan was the father of both. Chinese scholars take a resolutely negative view of this barbarian, and decline to examine his integrity or his sensibilities. Other scholars follow the Chinese view. Since the time of Confucius, educated Chinese have equated good government with good scholarship. Nomad rule in China caused some intellectual discomfort. Did the earthy Khans hold the Mandate of Heaven to institute civilized prosperity? During the reign of Kublai Khan, at least one Chinese playwright exhibited a troubled skepticism toward his society's long-presumed moral clockwork. However, later scholars had fewer doubts. Of Genghis Khan, history was written by the defeated. To him they conceded small integrity and few sensibilities. In his last years, the first Khan had seen and felt enough, he had triumphed enough, he no longer cared about his place in anyone's history, and this most willful of men lost the will to live.

Curious, that the very magnitude of his achievement should estrange him from it.

We take pride in our culture. Western societies have unlocked the secrets of nature, cured the sick, originated startling new technologies, produced sublime literature and art and music, conceived nuclear weapons and the systems to deliver them, polluted the planet, spread righteousness, and freed the mind of man. Above all, we have been our own sharpest critics. We have met the enemy and it is us.

Which human individual who ever lived, had the most subtle experience? How does an individual maximize the subtlety of his own life? None of us knows. If we did know, our experience could not be especially subtle. Perhaps we find coherence in the *general* features of subtle experience, and the subtle universe that facilitates it. But the massive and crucial detail, we will never fathom.

Western culture assigns merit to people who read widely, travel widely, cultivate wide interests, continually refine their sensibilities, continually refine their understanding of the world, ingeniously apply rational methods to diverse phenomena, pursue adventures ingeniously diverse, appreciate and cherish human diversity, find beauty in many forms. We have a very fine culture, so long as we do not misuse the merit it assigns to us. Our culture points to unlimited possibility, for any individual with sufficient interest. Perhaps an immortal being could not exhaust all the Western possibilities of being alive. A mere barbarian, even a rather intelligent barbarian like Genghis Khan, might appreciate much in his own way, but in our view, he must suffer from a more limited perception of possibility.

We take pride in our culture. Pride begets deception. What lies beyond unlimited possibility? Must we forever be excited puppy dogs, endlessly sniffing each new bush and lamppost, until time itself grows weary of our little wagging tails?

Lately my life subverts itself. Former pleasures become unendurable. With confusion and regret, I remember the world's shining seductions. Subtle beings lack a constitution suitable for immortality. If our lives find no other way to crush us, they finally turn upside down. According to the Gotama Buddha, serene indifference to being alive is the highest and final state of awareness before extinction. With no way back, we subtle beings can only hope to go forward that far.

And yet, for a short time, the earlier states of awareness did have their hypnotic glory.

The Murder of Mr. Smith

Prosecutor: Thirteen witnesses testified that they saw the defendant stab Mr. Smith with a knife, and heard Mr. Smith shout, "Murder!" Two police officers testified that they arrived at the scene, saw the defendant standing over the lifeless body with a dripping knife in his hand, and heard the defendant say, "I killed him and I'm glad." The defense has presented no evidence *against* murder. The jury must convict.

Defense Attorney: All this testimony has possible explanations other than murder. Perhaps the witnesses are playing a trick on us, just to see if they can get away with it. Who knows what their motives are? Can any of us see inside another person? Mr. Smith may have fallen on the knife accidentally, while my client happened by coincidence to be holding it. And even if my client did say, "I killed him and I'm glad," the reference might have been to his pet turtle.

P.: My esteemed colleague raises *possible* doubt. But I need only prove my case beyond all reasonable doubt. My explanation is simpler and less contorted than the defense attorney's. My colleague stoops even to strained coincidence. But the murder of Mr. Smith is a simple and natural explanation of the evidence. The evidence becomes difficult to explain, if and only if the defendant did not murder Mr. Smith. Any other explanation would be convoluted and contorted. For precisely this reason, my explanation meets the standard: beyond all reasonable doubt.

D.: "*Any* other explanation would be convoluted and contorted?" A bald assertion! Has the prosecutor reviewed *all* other explanations? Only a god could assemble them all. "My explanation is simpler?" Hopelessly vague! What makes one explanation "simpler" than another? "Mr. Smith killed himself," sounds short and simple to me. The prosecutor talks about simplicity, but doesn't tell us how to measure it. He just baldly asserts that his explanation is "simpler," by some mysterious standard he fails to specify. How can the jury apply that standard, or find it justified, when no one here in court can say what it is? Perhaps an enormously superior intelligence could justly decide this case. Perhaps a god could review *all* the explanations, and pick out the "simplest" by some defensible, objective standard. But we mere humans cannot.

P.: Yes, members of the jury, I agree, humans are fallible. All of us here in court today, fall well below the highest possible level of intelligence. Unfortunately, you happen to be the only jury we have. Superior intelligence isn't available to us. But don't be discouraged. You still have sufficient competence to decide this case. Each of you must weigh the evidence and ask himself, Do I know beyond all reasonable doubt, that the defendant murdered Mr. Smith? Even without the highest possible level of intelligence, you know how to interpret the evidence.

D.: (unable to repress a smile): Absolutely absurd! The prosecutor covers up vagueness with yet more vagueness. "Weigh" the evidence? You "know" how to interpret the evidence? Once again the prosecutor omits to define his terms. Rather convenient for him, that no one in this room can say exactly what he means. Without specifying *how* he wants you to "weigh" the evidence, the prosecutor tells you to "weigh" it *his* way! The jury must not obey these deceptive commands! Unless he tells you what his instructions mean, none of us can judge them sound or unsound. But he does not tell us. Therefore, as it stands, the prosecutor's case cannot be verified. The evidence counts neither against his case nor for it. The jury must acquit.

P.: (after mopping his brow and frowning at the floor in silence): My worthy colleague confuses the rigor of analysis with the rigor of jurisprudence. I argue to reasonable doubt, not to possible doubt. Yes, I ask the jury to "weigh" the evidence, to find one interpretation of the evidence "simpler" than all the others, and to "know" the defendant guilty. The rigor of jurisprudence makes no demand that I define these terms. Nor must I review every possible explanation of the evidence. For thousands of years, juries have weighed evidence, found the simplest explanations, and known defendants to be guilty beyond all reasonable doubt. The jury already understands these terms, notwithstanding that none of them have explicit definitions.

୧୬୭୫୭ଡ଼

In this book I argue that our universe stands guilty of being the best possible world. I argue as a prosecutor would do in a murder trial. I argue that a massive array of facts about our world, points with crushing effect to its guilt. I claim that *no* facts about our world point even feebly to its innocence. And then I ask the jury to find our universe guilty, beyond all reasonable doubt, of being the best world possible. You, good reader, are the jury.

My argument can be attacked at several points. My terms "subtlety" and "subtle experience" might be rather familiar to you by now, but they cannot be defined. They remain vague. Even if you understand my argument and my evidence anyway, you cannot consider *all* possible interpretations of that evidence. Moreover, if my own interpretation really is the "simplest" in some telling way, I cannot be specific about why. And nowhere do I consult a god or present the relevant opinions of a superior intelligence. In short, I do not remove all possible doubt.

Similar objections apply to almost any prosecutor's argument. They can be fatal or not fatal. If you the jury find my argument lucid and convincing despite such objections, then they fail.

The rigor of jurisprudence recognizes these competencies in human juries: They understand familiar but undefined terms, and they know how to interpret evidence justly. Accordingly, you the jury have the competence to find our universe not guilty by reason of insufficient evidence, or guilty beyond all reasonable doubt. As you read on, you yourself will know you have that competence.

Dialogue on Death

My longtime mentor is Hubert Dreyfus, professor of philosophy at the University of California at Berkeley. Sometimes he and I talked about death. I was not always so fluent with answers as represented. The following version of our conversations is condensed.

Prof. Dreyfus: If this is the best possible world, why do we have to grow old and die? Growing older, wiser, and more mature may be compensations, but are these compensations sufficient clear up to death?

I think I felt best when I was about your age, when I had enough experience to know what was worth doing and why, but still had lots of energy and lots of open possibilities. What distresses me now is that I get tired easily, so that I can't work and teach as hard as I used to. And I am only sixty-eight. My energy seems to be running down faster than my wisdom and satisfaction are going up. Also, I can't look into an open future in which I will go on learning new fields, writing new books, meeting new students, falling in love with new women, having new children, etc. I was just about your age when, one day as I was swimming in the pool, I realized that I was stuck with the life I have had. That I could no longer open a new field of research, learn a new language, or learn how to play the violin—not to mention no more skiing and other physical feats. I like my life and job and family very much, but I loved the openness that I felt until I was about your age, and don't feel anymore. I'm sorry to say that I don't feel that the wisdom, calm, and sense of satisfaction I have gained since I was fifty-one, make up for the energy and possibilities I have lost.

As for death, and the sadness of death, I don't see how your argument comprehends them. Insofar as I feel wiser and calmer and have new satisfactions, these advantages don't come from the sense that I am going to die. You think that death makes life more poignant. Perhaps it does, but I'm not sure that makes up for the fear and uncertainty it brings. I approach my own death with feelings of sadness and regret.

How does death benefit us? How does my death benefit me?

John: The benefits permeate most adult experience, often in surprising ways. The benefits are everywhere. If we had endless time, how valuable would our time be? Because our time is limited, we appreciate it more. The subtlety of our lives we appreciate more. At some point, usually after we reach our majority, we start to have a mortal attitude toward being alive.

For subtle agents, an existence with straightforward noncontradictory desires satisfied completely in straightforward ways, is incoherent. For us, evils and goods give size to each other. Without death to disturb and sadden us, our world would need some other evil just as big.

For us subtle agents, the world's goods and evils have automatic balance, whether or not we want them to, and whether or not we pay attention to the balance. The balance is there, even if we don't realize the balance is there. But after we pay attention, we can see the balance.

As the sovereign evil, death does have some advantages. We benefit from a ruthless biological evolution based on death and survival—based on new creatures and new behaviors replacing the old. Our evolution slowly pieces together a commensurable dilemma, complicated yet coherent. Our own death connects us to that well constructed dilemma.

As the sovereign evil, death takes away what we must lose anyway. You and I change over time. Eventually we each become someone else. Since we are impermanent anyway, why shouldn't the world use our impermanence to best advantage?

Death is at least a sound choice as the biggest evil balancing the good in our lives. The amount of our complaints indicates it may be an inspired choice: one locus of evil balancing many goods.

Prof. Dreyfus: I will concede that *some* goods and evils balance, and in that sense the evils have compensation. For example, virtues and vices measure each other, and many kinds of good fortune and bad fortune also have a relative balance. I concede that. But how does *death* have *balancing* compensation in this way? It might have the compensation of making life more poignant, but if it does, this compensation doesn't seem to be enough. Surely we could have subtle perceptions of our lives without actually having to give them up.

John: The travails and distresses related to old age and inevitable death, already have compensation when we are young. We don't wait until old age to have compensation for old age.

Part of the quality of your life in the past was that you were not yet old, that you were still a *comparatively* young man. Today your amount of energy and openness and time remaining fall at the lower end of a comparative scale. When you were younger, these amounts clocked in at more attractive points on a similar scale. They had their attraction by comparison, and part of the comparison was the conditions of older age, including proximity to death.

Prof. Dreyfus: Missing my energy and openness now was not a requirement for enjoying them then. For example, I enjoyed my body, but not because I was happy my joints didn't ache. I had no idea how it felt to be old. How could I measure the pleasures of youth by comparing it to an old age I had not yet experienced?

John: While we are still young, we already compare youth to old age. Becoming old ourselves does not initiate the comparison, but only changes it.

In fact we make numerous comparisons to experience we have never had ourselves. We compare our own experience to *other people's* experience.

A person suffering in a bad marriage may have little personal experience of what a good marriage is like. But she can still know her marriage is bad, by comparison to other people's marriages. She reads about other marriages, observes them, listens to what other people say about marriage. Later, if she gets into a good marriage herself, she has a more personal way to measure her former bad marriage. But she always measured bad marriage by comparison to good marriage.

When I was younger, I wanted to have more confidence in myself. However, I had little idea how it felt to be a lot more self-confident. I compared my lack of confidence to *other people's* more abundant confidence.

Today I feel a bit more at ease in the world. My comparative confidence now, and my previous heavy doubt, measure each other. They are counterparts.

Before I had this access of certainty, before I experienced the counterpart to self-doubt, I used a substitute: the confidence reported or observed in other people. I didn't really know what having confidence was like, I didn't have that experience, but I could still measure my lack of confidence, by comparison to other people. Later, when I felt more comfortable in the world, the counterpart relationship changed.

I always measured less confidence by comparison to more confidence. As I grew older, the comparison only changed. It became more personal. But one way or another, I always compared less to more.

During most of our younger adult lives, we typically do make the comparison to old age. I don't entirely know what it's like to be old until I get there. While I'm young, I compare my youth to *other people's* old age. When I'm old myself, I can make a comparison *within my own experience*. As I get older, I measure my youth in a different way. The inalterable past changes. But my youth always had value by comparison to old age.

When my own experience lacks one of the counterparts of a duality, I can use the substitute of other people's experience as a link to the counterpart. I can even seek out these substitutes, as a way to understand myself. Other people are similar to me and dissimilar to me, and both characteristics illuminate my own experience.

Prof. Dreyfus: Yes, if you so choose. But what if you happen to be uninterested in such comparisons? You might simply tune them out.

John: We can be oblivious to some comparisons, but not all. Our experience does fascinate us. We are *addicted* to experience, ours and other people's and fictional inventions. We all want to find out what will happen next. And part of our addiction arises from the complex structure of counterparts in our experience. The significance of my experience can be changed by your experience. Our present experience can be redefined by future experience. In a variety of ways, much of my past experience seems different to me now than when I lived it. *Everyone* feels these differences. The counterpart structure keeps changing and evolving.

We cannot help being fascinated by our own experience, by all the relationships and complexity it has, by the ways we find it predictable and surprising. We resemble people lost in some intricate computer game, unable and unwilling to break free. Few of us live long enough actually to get tired of being alive. The vast majority of humans want to move forward and find out what happens next. Sometimes we feel an intense need to go forward and discover the patterns of experience—even though moving forward, consuming yet more experience, must eventually bring physical deterioration and death. Fascination with experience has an unhappy counterpart: awareness that we have a limited amount. Because we must die, we can be spellbound all the more intensely by once-in-a-lifetime sensations. Because we must die, we pay more attention. Our obsession gets rewarded when present and past experience illuminate each other as striking counterparts. From time to time we feel the intoxication of striking departure from the past: the wonderful new adventure, the wonderful new film, the new day that might surprise us, the rite of passage, the astonishing new technology, the exhilarating new relationship. For awhile we are thrilled, then we want more.

And yet, we would pity the people who live forever but live without these vivid counterparts to death and dying, or without the counterparts to other evils just as great. They cannot play the game that fascinates us. We are addicted to a drug that destroys us. We do not wish to break free. We hate the destruction, but we crave the absorbing experience that brings destruction.

Prof. Dreyfus: Then perhaps I should take up heroin, another absorbing experience that brings destruction. How would addiction to heroin differ from the addiction to What happens next?

John: Some addictions are better than others. None of them are the same. They only share the same general structure.

A heroin addict loves the first effects of his drug, but hates the later effects. Some people love the intoxication of sexual adventure, but hate the morning after, when deeper needs have only grown more acute. The heroin addict and the sex addict have a way out. If they have enough resolution, they can forego the inferior form of bliss, grapple with the pain they sought to avoid, and emerge into a different bliss more satisfying and complete. But the larger bliss still addicts us. Always we are addicts somehow, and in various ways.

Our form of agency entails satisfaction measuring and measured by dissatisfaction. Every satisfaction has a price. If we have the satisfaction first, someone pays for it later. We cannot escape into an *endless* series of more complete and satisfying blisses, each accompanied by greater pain and destruction. At some point we reach the most subtle and interesting form of addiction available to us. At that point, we only want to escape the price, not the addiction itself, for we have located the highest accommodation we can make with our essential nature.

Prof. Dreyfus: You have talked in general ways about how our experience has counterparts that illuminate each other. You described how some of the counterparts can be outside one's own direct experience. These generalities sound plausible. Yes, I do feel addicted to life and to subtle experience. But somehow your general description does not quite convey to me the specifics of how we benefit from death. Specifically, how does the drama of death cause a person to love life when he is younger? I would like to hear you talk in more detail about old age and death as a counterpart that illuminates youth.

John: When you tell me about the sadness of old age and dying, it seems you are telling me you have had a good life somewhere along the line. If someone is *bitter* about dying, he must be thinking, Others have had a better life than mine, or, My life could have been less miserable, or, I never got what I wanted, or even, To hell with this crap. But if someone is *sad* about dying, then surely he is thinking, I am losing much.

Prof. Dreyfus: Yes. I have the good fortune to be sad, not bitter. I have liked my life.

John: For most of my life I have measured the present both by the past and the future. Awareness of my death has long affected my perception of life, whether intensely or in muted ways. When I was twenty-one, I felt the shadow of turning twenty-two, even though I did not understand what I understand now. I already knew that many people in the world were elderly and that they suffered from being old. When I was twenty-one, part of the quality of my life was: I am not old like they are; I have youth. Today I am aware of being not so spry as formerly, but more energetic than my future self. Since the age of twenty-one I have felt the gradual process of dying. At various times I was asleep or awake in the presence of death, but asleep or awake I still felt it.

We must pay a price for being alive. How can life be valuable unless someone somewhere pays a price for it? But not all of us pay the same price for being alive. And not all of us have good lives. Some of us have bad fortune. Some of us have smaller benefit from awareness of death. The middle of life gets measured by the future, but not by our own *unique* future. We don't always pay a fair price when the future arrives. We can be fortunate or unfortunate about the price we pay. Now you feel sad, but you are still alive at sixty-eight, and you have the good fortune to be sad rather than bitter. And you still enjoy your life. You have substantial distance from the category, "Tired of livin' *and* feared of dyin'." By another scale of comparison, you are doing well: Some older people look on their past with dissatisfaction, and/or find themselves discarded and lonely in the present. You compare well to your peers. Perhaps some older people find solace in this alternate comparison. Our systems for comparing satisfactions and dissatisfactions can be convoluted. Younger people can be lonely and frustrated, while their elders find friends and fulfillment. We simultaneously compare with each other in multiple ways, with the optimism of relative youth being only one of those ways. Sometimes the price we pay for being alive comes early, sometimes late, sometimes both. But someone somewhere pays a price for each of our lives. And the converse follows: The price each of us pays has compensation somewhere for someone. All of our distresses and satisfactions balance. They compare and balance in multiple, overlapping, complicated ways, but they balance. The comparisons themselves have comparisons and balance, but they balance. Somewhere, somehow, all of our distress has compensation. We are not always all of us sad.

I'm not handing you a perky, upbeat thesis. My argument can be described as, "This is the most there can be. We can't do better." Sorry about that. For the right reasons, I want to owe as much income tax as possible to the IRS, and I want to be as saddened as possible by my death. Both measure something positive.

Prof. Dreyfus: I understand how *your* awareness of old age measures *your* present appreciation of relative youth. But does everyone think this way? When I enjoyed my youth, I enjoyed it without thinking about old people. I never thought about death and old people. You did, but I didn't. I just enjoyed my energy and openness without realizing I had them. In what manner was *I* measuring the pleasures of *my* youth, by comparison to other people's old age?

John: Even when you're not thinking about old people, your mind can still make a comparison to old people.

The human mind constructs scales of comparison that simplify comparisons. Here's an example.

Suppose I take a walk in the park. If my usual occupations consist of mountain climbing, scuba diving, skiing, attending fabulous parties, driving race cars, etc., then I might find walking in the park dull or soothing. But I don't need to think explicitly about those other experiences to find my walk dull. From those previous experiences, my mind has constructed a scale of comparison, such that the walk seems dull *as measured by that scale*. In this way, I measure my walk in the park by comparison to numerous other experiences, without having to think consciously and explicitly about all the comparisons involved. My mind has constructed a convenient simplification: a scale of comparison.

If my usual occupations consist of lying in bed and watching TV, or working in a windowless office, or doing time in prison, then my mind constructs a different scale, and the same walk in the park might be quite exciting to me. Again, I can feel this excitement without explicitly and consciously reviewing all the comparisons involved.

Another example: A woman might be unsatisfied with her boyfriend, not because she has had better boyfriends, but because her girlfriends have told her about *their* boyfriends. She may have never met the boyfriends described to her. Indeed, her girlfriends may have described their boyfriends to her many years ago, and *she may have forgotten those descriptions*: She may have forgotten the specifics of the descriptions and the specific experiences of hearing the descriptions. Nevertheless, those forgotten descriptions of other women's boyfriends might cause her to be unsatisfied with her present boyfriend. She may forget the descriptions, but remember the scale of comparison they created. "I never have good boyfriends," she might say. "Why can't I have an honest, punctual, and attentive boyfriend. Why am I so unlucky?" Other people's experiences influence her present scale of measurement, even without conscious thought of those experiences.

In a similar manner, other people's experience of old age influences the scale by which you measure your own experience, including youthful experience, even though you are not actually thinking about old people when you enjoy the pleasures of youth.

And in fact, your particular life shows unusually strong influence from life's dilemma—from thoughts of death, disability, how helpless we are to overcome dilemma, how precarious is what we love, and how indifferent the world to our desires—because you spent much of your life discussing Kafka, Melville, and Kierkegaard with your students. You knew all along that you would die, and how terribly and completely you were always at risk.

When measuring and evaluating our experience, sometimes we think of the comparisons consciously and explicitly. But most of the time we use the convenient simplification of scales prefabricated in our minds. Our mental processes automatically construct and update these scales of comparison, as we have new experience. We need these scales as an intermediary to our comparisons. Otherwise, we would be constantly reviewing an enormous number of comparative relationships between our present experience and all the experiences described to us, witnessed by us, or directly experienced by us in the past. Using the scales as an intermediary also allows us to drop a lot of detail from our memories. Yet sometimes we do review the underlying comparisons explicitly—perhaps when we want to examine or modify the ways they influence us.

For many years I made a conscious effort to think about death explicitly, with various degrees of success, because I wanted the maximum advantage from understanding my mortality. I traveled in Southeast Asia and China because I knew my time and health were limited. Had I been less conscious of my death, I might have been content to be a potato. After all, my travels involved effort, discomfort, and risk for myself and for my wife. A potato avoids these annoyances. Uneasy awareness of death drove me out of the potato field. Sometimes I felt as if I were running away, with death following close behind, ready to harvest the potato crop. And I notice that you explored the world in your own energetic ways.

Prof. Dreyfus: Your scales of comparison sound correct. But surely we can avoid potatohood without awareness of death, even indirect awareness. Children and dogs often enjoy their lives, and often explore their world with enthusiasm. But how well do they understand that death awaits them?

John: Children and dogs have satisfactions and dissatisfactions different from ours. When I was a child, being required to sleep was sometimes a major disappointment, I hated my little companions appropriating my toys, and a routine scolding from my parents could reduce me to tears. I did not fear death, but other evils were larger than they are today. Now I have changed. I am not the same person I was then. I can no longer enjoy life entirely in the same ways. My satisfactions and dissatisfactions have changed. They have become more subtle. Today I would not want to be limited to the satisfactions of childhood. Not during all, but during some portions of my life, awareness of death has heightened my appreciation of being alive, and pushed me to explore my life in more subtle ways. Such appreciation and subtle exploration is compensation for death. I may have been short-changed or I may have been overcompensated, but I have had compensation for death. For the human race as a whole, goods and evils balance.

Prof. Dreyfus: I still don't see the balance. The French existentialist Jean-Paul Sartre could find *no* positive counterpart to the fact of death, his or anyone else's. Consider his short story "The Wall": A partisan of the Spanish Republic, captured by the Fascists, is convinced he will be stood up against a wall and shot, within a few hours' time. For the first time in his life, he *truly* knows he will die. This knowledge so devastates him, that he loses all interest in living. His former life seems remote to him, as if it had happened to someone else. Even after the sentence of death gets unexpectedly removed, his loss of interest remains. Had he *truly* known all along that he must die, he could never have cared about his life.

John: I agree, most of us do not really believe we will die, no matter how many funerals we attend. We believe it and yet we don't believe it, so terrible is this fact.

But Sartre apparently regarded his own response to the fact of death, as universal. It is not; his response was idiosyncratic, just as yours and mine are. A few outrageous people do not feel alive, unless they are clinging by their fingernails to some inverted mountain cliff, their feet dangling in space, no safety ropes, and the pieces of the cliff starting to crumble under their scrimpy grip. As to their more banal pursuits—shopping for new cleated boots, making conversation with their families, paying their income taxes, raising money for their next expedition—they endure as best they can, function like zombies, and wait for the passionate moments when death again is near.

My brother has this tendency. He describes his life as satisfying and fine, with no serious disappointments. But about a year ago, he *condescendingly* defied an armed mugger, who wanted his wallet and his wife's wedding ring. The mugger fired a shot past his ear, then pointed the gun directly at his nose. My brother reported feeling exalted. He stared past the muzzle of the gun and into the mugger's eyes, came within a millimeter of being shot, miraculously carried his point, and spent the next several hours in a state of high excitement—completely impervious to the distress of his loved ones. Most of the time, he seems to be quite sane.

Surely the most typical human response lies somewhere between Sartre and my brother: We are diagnosed with an incurable disease, given one week to live, discover three days later that the malignancy was just a smudge on the X-ray, and then we go outside and hear the birds chirping.

"The Wall" actually supports my thesis. Numerous *comparisons* appear throughout that story. I claim that we measure our experience by comparison. Sartre's about-to-be-shot protagonist describes his present feelings of indifference toward his life, by *comparing them* to past feelings quite different. Each attitude measures the other—even for Jean-Paul Sartre.

In *The Stranger*, Albert Camus also plays off a comparison: his protagonist's indifference toward the death sentence, where you and I would take the easy acquittal.

If a cold wind blows from the future, then what is warm by comparison? If some people feel indifference toward life and scant compensation for death, then other peoples' relish for life becomes larger by comparison. Their compensation for death becomes larger by comparison. Sartre and Camus can rearrange the comparisons, but they cannot evade comparison as our measure of experience.

Prof. Dreyfus: That sounds right. Your argument doesn't require that *everyone* have compensation for death, much less that everyone have exactly the same compensation.

But I still don't see an exact balance. What about people who believe they will go to heaven, that death releases them into a better life to come? How does death benefit them?

John: Conceptions of an afterlife can be beautiful and motivating in their own way. Part of the subtlety of our world is that mortality affects us in so many different ways, and to so many different degrees. Some of us are luckier than others. You and I are frightened. Sometimes fear of death has the beneficial effect of helping us love our lives, and helping us live them better. Perhaps you and I have been lucky in this way. But fear of death can have other effects also, and awareness of death can have effects other than simple fear. Some people do believe in a beautiful afterlife.

You and I regard them as living in denial, but they are able to do it, and *they* regard *us* as deluded. Their satisfactions and dissatisfactions differ substantially from yours and mine, and this variety makes the world more subtle.

Often our beliefs about death are far from straightforward. You and I are struggling mightily with an Awful Fact. But religious people can also have complicated feelings, perhaps more complicated than ours, if only because they have various degrees of faith. Some religious people work hard at controlling their doubts. Sometimes their fervor measures the persistence of sneaking uncertainty.

Recently I talked to a friend with cancer, thirty-six hours before he died. He was a devout Presbyterian, at least in the sense that he was quite active in his church, and thanked God before every meal. As far as I could tell, he sort of believed he was going to heaven, and he sort of didn't. His life of church-sponsored good works may have constituted his preparation for heaven, but all the same, he didn't seem exactly overjoyed that his earthly life was about to end. Presbyterian heaven gives you a brand new body, but this man talked sadly about how healthy he had been, and how suddenly his health had evaporated. He looked at me and at his other visitors with a haunting, sad, detached gaze. He said "Goodbye," rather than, "See you later."

His religious faith and his emphasis on good works show a different kind of influence from approaching death. He took pleasure in his health *and* in his work for the church—a complicated response to his mortality.

And we have still other responses. Mortality motivates some people to have children, or teach, or write a novel, or otherwise try to leave their mark on the world. In my case, it motivated me to travel.

We believe in an afterlife, or want to believe in it, because we want to escape the dilemma of being alive precariously. We believe in many kinds of afterlife, presided over by many kinds of Supreme Being. We believe with various degrees of certainty and expectation. This variety helps make the world subtle. But rarely is the afterlife a calm fact calmly accepted. Usually the *certain* afterlife arouses emotion, sometimes to the point that we kill each other over the details. Surely these fierce emotions are really aroused by our original longing that we continue to exist. The exultation of feeling alive and well when existence is precarious, and the exultation of glorifying God, are surely related. Which is the superior compensation for death, I cannot say.

Prof. Dreyfus: I understand how your argument comprehends death. You give a good variety of examples and they sound right. But how can you generalize from *some* examples, even a lot of good examples, to *all* examples?

John: I don't have a logical deduction proving perfection in our world beyond all *possible* doubt. I only have a plausibility argument. But if the concept of subtlety, and the related thesis that our world is the best possible, have enough coherence, if they answer a number of questions about our existence that otherwise would be quite puzzling, and if they explain and unify a sufficiently large amount of phenomena in our lives, then surely their plausibility increases beyond *reasonable* doubt. Each example and each observation is another piece of evidence. My argument takes the form of accumulating evidence beyond a reasonable doubt, as a prosecutor would argue in a murder trial.

Prof. Dreyfus: I see. Then my role has been to propose counterexamples to your thesis, to determine whether you can explain them, and whether your explanations fit in easily, without contortions. And I have to admit, each time I tried to puncture your thesis, your explanation made it more plausible, not less. At this point I'm convinced that our world really is the best possible. If I were on the jury, I would vote with the prosecution. And that's a strange opinion for me to have. In a sense, you and I are the defendants, and neither of us wants to be guilty.

Part Seven

MORAL
RESPONSIBILITY

Why We Exist

The reason why we exist proceeds from (1) the evidence for perfection in the world and (2) the logical structure of explanation.

The explanation, "My shirt is dirty today because I didn't do the laundry" connects together two propositions: the *explanandum* "My shirt is dirty today" and the *explanans* "I didn't do the laundry."

If it happens to be a true proposition, then "My shirt is dirty today" is true but logically contingent. It doesn't have to be true. In logical possibility, my shirt could have been clean today.

"Human beings exist as we do and have the adventures we have in a Big Bang universe" is a true but logically contingent proposition. This is our grand explanandum. In logical possibility it doesn't have to be true. But it is true.

We're looking for an illuminating and appropriate explanans. We want to know the reason why our explanandum is true.

Any true explanation of why human beings exist as we do, takes the form, "We exist as we do because X," where the explanans X is a true but logically contingent proposition.

If the explanans X itself has a further explanans Y—"X because Y"—then Y must again be true but logically contingent. If Y has the explanans Z, then Z must be logically contingent. And so on.

Any true explanation of why we exist as we do, must stop somewhere with a "final" explanans: a true but logically contingent proposition that itself has no further explanans. There the explanation rests.

A final explanans accounts for us being here in a Big Bang universe and having the adventures we have. That's the original explanandum.

("We exist as we do for no reason" is the case where the explanandum and the final explanans are identical.)

Whatever final explanans we fix upon, even if we know it is true, we humans will find it mysterious. Why it is true will be puzzling. Whatever final explanans we fix upon, it will be contingent, it could have been false, and why it is true will remain unexplained.

We're looking for a final explanans that's not too puzzling, but still illuminates the explanandum.

Some candidates for final explanans fail to be accurate. They have inconsistencies with the facts of existence. For example, "Existence is a random state of chaos" doesn't accord with the facts. Your daily life and mine have a lot of coherence.

Other candidates fall short of a full accounting. For example, the Big Bang makes a poor final explanans for what exists, because it fails to answer for everything that actually happens. The Big Bang fails to explain certain actual facts: conscious awareness, free will, the world's elusive nature just outside our grasp, the world doing better for us than we can do for ourselves.

One candidate for final explanans of what exists, goes bankrupt for remarkable reasons. "Every possible world is an actual world" will turn out to be a flawed accounting for your existence and mine. The next two chapters touch upon why it doesn't work. This explanans entails a state of existence both repugnant and absurd. Moreover, it fails to answer for everything that actually happens in our world. But most enlightening, it has further defects related to free will and moral responsibility. Over the course of the next two chapters, I hope, all these defects will be clear.

"Existence conforms to a principle of goodness" has decisive advantages as final explanans. First, it's logically contingent, as required. In logical possibility it could have been false.

Second, it's accurate. It accords with natural phenomena. On the evidence for perfection in the world, it's a true statement.

Third, it does answer quite well for our world's structure—as we will see in the next two chapters. In particular, this explanans accounts for conscious awareness, our status as moral players, and our genuine free will in a determined world. And as we will see, the accounting is simple and insightful.

"Existence conforms to a principle of goodness" has a fourth advantage, as final explanans for the state of existence. This particular explanans stops at a natural point of rest. It goes far enough but not too far. Thus:

Any further explanans X—"Existence conforms to a principle of goodness because X"—would raise more questions than it answered. A further explanans X would add difficulties to the original explanandum, without compensating enlightenment.

For example, "Existence conforms to a principle of goodness, because a Supreme Being wills it to be so," only complicates the original explanandum. The additional explanans raises more questions than it answers. Not only do we have natural phenomena to explain, we add new supernatural phenomena that also want explaining.

Moreover, if that further explanans were somehow true, then we would have at least two coherent, mutually exclusive structures for the Supreme Being. Whichever structure the Supreme Being actually had, the structure would be arbitrary. More on this in "The Alien Presence" (p. 356).

An explanans that goes beyond "Existence conforms to a principle of goodness" adds absolutely no accuracy to the explanation of natural phenomena. Any further explanans just adds complication. It raises more questions than it answers.

"Existence conforms to a principle of goodness" illuminates the original explanandum without complicating it. This explanans keeps the explanation complete but simple. It's a natural place for the explanation to rest.

"Existence conforms to a principle of goodness" is contingent but true, it accounts for all the facts of existence, and it doesn't add complications to the explanandum. This is the reason why we are here in a Big Bang universe having the adventures we have. This is the reason why we exist.

Not even an omniscient being could supply a final explanans that humans would find less mysterious. *Any* true explanation of why we exist as we do, must have a puzzling final explanans, not because information is hidden from us, but because explanation has a particular logical structure. The mystery of our existence hides in plain sight.

"We are here in a Big Bang universe having the adventures we have, because existence conforms to a principle of goodness." That's the most insightful explanation we can understand, for why we exist as we do. The explanation stops at its natural point of rest. All further mystery is irreducible.

The World's Peculiar Structure

The very best world contains unique moral perceptions, I believe. Highly subtle inhabitants of the best possible world, have substantially different moral perceptions than highly subtle inhabitants of merely good worlds. Here's why I think so.

In the last chapter, you and I identified the final explanans for why we exist: Existence conforms to a principle of goodness.

Why existence does that, no one will ever know. The final explanans has irreducible mystery. Not even an omniscient being could further reduce the mystery. It hides in plain sight.

But at least we have a final explanans. The reason why we exist stands revealed:

You and I inhabit the best possible world for subtle agents. We are here in a Big Bang universe, in a world both seductive and fatal, having the temporary adventures we have—because existence conforms to a principle of goodness.

In light of that explanation, you and I may look at our world in a new way. If all the world's phenomena conform to a principle of goodness, then causal patterns in those phenomena don't finally explain why the inhabitants exist. The Big Bang, the subsequent evolution of galaxies and planets, the evolution of life on Earth—such happenings fail to be the final explanans for human existence. Instead, those phenomena themselves have an explanation that illuminates them. The structure of our universe has a new significance. I'm going to tell you about it.

In a world conforming to a principle of goodness, the Big Bang and its subsequent evolution have broadly useful functions. They don't explain our existence, but they have other jobs to do. I will quickly describe one such broadly useful function: giving the subtle inhabitants a means of perception, including moral perception.

You and I can follow out a big chunk of history in our universe, from the Big Bang to people. Our universe assembles agents with high idiosyncrasy and complex structure, yet all this intricacy has strong coherence in each of us. Our universe produces a human dilemma with high quality randomness and labyrinthine structure, yet for each of us this dilemma has a consummate commensurability—sometimes a sublime commensurability. Our universe does well making us. It works hard. *And it stays intelligible.* You and I can see how we are put together. We live inside a transparent process that assembles us and assembles our experience.

To stay intelligible to the inhabitants, our universe relies on its size, its age, its versatile physical law with reusable structures, and its falling-down progress toward lightness and structure in tandem. Simple yet potent.

In this manner, much about our giant universe connects visibly to our own nature, and the nature of our daily experience.

We are able to explore that connection. The Big Bang generates agents who gradually understand the Big Bang. Evolution generates a curiosity that investigates evolution. We have something interesting to do. And we see ourselves as embedded in large, intelligible, illuminating processes.

Such perspectives give us a variety of information about ourselves and the world, in curious stages throughout our history. Such perspectives prod us to consider a variety of questions, some of them metaphysical, some of them moral.

Sometimes we don't know we like something until we know what it is. By giving us perspective on our lives, Big Bang evolution enlarges our ability to understand good experience. It even helps us understand our own standards of good experience. Thus:

In modern times, physical process casts light on our lives. We don't live in a flat painting. Very much the contrary. The balance in our experience, that we know what will happen each day and we do not know, has high quality. Our lives surprise us in subtle ways. Moreover, we can explore the idiosyncrasies in our daily experience, to a tremendous depth and dimension. We are coherent agents and our never-ending dilemma remains vastly commensurable. These features and more, sharpen under the illumination of Big Bang evolution.

By noticing how our universe does well constructing our experience, we gain a new understanding of how our lives are good; how they have a coherent subtlety.

We thereby gain insight into our own standard of good experience. We have a new perception of goodness.

In short, Big Bang evolution helps us understand what is good.

Evolution has done that for us since the dawn of our species. When first we became human, we already felt worship for an intimate process greater than ourselves. More on this in a bit.

The world's reflexive causal pattern—its Big Bang generates idiosyncratic agents who investigate and gradually understand the Big Bang—constitutes an exacting technical achievement. Only profound ingenuity makes physical law both intelligible to our understanding and sufficiently versatile to evolve us. In consequence, the inhabitants have full perspective. Thus:

Suppose human idiosyncrasies and human experience happened by fiat, with no embedding processes to illuminate them. Suppose, in an alternate world, human beings had the same structure-with-idiosyncrasy in their personalities as actual humans, but everything else was simplified. The entire world consists of a large flat piece of land with a motionless sun overhead that turns on for twelve hours and then off for twelve hours. Anyone who falls off land's edge simply vanishes. Rain comes every fifth day, soaks into the ground, and vanishes. All nonhuman life consists of crops, eight different kinds. The crops produce no seeds; they propagate when humans take a mature leaf and stick it into wet ground. Atoms are indivisible. Metals are unknown. Glass and electricity cannot be made. The inhabitants can discover no particular reason why the sun shines or why it remains suspended in the sky. It just does. They can invent a reason, but they cannot discover one. In like manner, no one knows where the rain comes from. The night sky has three thousand motionless points of light, all equally dim. No one knows why. The soil underfoot contains no fossils, no geological layers, no useful deposits. The weather repeats itself in an endless five-day cycle. No amount of prayer to unseen deities causes any deviation in those patterns.

Human beings in that world could still have subtle lives. Their full idiosyncrasy would be present by fiat. They could have social relations, create art, mourn their dead, make war, tell stories, fall in love, raise children. They could plot and scheme. In very simple ways they could wonder why they exist. But those humans could not make discoveries about their surroundings, that illuminate their own nature. Their world's fiat character would reduce their insight into themselves. I believe that in consequence, their moral perceptions would never rise above immediate connections to their daily lives.

Nor must fiat worlds be so simple and predictable. Suppose the sun turns on and off at unpredictable times, for no particular reason that the inhabitants can discover. It just does. Suppose that any mature leaf planted in wet ground, might develop as any one of the eight crops, for no particular reason. Which it turns out to be, is unpredictable. Suppose that the stars have a different color each night for no particular reason. And so on.

The environment becomes unpredictable, perhaps even intriguing. If well constructed, it might even contribute to a good balance between the expected and the unexpected. But the humans still cannot make discoveries about their fiat environment, that cast light on their own nature as humans. In that respect, they live in a blank world.

By contrast, actual human beings inhabit a highly reflexive causality. One hundred and sixty thousand years ago, at the dawn of our species, we could already see ourselves reflected in the world around us. Many other creatures were echoes of us. They ate, defecated, breathed, and bled like we did. They had bodies and faces, limbs, ears, and eyes like we did. They gave birth, raised young, and died like we did. Animism, a straightforward elaboration of those echoes, appeared early among homo sapiens. We began to theorize about coherence in our world. And our theories led to investigation and to new theories. We started down a path that beckoned. The more we analyzed our surroundings, the more coherence we discovered. Eventually our surroundings ballooned into 250 billion galaxies in a cosmos 13.7 billion years old—that illuminates what we are. We have gained penetrating perspectives on ourselves and the world.

At the dawn of our species, we and our world reflected each other in a way that intrigued us. We already saw ourselves as connected to the world in some deep mysterious way. We already felt worship for an *intimate* process greater than ourselves. Wonder at our reflexive world already figured into our standards of good experience.

In future, the structure of the world might enlighten us in unexpected ways.

In contemporary times we have gained penetrating perspectives on ourselves and the world. The next chapter talks about these moral perspectives: how our moral status has coherence and idiosyncrasy, how our world "behaves well" toward us outside our own standards of right behavior, the nature of subtlety and goodness, how our moral choices affect the world's goodness, and the relationship between moral status and existence. These perspectives and others are part of the view in our Big Bang reflexive world. Our moral perceptions become radically different than they would be in a fiat world.

That our world conforms to a principle of goodness, enhances our ability to understand goodness.

The structure of our universe casts light on human nature and on human standards of goodness. Indeed, it casts light on the nature of any subtle being, actual or possible, and on subtle but nonhuman standards of goodness. More on this in the next chapter.

One last comment on the world's structure.

Reflexive causality is the world revealing itself to our understanding. Amazing grace is the world operating outside our understanding. This balance in our lives puts our Big Bang itself into perspective. Let's take a look.

The Big Bang and physical evolution fail to account for what exists. They account for neither consciousness, nor free will, nor the elusive nature of all human experience, nor the world's consistent ability to give us different and better than we could wish to have.

The world operates not quite always within our understanding. The world keeps our ambitions subtly elusive. It does that for everyone. It sneaks past our banal desires and our incoherent ideals. It sounds us. It changes us. It gives us sublime moments we cannot strive to have, nor even imagine in advance. In its own way, the world knows what to do with us better than we do. By its own mysterious and alien agenda, the world refines our lives. We don't quite see all the world's structure.

The world's *overt* structure has broadly useful functions. The world's visible structure allows us to find order in our experience, to explore and discover, to interact with each other, to have moral status and to have perspective on ourselves. And it has another broadly useful function: the world's visible but blind evolution of lightness and idiosyncrasy, adapts well to a fine tuning that leaves the other functions intact. The visible structure and the transcendent structure work well together.

The world uses that fact to advantage. It hides inside an opaque randomness. The world hides inside its own unpredictability. We don't get what we want, and yet our lives are well worth living. Consistently we strive to have steak and consistently we receive linguini. We experience, not just any randomness, but a cunning randomness beyond the overt effect of physical evolution.

And that conclusion should be unsurprising. The final explanans for why we exist as we do, is a principle of goodness, not a principle of physics.

Moral Status

Four questions about moral responsibility, have interconnected answers.

1. If happiness and unhappiness remain always in balance, why should I bother to help anyone be happy? My efforts would not change the world's proportion of happiness to unhappiness.

2. The best world needs good people and bad people together. Where would the world's subtlety be, without diabolical schemes? May I not contribute by doing evil?

3. How can I improve the best possible world? How can I harm it? No matter what I do, this world remains the best it can possibly be. Why, then, should I try to better the world?

4. "Moral imperatives" are impulses that had survival value during evolution. In a Godless unjust universe, why should I heed them as anything more?

If this world is the best possible as described, then the last question has a particularly telling answer. But let's first untangle the other three.

QUESTION ONE goes to the causal consequences of our good deeds. We're not asking *why* we should improve the world's happiness, but how.

Yes, it's true, fifty percent of human experience must fall below average. Unhappiness must balance happiness. None of our good deeds can change that fact. But good deeds generally improve the subtle quality of life. We can help other people be happy and unhappy at higher levels of subtlety.

Human beings are choosy about happiness. We don't want just any sort of happiness. We don't want to be glowworms. We want subtle happiness, or happiness in a subtle context.

Causing someone to be *un*subtly happy, degrades that person's "potential in life." Making someone happy by giving him a lobotomy, or addicting him to heroin, does not qualify as a good deed, except when lots of pain gets relieved—pain so intense that life was not worth living.

A lobotomy or heroin addiction may cause a person to be happier, but probably it will also cause his experience to be less subtle.

The examples following are evidence for this assertion: We feel a moral duty to help other people's "potential in life"—their potential to have, not just happy experience, but subtle experience.

Even when we don't explicitly think about that duty, our moral sensibilities tend to reflect it. One way or another, right and wrong for us relate to subtlety.

When Mr. Edison invented the light bulb, he did not expect his invention to create a world without problems. But he could have reasonably expected his light bulb to create a world with new and different problems. And he could have expected the new problems to be better than the old, in this sense:

Human life today appears to be more subtle than it was forty thousand years ago. The light bulb, the internal combustion engine, antibiotics, the motion picture, the printing press—none of these change the balance of happiness. But in the long sweep of history, they do make our lives different and apparently more subtle.

That fact encourages us to invent and discover things, with the expectation of making the world new, different, and more subtle.

If I buy breakfast and a new suit for a homeless person, I might hope that he will enter the workforce. There he will be constrained to meet deadlines and find his boss's jokes funny. Other working people, whose self-image as fortunate or successful may have been reinforced each time they passed his derelict prostrate form, will now be competing with him. Problems in the world will persist. Unhappiness will still balance happiness. But the problems will be new and different, perhaps less basic. Competition might move to a higher level. I can reasonably hope that this man, and maybe the world generally, will go on to more subtle problems. Past history in the world does support such hopes.

If I smile encouragement to a passing stranger, just because he seems downhearted, I can reasonably hope to strengthen him. He may be able to do more with his life.

If no one in the world could read or write, happiness and unhappiness would still balance. But our lives would surely be less subtle. If I support a child who wants to go to school and learn to read, I have expectations about the consequences. She may rise above the problem of digging ditches without getting bored, to the problems faced by a university professor or a corporate executive. She may become happy and unhappy at higher levels of subtlety.

I'm not giving a complete account of human motivation. In fact we do care about the level of happiness in others. Sometimes we have the incoherent goal of making everyone everywhere happier always. Quite often we just want certain particular people to be happy, without reviewing the consequences for humanity in general.

But, one way or another, our solicitude for subtlety remains. Even when we have a simple benign intent just to make someone happy, we still feel a duty, and we often take care, not to damage their potential for subtle experience. Before I gift my nephew with an entertaining video game, I check for unintended consequences. Is the video game *too* entertaining?

In some circumstances, we need only minimal reflection about subtlety. Without even thinking about subtlety, we feel it's a dirty trick to give someone a happy lobotomy. Our instinctive moral sensibilities tend to reflect the duty we feel, to promote *subtle* happiness.

Thus, one way or another, solicitude for subtlety figures into our good deeds. Right and wrong for us relate to subtlety, not just happiness.

Sometimes a good deed actually attacks the happiness of another, to improve his potential for subtle experience. A bleary-eyed man who never stops singing, might be less happy after I pour out all his bottles into the river. But he might find his new life more interesting.

How can I improve the world at hand? What causal effects do I expect from my good deeds? I hope that people will be longer-lived, healthier, stronger in character, more untroubled by low concerns, more knowledgeable, more fascinated by their lives, and more empowered—able to confront new and more subtle problems. Those are my realistic expectations for good deeds in the actual world.

I can have those expectations, even if I know that happiness and unhappiness in the world must always balance.

Not all moral acts are good deeds with solicitude for subtlety. Choosing death before dishonor, for example, can be a moral act without being a good deed. Choosing death before dishonor can destroy one's own potential for subtlety, and still be a moral act. But now we have moved beyond the first question.

QUESTION TWO: The best world needs good people and bad people together. Where would the world's subtlety be, without diabolical schemes? May I not contribute by doing evil?

This question conflates two different meanings of "contributing to the world." Let's consider an analogy.

Suppose that we have a landscape full of litter, and a manager who directs a campaign to clean up the litter. The manager hires people to constitute cleanup teams, which go out onto the landscape and pick up litter. For these teams the manager may hire two types of people: Picker Uppers and Litterbugs.

Picker Uppers believe in a litter-free landscape. They will exert themselves to pick up litter.

Litterbugs don't care whether the landscape has litter or not. And they are lazy. They only pick up litter when other people glare at them and make abusive comments. More often they simply drop their candy bar wrappers and empty plastic water bottles right on the ground, making a mess for someone else to clean up.

The manager has discovered that Litterbugs motivate Picker Uppers. When they see Litterbugs being lazy and careless with litter, Picker Uppers become outraged. They work three times as hard to pick up litter. Also, they glare at the Litterbugs and make abusive comments. The manager has discovered that cleanup teams with just the right mixture of Picker Uppers and Litterbugs, pick up more litter than teams of all Picker Uppers.

One day a Litterbug starts bragging. "Litterbugs like me are vital to the cleanup effort," he says. "Without us, litter would be everywhere. We Litterbugs contribute just as much to a clean landscape as the Picker Uppers." And he throws another candy bar wrapper on the ground.

But a Picker Upper says, "Yes, in a sense you do contribute. Thanks to an excellent manager who chooses the best possible cleanup teams, your vile habits get subverted and turned to good use. But you don't help in the same way we do. To make the landscape clean, someone must bear a burden. We bear the burden, you make it heavier. In that sense, you do the opposite of contribute."

In the landscape cleanup effort, actions that help bear the burden are moral. Actions that exacerbate the burden are immoral.

The cleanup analogy shows that "contributing to the world" can have at least two meanings.

One element of the best world is a certain amount of trying unselfishly to help others. Our world would not be the most subtle possible, if human beings were entirely selfish and never took care for other people's subtlety-potential.

But another element of the best world is a certain amount of deliberately harming other people's potential, for selfish reasons.

The best possible world is not a thinking entity like you and I, but it is a good management of all the elements of high subtlety. In particular, the best world subverts deliberate harm to others. In the best world, selfishness does well giving size and subtlety to altruism, and vice verse. In ways unexpected and sometimes mysterious to you and me, harming other people's potential for subtlety, actually contributes to the inhabitants' high subtlety.

As in the litter cleanup analogy, good management makes good use of bad deeds.

Nevertheless, the best world still relies rather heavily on that first element: people unselfishly trying to help the subtlety-potential of others. Someone must make that effort. Someone must bear that burden. Although a wide variety of actions figure into high subtlety, only some actions contribute to bearing the burden. Other actions exacerbate the burden. Hence moral and immoral choices and actions.

QUESTION THREE: How can I improve the best possible world? How can I harm it? *No matter what I do, this world remains the best it can possibly be.* Why, then, should I try to better the world? Why should I do what's right?

The statement in italics covertly conflates two different descriptions of the world. We get a good view of this conflation if we elaborate a bit on Question Three. Good reader, this is our chance to talk about free will in a determined world.

Throughout this chapter, I assume that genuine free will is coherent, that it really can happen in a possible world. If in fact free will is *in*coherent, if it can't happen in a possible world, then free will doesn't happen in the best world. But I happen to believe it does happen in the best world.

My own personal experience of weighing alternatives and making choices as a conscious being, leads me to believe that genuine free will is coherent. I seem to feel how genuine free will would operate coherently.

Even if my free will is illusory, just a false appearance, I would still understand how it could have been authentic, I believe. Even if each choice I make was already written in stone before I was born, even if I have only the illusion of making decisions and choices, then the illusion still shows me how my free will could have been real. That happens to be my opinion.

If free will really is an incoherent notion, then Question Three has a short and unpleasant answer, an uninteresting answer that leaves the best-world thesis intact. You and I are looking for problems. Accordingly, as we answer Question Three, let's assume that free will is coherent, that it can happen in a possible world, that free will in our own world might be genuine. Let's find out whether those assumptions lead to problems with Question Three.

If my free will *could* be genuine, then in fact it *is* genuine. The world's principle of goodness says it is. The composition of the best world is just the mandate of the united opinion of all possible subtle agents, as per "Opinions and Spiders" (p. 107). The united opinion prefers genuine free will to fake free will, as a component of the best world. We will see why shortly. Therefore, on the evidence for perfection in the actual world, I have genuine free will.

Good reader, you, too, are in luck. I know you have consciousness and free will like I do. Don't try to deny it. The united opinion wants you and me both to have genuine free will.

Suppose you and I could build a machine able to reason, emote, and make choices. Suppose we could endow our machine with a complicated personality, highly idiosyncratic yet highly coherent. We can't, maybe we never can, but suppose we could. Then the united opinion might want our machine to have consciousness and authentic free will, not the illusion of free will.

But now we have some puzzlements. Perhaps the machine would make the choices we program it to make. How could it *freely* make the choices we arrange for it in advance? How could it be responsible for its choices?

Moreover, you and I ourselves correspond to a kind of machine. We have brains with synapses and cortexes and other grey stuff. The grey stuff follows its own rules. You and I didn't make those rules.

Our grey matter operates under the laws and constraints of physical process—just like all the other physical matter in the universe. Those laws and constraints have neither consciousness nor free will. If you choose to watch your neighbor's kids when she has an emergency, you exercise free will. But the same decision can be explained as your brain's molecules reacting to stimuli according to the laws of physical process, almost like billiard balls. How your brain reacts seems determined by the rules—not by free will.

Thus we have two different accountings for the same choices. We have grey stuff rattling around our heads according to rules we never made, and we have genuine free will. Puzzling.

It gets worse. I've been telling you that the actual world conforms to a principle of goodness. Whatever phenomena constitute the best possible world, obtain. Whatever causal patterns those phenomena would have in the best possible world, obtain. In that manner, a principle of goodness *determines* the entire causal pattern of the world. In every significant detail, the causal pattern is predetermined before it begins. Every choice you and I make, was already determined before we were born.

We have two accountings for each choice we make. And each choice we make was already written in stone before we were born.

What happened to our free will? Is it fake? How are we responsible for our choices? Do we have only the illusion of making selections and decisions?

Good reader, I've kept you in suspense long enough. These puzzlements have a simple resolution.

A principle of goodness determines the world's entire causal pattern, including all the choices we make. Yet we make our choices freely. The united opinion tells us how:

Among all possible worlds, one possible world contains a population freely expressing their free will, where their choices happen to be just right for the principle of goodness. By coincidence, all their free choices happen to fit optimum collective subtlety. In one possible world, free choice and the best possible causal progress, happen to be identical. They are the same in every significant detail. The inhabitants exercise their genuine free will, but each free choice they make coincides exactly with the predetermined master plan mandated by the united opinion.

That's a vast coincidence. But that's also a possible world, and indeed, the best possible world. The united opinion prefers it above every alternative.

Yes, we're talking about a coincidence very large. But the number of possible worlds is also very large. One of those worlds does have exactly the perfect coincidence, right down to the last detail. If our world is that world, then my decision this morning to flick a speck of dust from my sleeve, fits a pattern of optimal causality.

This is how the world ought to be. This is the world mandated by the united opinion. On the evidence for perfection, this is the actual world.

In the best world possible, all causality is just what the united opinion wants it to be. In particular, what your grey matter does and what mine does, are what the united opinion wants them to do. All our lobes and synapses conform to the principle of goodness mandated by the united opinion.

Apparently the united opinion wants a correspondence between our free choices and grey matter activity. And we can see why:

Our brains replicating our conscious awareness, confers many benefits. A universe with predetermined causal copies of its free will, confers benefits. For the same choices we get two different accountings.

One of the accountings involves the Big Bang and the laws of physics. We can understand our personalities as evolved and structured. My conscious awareness and yours, my free choices and yours, connect to biological evolution, to the rules of chemistry, the composition of living cells, photosynthesis, oxidation, eating and sleeping, the growth of infants into adults, the arrangement of lobes and cortexes and hormones and synapses, the evolution of life from the Big Bang. This second description of free choice, gives us considerable insight into ourselves and each other. We study ourselves when we study the world around us. We gain the insight of reflexive causality.

We also gain a causal context for our free will. The world replicates our free choices within a thoroughly detailed, highly coherent causal pattern we can understand and use. Their causal context gives coherence and significance to our choices. We become efficacious as agents in a causal world, and our world has causal influence on us.

Our world replicates our free choices as causally determined within a causal context. We benefit in many ways. This is how the world ought to be. This is the world with the most subtle experience. The united opinion wants the world to have predetermined causal copies of free choice. And so we do.

Thus a principle of goodness explains the correspondence between free choice and predetermined causal progress, including the causal progress of grey stuff inside our head-bones.

(As to the personality machine, with high idiosyncrasy yet high coherence, which we may never be able to build: Does the united opinion want our machine to be a copy of conscious free will?

(If the machine has moral status, then I suppose the answer is yes. If our machine has moral status, then it can rebel against its formative influences. My publisher having limited me to one hundred thousand words, I will speculate no further.)

As I've been telling you, the nature of existence has an explanans with irreducible mystery. We identified the final explanans as a principle of goodness, not a principle of physics. I ticked off some phenomena which physical principle cannot explain: consciousness, free will, our elusive world operating just outside our reach, our mysterious universe doing better for us than we could do for ourselves. Now we have another phenomenon that physics cannot explain: the correspondence between genuine free choice and brain activity following its own rules.

We explain this correspondence as a prodigious coincidence mandated by the united opinion.

Are we *introducing* vast coincidence as a new phenomenon? No. We're only trying to understand the exact nature of the coincidence. Whether or not our world is the best possible, it has prodigious coincidence anyway. Any final explanans for why we exist, must account for large coincidence. Thus:

Good reader, you and I inhabit a highly coherent world. Indeed, our world has far more coherence than logically required to support intelligent beings. But this coherence just amounts to many constituent elements *coinciding* well. Our world's high coherence—the daily coherence of your life and mine—is a prodigious coincidence. Whether or not our world is the best possible, it still has high coherence and therefore vast coincidence.

If our world is *not* the best possible, then a prodigious coincidence cries out for some other explanation.

According to usual practice, coherence in our universe gets explained as a causal consequence of the Big Bang and orderly physical law, with perhaps some fortuitous "random" factors thrown in.

This explanation fails to account for consciousness and actually excludes genuine free will. On this explanation of coincidence in the world, our free will is fake. We have only the illusion of making decisions and choices.

But the prodigious coincidence of high coherence in our world, can also be explained by a principle of goodness. This explanation accounts for more features of our actual daily experience, it accounts for consciousness, and it gives us genuine free will.

Some people do have another explanation for large coincidence in the world. It goes like this:

Every possible world exists. Some possible worlds are highly coherent, and some are not. You and I should feel no surprise to find ourselves inhabiting one of the more coherent worlds. Without quite a lot of coherence, conscious intelligence cannot function. Only the highly coherent worlds contain people able to wonder why their world is coherent.

Nifty. But it doesn't work.

First off, this explanation fails to account for our Big Bang and our efficient physical law. As discussed in "The World's Peculiar Structure" (p. 271), people can be conscious, intelligent, and even subtle, without reflexive causality. Yet the actual world has a very good reflexive causality, emanating from its Big Bang and its potent yet simple physical law.

Second, this explanation takes no position on whether our free will is genuine or fake. It could be either. We might have moral responsibility and we might not.

Third, this explanation fails to account for the elusive nature of our world, operating just beyond our reach. It fails to account for our world doing better for us than we can do for ourselves. Even without those advantages, we could still be intelligent beings wondering why our world has coherence.

Finally, the explanation for existence, that everything possible is actual, has a fourth flaw, perhaps the most serious.

The realm of possibility contains multitudes. It contains all the possible worlds and all the possible people.

In one possible world, none of the residents wear pants. None of them have genitals. They never use bad language. They eat, but they don't excrete. When they see something exciting, their eyeballs literally pop out of their heads. If they walk off a cliff, they don't fall until they look down. When they do fall, they get bent out of shape for a few moments, then resume their former good health.

Some people say that every possible world exists. But I doubt they would claim that Daffy Duck World exists.

Another possible world has an infinite number of intelligent, sentient, immortal inhabitants, each turning slowly on a spit inside a hot oven forever. Nothing much happens, just the endless cooking and the parties being cooked having thoughts and feelings.

Yes, some people do claim that every possible world exists. But I doubt they would claim that Total Torture World exists.

What excludes Daffy Duck World and Total Torture World from existence? Those worlds violate principles of goodness. Whatever else they are, existing worlds must not be entirely cruel and they must not be absurd. Those are principles of goodness.

Apparently you and I have the intuition that principles of goodness govern existence. If we explain existence by saying that every possible world exists, we would want to modify that explanation by introducing a principle of goodness somewhere.

If we want the principle of goodness to explain *all* the coherence in the actual world, including conscious awareness, elusive causality and reflexive, efficient physical law, then we end up with the mandate of the united opinion: What ought to exist does exist, including genuine free will.

Our world conforming to a principle of goodness, is quite different from our world conforming merely to a Big Bang. Quite different. Let's take a look.

In the best world, an entire causal progress supports the optimum collective subtlety. Every significant element of the causal pattern—the Big Bang, the nature of physical law, any "randomness" in physical law, any covert exceptions to physical law, causal progress in the universe, the precise operation of the grey matter in my head, the color of my socks today, the words I utter, and the free choices I make—all significant elements of the causal pattern are logical consequences of the optimization. All our own actions, and all the world's actions upon us both open and covert, are logical consequences of the optimization.

The world around us becomes a living sea with its own subtle agenda—as our experience sometimes shows it to be. We have control and we don't have control.

Causality itself in our world, is a logical consequence of the optimization. We have cause and effect because the world is optimized. We need cause and effect according to orderly rules, to make our experience intelligible and subtle. Causality obtains and takes the particular form it takes, because of the ensuing benefits to our subtle agency. The Big Bang and the entire causal pattern obtain because they serve our agency.

In other words, the Big Bang happens because we subtle agents exist and have the experience we have and make the choices we make—*not the other way around.*

My brainy grey matter and yours, rattle around in just certain patterns, because we make certain choices—*not the other way around.*

This arrangement of the world gives the inhabitants many, many advantages. This is how the united opinion wants the world to be.

And surely the most important advantage is this:

In the mandated best world, you and I are responsible for what we do. No Big Bang, no physical process, no random accident, and no supernatural entity bears responsibility for my choices because it created me and made me what I am. That's not the case. Here's why.

Among all the possible subtle agents with free will, only a tiny minority gain existence in the highest world. The best possible world fits possible agents together like a jigsaw puzzle. You and I as possible agents, gain existence because we happen to fit the puzzle. In virtue of the particular choices we happen to make, and the particular reactions we happen to have, from the beginning to the end of our lives, we gain existence. *In virtue of how we exercise our free will* throughout our lives, we exist.

In light of that circumstance, you and I are responsible ourselves for the choices we make. We are moral players. We have moral status.

Moral status is the reason why the united opinion prefers genuine free will to fake, as a component of the best world.

The united opinion likes the game played so subtly in the best world: We are alive, we have desires, we learn, we are mortal, we grow and decay, we strive within a causality highly subtle and elusive, we make our choices, sometimes our choices are difficult, *we bear responsibility for our choices*, sometimes we feel shame or satisfaction for the choices we make.

The united opinion doesn't want us to feel shame for choices we don't actually make. That state of affairs would be uselessly unjust—especially in the difficult best world. The united opinion wants us actually to make the choices for which we feel responsible.

We have genuine free will because the world is better that way. We have a second description of our free will—a causal replication—because the world is better that way, too. On the evidence for perfection, the actual world has that superior arrangement.

And the superior arrangement accords with common sense. You and I know our free will is genuine. We know the world doesn't give us an elaborate sham.

Our free will notwithstanding, we have a predetermined world—but not a predictable world. Predetermined and predictable are different. Even though the world's causal pattern was predetermined in every significant detail before it began, we who live within the causal pattern don't always know what will happen. We experience the world as surprising and unpredictable, yet subject to our influence.

In that manner, two descriptions of the causal pattern are mutually consistent. The world is predetermined, and the world is unpredictable but subject to our influence. No contradiction.

In the best world, both descriptions are true. If the final explanans is a principle of goodness, not a principle of physics, then both descriptions apply.

In consequence, all these statements are true: No matter what we do, our world is the best possible. If we try to make the world better, it might very well get better. The world is predetermined, we change it, and sometimes we deliberately change it for the better.

And so, consider these two statements:

No matter what I do, this world remains the best it can possibly be.

No matter what I do, this world neither suffers nor benefits.

The first statement is true. The second is false. Question Three conflates them.

Let's review where you and I and the other people stand in the world.

Predetermination of the world's causal pattern, and predictability in the pattern, are different. The best possible world has a causal progress predetermined in great detail, to give maximum support to our agency, including the exercise of our free will. From our perspective as agents operating in the world, the causal pattern balances predictability with unpredictability. That balance supports our agency. On the one hand, we can reasonably expect certain of our actions to help subtlety potential, and others to harm it. Certain of our decisions count as moral choices. On the other hand, our actions have unintended consequences, sometimes mysterious consequences. We have good reason to be alive and find out what happens. For us who make choices and try to influence the world, the causal pattern combines predictability with unpredictability. Both elements are needed to give us the status of living moral agents. Even the unpredictability is predetermined in detail.

You and I might think of our situation like this: We are finding out how good is the unpredictable best world. How good it turns out to be—how subtle the inhabitants and their lives—depends in significant ways on the decisions we make to be selfish and altruistic.

The dependence isn't entirely straightforward. That would be unsubtle. But the dependence is sufficiently strong that in fact we are moral players, and many of our decisions count as moral choices.

Why existence is what it is, remains mysterious. And the mystery is irreducible. No one actual or possible, however omniscient, can know why existence conforms to its principle of goodness—on pain of incoherence. This fact follows from the logical structure of explanation.

On the evidence for perfection in the world, the irreducible mystery is just this: all the possible subtle beings with genuine free will who happen to fit the best possible pattern of causality—these are the beings who gain existence. The evidence shows these facts, but no reason why explains. We can only feel wonder.

The irreducible mystery is strange indeed. The united opinion of all *possible* subtle agents, somehow governs what *actually* exists. Somehow, the ghostly realm of possibility governs the vivid realm of actuality.

Owing to this strange relationship, you and I have a form of immortality, in this fashion:

The causal pattern is determined by a principle of optimum subtlety. The causal pattern is subject to our influence. Under both of those descriptions, our lives have a temporal organization, and we are extinguished. But the optimum pattern of causality has its logical determination outside time and causality. Rather like the Pythagorean Theorem, your contribution and mine to the best possible world, have a certain immortality.

In large measure, the world is what we make it. In large measure, the world's value depends on how we conduct our lives. And every detail of how we freely conduct our lives, has in logic its immortality.

QUESTION FOUR: "Moral imperatives" are impulses that had survival value during evolution. In a Godless unjust universe, why should I heed them as anything more?

This question as worded, expresses two false presumptions: Evolution is unholy, and a "righteous universe" would reward a person of virtue.

Does the actual universe visibly reward a person for moral behavior? Does our world reward virtue without fail and without doubt? No.

Why, then, should we be moral? A circular answer would be: Following our moral impulses generally makes the world better for everyone.

That answer only points to the causal consequences of good deeds. It leaves unanswered the questions: Why should I care about the causal consequences of my good deeds? Why should I care about the world beyond my own welfare? Why should I perform any moral act, except in the hope of reward?

The non-circular answer: A being who cannot feel shame, cannot find value in his existence. Thus:

Subtle beings are moral players by logical necessity. Unless an agent has the essential components of moral status, her comparisons collapse to a limited range. Her existence descends to mere calculation. She becomes a spider.

One essential component of moral status and subtle agency is this: The agent views the self and the world in moral terms. She cannot separate her moral perceptions from herself. She cannot make the decision to continue being a subtle agent as before, but without feeling what is right and wrong.

The first three questions and their answers, already discover a connection between what is good and what is subtle. The connection between goodness and subtlety already has these discovered elements: The principle of goodness to which the world's phenomena conform, is a principle of optimum subtlety. To better the world by right behavior, is to bear the burden of promoting the subtlety-potential of others. And moral status is the reason why our subtle free will is and ought to be genuine.

We should not be surprised that the connection goes further. It goes much further. In our daily lives, in great detail throughout human activity, and in profound ways, how we are good relates to how we are subtle. Some examples:

Falling in love is a big part of human affairs. If humans were not moral players, then the idea of another person's goodness would lose dimension. So also would these lose dimension: our ability to protect and encourage another's goodness, to care for another person, to love and be loved. Our capacities for love and for hate would contract to machine-like imperatives.

Achieving success is another big part of human affairs. The satisfaction of success relates to deserving success, which is a moral concept. For us, moral overtones give dimension to triumph, defeat, admiration, jealousy, generosity, bitterness, outrage, dedication, disillusion, allegiance, betrayal, guilt, despair, hope, struggle. If humans were not moral players, then our daily satisfactions and disappointments would have severely limited dimension. Our motivations would reduce to spider-style basics. With mechanical efficiency we would survive and reproduce and protect our offspring. The successes and failures thereof would inspire no complicated emotions.

When we go to war and when we make peace, we are moral players. When we search for new medicines, we are moral players. When we search for technologies that free the human spirit from drudgery, thereby making life more subtle, we are moral players. When we set out on a voyage of discovery, to add to the wonders of the world and thereby make life more subtle, we are moral players. Our daily interactions relate to principles of fair play. We engage in societies, friendships, competitions governed by rules of fair play. When we trudge off to work each day, to secure for our children a greater potential to have subtle lives, we are moral players.

Almost everything humans think about relates to our moral status one way or another. The human mind, automatically making comparisons, pursues those relationships. It compares its comparisons. It makes comparisons direct and indirect, primary and derivative. The comparisons reverberate and feed on each other. In tangled ways they begin to contradict each other. As moral players we have well dimensioned experience, sometimes sublime experience, and sometimes a complicated inner struggle.

Without moral status, those comparisons would collapse to a restricted range. We would operate in a grey, spidery world of single-minded calculation.

Similar reasoning applies to any possible subtle agency. To have a life worth living, human or otherwise, requires a view of the self and the world in moral terms. Unless an agent can feel shame, it finds no value in its life.

Our universe does much to promote our moral dilemmas and intensify our moral perceptions. Let's focus now on exactly how our Big Bang universe operates as a "righteous world": how it assembles the ingredients of our moral status.

Viable moral status has minimum requirements. For starters, interacting agents must have the power to enhance and destroy each other.

Consistent with high subtlety, we humans well exceed that particular minimum requirement. We are mortal beings able to effect each other's death. We can enhance and destroy each other in countless ways large and small. Our power over each other's well being, comes near to being complete and absolute.

But viable moral status has further minimum requirements. A moral player must see others in her power as agents like herself—and therefore as moral players like herself. Otherwise, all her altruism collapses to tending a garden, or an ant nest, or a spider web—according to spider-style imperatives. Thus:

The agents interacting in a community must share a common moral knowledge. They must feel both responsibility and resistance to that knowledge.

Understanding right behavior is not enough. The interacting community must respond to moral knowledge with inconsistent attitudes: zeal, indifference, denial, rebellion, and complicated mixtures of all four.

Moral status requires a particular kernel of inner struggle. If we understood right behavior, but we uniformly conformed or uniformly resisted with no inner conflict, then we would be ants. An ant can give satisfaction or dissatisfaction, but an ant has no moral responsibilities. An ant lives in a grey world.

Moral status requires an "indifferent universe." If happiness in the world attached only to moral behavior, without fail and without doubt, then we would have a fatally wounded inner struggle. We would be spiders. If happiness so attached only to selfish behavior, again we would be spiders. An "indifferent universe" remains neutral between moral and selfish impulses.

Consistent with high subtlety, human existence well exceeds the minimum requirements for moral status. For example:

Some humans believe that eternal happiness does attach to certain people who qualify. But these believers have not become spiders bereft of inner struggle. They are not ants single-mindedly following the trail to heaven. A human being can believe in righteousness and still plot against his fellows. We can have more faith one day and less faith the next. We can be torn. We can become shrill, as if pretending not to be torn. Our religious convictions, even for those who repudiate them, only change the inner struggle and add to its scope.

Our universe gives us more than a technically sufficient, minimum neutrality required to support moral status. Our universe maintains an agile, cunning, comprehensive neutrality consistent with highly subtle moral status. Most everything we strive to have, our world keeps elusive. Even if we deserve to have it, we cannot always succeed in grasping it. This unjust world has an agenda different from ours. Let's take a look.

Good people seem to be just as happy and unhappy as bad people. But the world's neutrality goes further. So far as we can see—and we have looked rather hard—no particular approach to life is the reliable key to happiness. Wearing clothes and eating food have largely been good ideas, but most of our policies lead just as readily to misery as to happiness. We know and we don't know how to be happy. This world tends to tantalize our pedestrian desires and our plodding ambitions. This world excels at surprising us. Our most sublime moments we can neither predict nor imagine in advance, much less grasp intentionally.

In consequence, our existence rises far above mere calculation. We are not spiders that only follow set procedures. We do not find happiness without fail and without doubt, by the simple manipulation of making sure we deserve it—nor by any other manipulation whatsoever. We have control and we don't have control. Because our universe remains "indifferent" to our grasping desires, in an agile and cunning way, a more surprising happiness can sometimes find us.

Our universe goes beyond sufficient neutrality to ingenious neutrality. It does better for us than we can do or even imagine for ourselves.

Even our understanding of right behavior exceeds the minimum requirement for moral status. Here is how:

A previous chapter, "The Human Style of Interpreting the World" (p. 65), included this discussion: A biological evolution of agents—an evolution slow and competitive—has an advantage over the construction of agents by fiat. Our own evolution used slow accretion to construct agents more and more idiosyncratic. Meanwhile, competitive pressures kept all that idiosyncrasy coherent. Human personalities ended up highly idiosyncratic yet highly coherent.

In particular, a combination of idiosyncrasy and coherence infuses our understanding of right behavior.

A Chinese proverb says, "Your neighbor's crops are always better than your crops, but your children are always better than your neighbor's children." Our evolution does more than give us straightforward moral knowledge felt and resisted. It gives us capacities for self-deception and transcendent insight about what is right and wrong. On moral issues we differ and we change our minds. Yet our moral knowledge has an underlying coherence that most everyone understands. Our evolution gives us highly idiosyncratic variations on a common moral knowledge. Our inner struggle rises well above the simple minimum for moral status, yet remains coherent.

High moral status with every essential component, is a profound technical achievement. Its causal ingredients are meticulous and legion. This universe supplies them all.

High moral status and high subtlety need each other. They feed on each other. What is good and what is subtle have a close relationship with several facets: The principle of goodness to which the world's phenomena conform, is a principle of optimum subtlety. To better the world by right behavior, is to bear the burden of promoting the subtlety-potential of others. Moral status is the reason why our subtle free will is and ought to be genuine. And moral status forms the kernel of subtle experience. Neither can obtain without the other.

Why should we be moral? Why should we do what's right? Because moral perceptions are needed to raise us above spiders. If we cannot feel shame, then our lives are not worth living.

In the face of our world's perfect goodness, surely our shame must be larger.

Harry Lime

"In Italy for thirty years under the Borgias they had warfare, terror, murder, bloodshed. They produced Michaelangelo, Leonardo da Vinci, and the Renaissance. In Switzerland they had brotherly love, five hundred years of democracy and peace. And what did that produce? The cuckoo clock."

So speaks Harry Lime, defending his crimes.

Harry Lime, played by Orson Welles, is villain of *The Third Man* (directed by Carol Reed, starring Joseph Cotton, Alida Valli, Trevor Howard, and Orson Welles), a 1949 black and white film about occupied Vienna in 1946.

Just after the war, Vienna has ruined buildings, an impoverished population, and wholesale health problems. People are desperate for medicine. Mr. Lime steals penicillin from military hospitals, dilutes it, and sells it as full strength on the black market. In consequence, people die horribly and Mr. Lime makes money.

Gentle reader, I've been telling you that moral behavior generally improves the world, and immoral behavior generally degrades it.

Harry Lime appears to believe differently. For him, selling diluted penicillin to desperate Viennese, might promote Vienna's artistic creativity. He produces an argument to that effect.

Some people, while disinclined to excuse Harry Lime, still wonder whether his argument has a grain of truth; whether moral imperatives might be less straightforward than they seem on first inspection.

Good reader, I'm on a tight budget. My publisher limits me to 100,000 words. But Mr. Lime's statement is sufficiently egregious, that I will take time to stomp on it as best I can. I hope to leave not even a grain of truth. Moral issues can be complicated, but nowhere near as complicated as Mr. Lime implies.

Harry Lime conflates correlation with causation. Since Italian terror correlated with Italian innovation, one must have caused the other, he suggests.

But two phenomena may correlate without either causing the other. A correlation between murderous behavior and creativity, doesn't show that murder causes creativity. Instead, a third phenomenon may be the cause of both.

Mr. Lime's reasoning—the Borgias in Italy when the Renaissance flowered—relies on guesswork about what caused what. He contrasts Italy's terror and creativity with Switzerland's dull brotherly love, and draws a facile conclusion.

But surely a third phenomenon—perhaps Switzerland's comparative insularity—caused both its tranquil politics and its tranquil creativity. The antidote would be opening up the country to outside influence, not poisoning the citizens.

Mr. Lime suggests that the Borgias' murderous ways produced a heightened creativity in Italy. Unlikely. In that period, according to my encyclopedia, Italy benefited from its central position on trade routes, its contact with the Muslim world, its general prosperity, and from the absence of pervasive political authority. Those conditions helped the play of ideas.

In that period Italy had lots of remarkable people, including members of the Borgia family. Apparently that family's murders did not actually cause the Italian Renaissance. Rather, a third phenomenon—the freewheeling tenor of the times—was conducive both to da Vinci's creativity and the Borgias'.

The Borgias seemed most helpful to the Renaissance in the person of Lucrezia, after she married a duke and moved away from her scheming family. The nasty stories told about her were never substantiated. They appear to be fabrications based on her family's reputation. Apparently she was, or became, a kind lady who set up a rather brilliant court, subsidized artists, and thereby contributed to the Renaissance. Mr. Lime may have believed that she terrorized people into becoming outstanding poets and painters.

Harry Lime does not face a knotty or difficult moral dilemma. He's not dealing with a grey area. Certain of the Borgias assassinated innocent people for simple, straightforward personal gain. Harry Lime did likewise.

As discussed last chapter, humans feel a moral duty to help other people's "potential in life." Even when we don't think explicitly about that duty, our moral sensibilities tend to reflect it. Thus, Harry Lime's *immoral* choices snuffed out *human potential* in Vienna. Such potential generally operates as one of the causal factors affecting subtle human experience. Hence a causal connection between moral choices and better subtlety.

Harry Lime could not simply pass bad medicine without comment, as a spider could. Harry felt a need to justify his actions, to say something in his own defense. He betrayed but felt a moral imperative.

Gentle reader, I have visited neither Vienna nor Switzerland. My loss, of course. But I do have experience with both Singapore and the United States. In Harry Lime's argument, those two would correspond to Switzerland and Italy.

According to its own government—which keeps a lot of statistics—Singapore has creativity and innovation in short supply.

Modern-day Singapore does have a low crime rate and high public safety. I lived there off and on for seven months total, including a four-month stint in 1997.

Good reader, I want to show you, by the detailed example of Singapore, how Harry Lime's argument is bogus. I want to show you in detail, low rates of creativity and low rates of crime coexisting without either causing the other.

Singapore outlaws chewing gum. The government doesn't know what you're going to do with that piece of gum, when you're ready to discard it. In Singapore, possession of chewing gum is a misdemeanor. Dealing in chewing gum is a felony.

Possession of marijuana, even in small quantities, carries an automatic death penalty. You can appeal to the prime minister for clemency, but he grants it almost never. If convicted, you have no other appeal. Your trial and your execution happen within a few months of your arrest, according to one of the residents.

Malicious mischief, such as marking public property with graffiti, carries the penalty of public caning. Humiliating and very painful, I was told. Five strokes of the cane, before an audience in person and on television, is an unforgettable experience that incapacitates for many months. Singapore pretty much has no flies, no mosquitoes, no litter, and no graffiti.

Singapore's street lampposts bristle with cameras, that record every instance of running a red light, and most instances of speeding. A computer knows your license and your address. It sends you your traffic ticket in the mail.

In Singapore I never saw jaywalking. Never. Great throngs of pedestrians waited obediently for their appointed time to cross the street, even when an illegal crossing would be totally safe. Pedestrians never jumped the walk sign by even one second, and never strayed outside the crosswalk by even one inch. The cameras were watching and the people complied.

Government officials get rather enormous salaries, to reduce the temptation of accepting bribes—which carries the death penalty.

One night on the evening news, the lead story described a purse-snatching. Singapore police coordinated their pursuit by radio, converged on the perpetrator from several directions, and gang-tackled him nine blocks from the crime scene. As I write this, eleven years later, he might still be serving his sentence.

Singapore maintains excellent streets and highways. Their subway is the safest and most comfortable I've seen. Ditto for their low-income housing. Singapore has beautiful buildings, spacious sidewalks, clean beaches, wonderful public parks, and no slums.

The climate: perpetual summer. Singapore sits almost astride the equator.

Like the former independent Swiss cantons, Singapore is a small political entity with large neighbors. Singapore's foreign policy: be inconspicuous. The country never takes sides in the disputes of others, and tries not to be disputatious itself. Rather like modern Switzerland and the small Swiss cantons formerly.

In 1997, the Singapore Air Force consisted of two obsolete fighter jets. As one citizen put it, "If Malaysia ever decided to invade us, we could hold them off for about ten minutes." Singapore doesn't get into arguments.

In 1997, Indonesia had large forest fires upwind from Singapore. I remember some two weeks of choking smoke day and night. So far as I could tell, neither the Singapore government nor the citizenry complained. They simply stayed indoors as much as possible, waiting for the wind to shift or their neighbor's fires to burn out. And that seemed the best policy.

In 1997, Singapore's public billboards encouraged men to get married and have children. Singapore frowned upon irresponsible young males.

Also, public billboards encouraged the citizens to learn foreign languages, especially Mandarin, which was good for business.

The official language was English. "The less educated" embellished it with Cantonese inflections. Singapore English had very little slang. Even the language lacked creativity.

In theory, Singapore has an elected legislature and an elected prime minister. The two contests for prime minister, previous to my 1997 visit, had similar results. In each case, the challenger made campaign statements implying that the incumbent was less than truthful. In each case, the challenger was immediately sued for slander, immediately stripped of all personal and business assets, encouraged to skip the country one step ahead of arrest, and tried in absentia. In 1997, the evening news reported the outcome of the latest such trial: not guilty on some counts of slander, guilty on all the counts that mattered. In the sense that they split their decisions, the court rose above mere rubber stamp. But the court endorsed the confiscation of assets, and the former challenger faces a heavy prison sentence should he ever set foot in Singapore again.

When running for office, a challenger may not suggest that the incumbent has deviated from his promises. That would be slander bringing immediate punishment, to be reviewed by the courts later.

As an independent nation with its own government, Singapore was born in 1959. Since then, exactly three prime ministers have ruled the country. The initial prime minister held office for thirty-one years. He chose his own successor, who served for fourteen years, then retired. The current prime minister took office in 2004. All three belong to the People's Action Party.

However, I don't know that any of the three profited unduly from his position.

American expatriates have dubbed Singapore, "Disneyland with the death penalty." Many people from Asian cultures consider Singapore heavenly. The business climate is most excellent, even for people without connections. Although I knew certain college students fairly well, I never heard a native grumble about his government.

Some of the Western expatriates, however, were bored out of their minds. No way to let off steam. Ladies of the evening were nowhere visible, and public intoxication was a felony.

In one evening news broadcast, the feature story dealt with "low creativity" in Singapore. The story did not explain in what manner Singaporeans failed to be creative. Instead, it described a blue-ribbon government commission formed to study the problem.

We can imagine a discussion among the commissioners. One of them says, "Singaporeans are too conformist. We need our people to follow the rules less often, to be less slavish to what society expects. We need a better play of ideas. Maybe we should put up billboards that say, 'Think for yourself.'"

But another says, "Wouldn't all that independent thinking lead to destructive behavior? Why disturb our little heaven? Let's just be comfortable, make our money honestly, and let the rest of the world worry about creativity."

That would be a reasonable policy discussion. A clear choice can be made about the nature of society, with disadvantages to each option.

In Singapore, both low rates of crime and low rates of artistic and technical innovation, appear to be caused by a third phenomenon: a species of complacent, insular, nonconfrontational, conformist thinking. That's the tenor of the times, as it were.

Except for Western expatriates, the people are generally content to make money and live in peace.

Neither the low crime nor the skimpy innovation appear to cause each other. They only correlate, as effects of the third phenomenon. Unreasonable for a Singaporean to say, "We don't have enough artistic innovation around here. I'm going to help my compatriots by passing off worthless diluted penicillin as genuine, when they're desperate for medicine."

But Harry Lime would say that, if there were money in it.

I don't really know how far Singapore parallels the old Swiss cantons. I read somewhere that Swiss democracy evolved into a more or less benign oligarchy. Singapore's 1997 democracy was in fact a more or less benign oligarchy. The landlocked Swiss mountains did provide insulation from the trade routes that roiled Italy. Maybe the Swiss cantons also generally accepted the way things were, like modern Singapore. That contentment, or complacency, appears to cause both a disinterest in innovation and a disinterest in criminal activity.

Conversely, in the United States, a perception of possibility, a sense that anyone can dramatically change his circumstances, appears to cause an abundance of both crime and invention.

Last chapter I made these assertions: Moral acts generally help the world's subtlety. Generally. Not always, not reliably, not with total visibility about the consequences of our actions—but enough to support reasonable hopes and expectations for the effects of good deeds.

Moral acts generally help the world's subtlety. That's an observable fact about our world. I believe it's a fact in Switzerland and Italy, in Singapore and the United States. In countries with limited crime and in countries with abundant crime, moral acts generally help subtlety, while immoral acts often degrade subtlety. Cause and effect work that way in the actual world.

Diluting the penicillin is heinous. Secretly withholding the penicillin is heinous. Harry Lime's pretensions to helping the world strangely by immoral acts, are bogus. In part by his hand, subtle experience in Vienna recedes toward a spider-style, bare struggle for survival. The tricky Mr. Lime helps reduce his customers to living by bread and medicine alone. They need more effort just to survive—if they do survive. His customers have little chance to reach a higher human potential. Mr. Lime has profited from and exacerbated the effects of a grinding, lost war on vulnerable civilians. Of course he has made the world worse.

Mr. Lime knows and does not know that he is horrible. He turns his face away. He does not let himself see. The woman who loves him does not let herself see. But the audience sees. Harry Lime gives his self-justification on a Ferris wheel that goes round and round in a lofty circle. From the top, he looks down upon people insignificant to him. But in fact, he gets hunted, cornered, and finally shot down in his true habitat: an underground sewer. Even when he sincerely wants to, he cannot climb out.

The Blind Masseuse
of Tsingtao

The heavy '83 Chevy pickup, all-steel construction, was fully loaded with dirt. It struck our little Altima squarely in the rear. It knocked us nine feet forward with our brakes on. Wife and self were idling at the stoplight, thinking our idle thoughts, when a power greater than ourselves shoved us through space, to the sound of shattering glass.

This happened in downtown Los Angeles, the day after Christmas, 2005.

The following spring, Lee Ming and I went to China, to her parents' apartment in Beijing. We intended to get massage therapy and to adopt a baby.

The second plan quickly fell apart. We found the baby-orphanage criminal, and our dealings with them unsatisfactory.

In Beijing we heard about Dr. Han. He's a talented masseuse, people said. We would find him in Tsingtao, a port city on the Yellow Sea.

To find Dr. Han, we went first to the hospital where he worked. We found an ancient building with the hospital name carved in stone above the main entrance. The building was decrepit and long abandoned.

After walking around the neighborhood for twenty minutes, we happened upon an older six-story apartment building, with several elderly people sitting in chairs just outside the front door.

These individuals were well informed. They gave us directions to Dr. Han's residence.

We stayed a month at the Tsingtao Ocean University Academic Exchange Center, a two-dollar cab ride from Dr. Han.

The Ocean University occupies sturdy buildings raised more than a century ago by German colonists. Today these old structures show well in new yellow paint and brown trim.

The Germans also planted trees, mostly parasol trees, which look a bit like maples. After one hundred years and more, the trees have grown into giants. They forest the university campus.

And the Germans set up a brewery in Tsingtao.

On Friday and Saturday nights, open-air vendors appear on the streets surrounding the university, selling draft beer. Young men come in pairs to buy it. After accepting payment, the vendor fills up a large transparent plastic bag, two feet across. The vendor fills the bag to a depth of nine or ten inches, while the two buyers support it carefully, each with one hand underneath and one hand holding the top. Then, moving slowly, the young men carry this prize back to their quarters and their comrades.

The Chinese central government rates hotel quality as three, four, or five stars. In some cities, but not in Tsingtao, a few grubby hotels have a two-star rating. Foreign nationals are forbidden by law to stay in non-rated hotels. The rating appears on a big brass plaque above the check-in desk. Rated hotels are required to have some English-speaking staff.

The academic exchange center being technically not a hotel, the law on where foreigners may stay does not apply to it. Lee Ming and I squashed in with all manner of visitors to the university, domestic and foreign, some of them college age, some of them older and professional.

In contrast to a rated hotel, none of the staff spoke English.

I would describe our quarters as a four-star room with two-star plumbing and one-star hot water. The bathroom sink spigot, rusty and ancient, required two strong hands to open or shut.

After flushing, the toilet tank needed fifteen minutes to refill. The shower pipe had no shower head, but otherwise it worked okay. Between seven and nine in the evenings, when the hotel fired up its boiler, we could take a lukewarm shower.

We did have access to a washing machine. It was located inside the public men's room on the first floor, perched in one of the toilet stalls above a squat-style toilet frequently unclean. We preferred to wash our clothes in our own bathroom sink and hang them around the room to dry.

The academic exchange center was formerly a German hotel with an impressive marble lobby. Except for the plumbing, the building has been kept up. It sits near the top of a big hill, which slopes down to the ocean about two miles away. From our third floor window, we could see the ocean and the fog creeping up the hill.

The academic exchange center served a complimentary breakfast for residents, featuring watermelon, one boiled egg per customer, and all the rice gruel we cared to eat.

For lunch and dinner we often relied on the student cafeterias. These were housed in a Chinese construction, a squat pile of stone, the exterior darkened by eighty years of grime. Downstairs was the cheap cafeteria, directly upstairs the more deluxe version.

Each student dining hall was a large square room crowded with plastic tables and chairs. Against one wall were spigots, sink, and soap for washing hands. Along the other three walls were the food stations, cafeteria style. Middle-aged women in white uniforms, bored with their lives, ladled out the delicacies. Each matron used a little machine to accept payment by debit card. We the patrons grabbed chopsticks and shiny metal trays from the stacks provided, got out our debit cards, then made the rounds of our favorite foodstuffs. At meal's end, we bussed our tables and presented our used trays to the young man charged with cleaning them.

The students swarming everywhere were young. They seemed like a different species.

Many physical therapists live and work in Tsingtao. Having a moderate seaside climate, and offshore breezes to combat air pollution, Tsingtao attracts retirees and visitors seeking long-term medical care. The city has a number of hospital-hotels.

Wife and self underwent Dr. Han's therapy program for twenty-two consecutive days, mornings, afternoons, and evenings.

Dr. Han discounted his fee, in return for my giving English and piano lessons to his six-year-old granddaughter.

Almost the first words we heard from the doctor's mouth, were personal questions. "How long have you been married? Any children? What are you doing in China? Where is your family? Why did you come to Tsingtao?" The doctor discovered that we would be unable to have children. While extracting this information, the doctor worked nonstop on another patient already on the table.

Dr. Han kept his overhead to the bare minimum. His therapy and waiting rooms were combined into one small room, which also functioned as a laundry room. Sometimes we found the morning wash still drying on the lines strung across the room near the ceiling. Patients waited for the doctor on a couch several decades old, under the clotheslines, cheek by jowl with the two therapy tables. After lunch, the doctor and his granddaughter napped on the tables. In the evenings, his family sat on the waiting couch and watched TV. At night, the tables and the couch served as beds for the doctor's son, daughter-in-law, and granddaughter. This room was multipurpose.

Dr. Han did no advertising. He had not invested in a sign outside his apartment. All of his business came to him by word of mouth.

The doctor's rules and procedures were informal. He had no billing personnel, no secretaries, no staff at all. All payments to him were cash at the time of service. The doctor, blind from birth, trusted us to give him paper currency in the correct denominations.

Our duties as patients included answering the doorbell and the telephone when not on the table, and on one occasion, stirring a pot on the doctor's stove.

Dr. Han still used the business cards and the white uniforms inherited from his years as a staff physician, at the hospital now defunct. He worked out of his small basement apartment in a seven-story, concrete-slab building. His furnishings appeared to be fifty years old. The wood floor had long ago seen its finish scuffed away. Dr. Han had no gym and no exercise equipment. His patients brought their own drinking water and their own towels to cover the therapy table. His patients refrained from using his family's tiny bathroom, except when absolutely necessary. Instead, we used the public toilets in "The Old Man Center"—a recreation center for retirees—about one hundred yards away.

Dr. Han was seventy years old, five feet tall, with a slender build and thick, short, white hair. We watched him read a kind of Chinese Braille with his fingers. He had unusually strong arms and hands.

The doctor had an acute sense of time. A 1950s steel clock on his wall chimed the hour and the half-hour. He had no other time references. Even when interrupted by an emergency patient, he gave us each precisely forty minutes on the table. If he started at 3:18, he quit at 3:58. On occasion when no one was waiting, he gave us extra time. Now and then he gave some of my time to Lee Ming, who was injured more seriously. At precisely 4:10 most afternoons, he turned on his transistor radio and listened to kung-fu stories told by a professional storyteller.

Dr. Han held office hours from three to six in the afternoon, seven days per week. His waiting couch was usually full. The small room never lacked for conversation.

On two occasions, the doctor interrupted our sessions to take emergency cases, each a middle-aged man who had dislocated something and could not walk without a lot of pain. Each time, the emergency patient came with strong friends, who assisted Dr. Han. The patient was helped to lie on a table. The strong friends held his feet. Dr. Han gripped his armpits and counted to three. The patient was suddenly pulled apart and snapped into alignment.

On two additional occasions, parents brought in a sick young child. Dr. Han questioned the parents and gave his diagnosis and his prescription, without pausing in the massage he was giving us.

One of the young children, a boy, found his visit to the doctor too lengthy. In protest, he dropped his pants and peed on the therapy room floor. His parents quickly cleaned up the puddle, but another stain was added to the ancient wood.

Dr. Han insisted that we give ourselves completely to his therapy program, that we put all other activities on the back burner. "Nothing else really needs attention right now," he said.

The doctor filled up our time with routine: morning walks, afternoon massages, thrice daily the therapy exercises he taught us, evenings with a heating pad on our backs, relaxation exercises before sleep. For some reason, we followed his program faithfully, day after day after day.

The doctor ordered us to walk every morning for two hours on flat ground. He specified Tsingtao's shoreline pathway, forty-one kilometers long, studded with benches where we could rest, paved with wood for easy impact, and passing through a beautiful public park. Each morning, under strict orders, we walked by the sea.

Each afternoon Dr. Han gave us forty minutes apiece on the table. While working on us, he talked sometimes about his "Let it be" philosophy of life. Usually his granddaughter was present. When waiting our turn on the table, we sometimes sang in English with the granddaughter. We sang, "There was a farmer had a dog" and "The wheels on the bus go round and round." Sometimes the granddaughter sat at my feet, right on the table where I was prostrate.

After feeling our backs with his hands, the doctor went straight to the area most sore. There he worked harder and harder, and slowly spread out. He worked with strength and confidence, always in vigorous motion. He was relentless.

The world was governed by a principle of goodness. We began to yield, to grieve, to surrender control. The days in their rhythm continued one by one, as if they would never end.

The United Opinion

Good reader, we have loose ends to tie down. Many times I mentioned the *united* opinion of all possible subtle agents. The united opinion wants this, I said, and the united opinion wants that. But how do we know the opinion is united? In what way do all possible subtle agents agree?

Previously we did talk about the sense in which they agree. In its own experience, any subtle agent implicitly likes higher subtlety better than low. You and I can see that each of those individual preferences instantiates the same general proposition: higher subtlety always betters low. That opinion is implicit and idiosyncratic for each possible subtle agent, but ubiquitous among all of them. Thus, the *same* general proposition—higher subtlety always betters low—gets reflected in each agent's preferences, as you and I can see. In that manner, their opinion is united. And from their united opinion it follows that the highest subtlety is best of all.

However, our analysis rested on several assumptions not yet discussed. We need to address them. Here they are, one by one:

SUBTLETY IS A COHERENT CONCEPT

Three chapters ago (p. 277), we discovered that only an agent with moral status can be a subtle agent. An agent with moral status understands subtlety-potential in other agents.

Almost every human has moral status. You and I have moral

status. You and I have a coherent notion of how to act rightly. We cannot have that understanding unless we understand subtlety-potential in others. You and I cannot take care for the subtle experience other humans have, as in fact we do, unless you and I perceive a coherent subtlety in human experience.

We can't define the terms "subtle" and "subtlety," but we know they refer to a coherent feature in human experience. (The familiar terms "knowledge," "belief," "justice," and "love" have a similar status. We can't define them, but we know they refer to coherent features in our lives.)

The coherent structure of subtlety in human experience has coherent counterparts in a mouse's experience and in any subtle agent's experience. You and I can perceive this relationship: Subtle experience being a coherent notion in human experience, it must also be a coherent notion in the experience of many, many possible subtle agents.

The structure of our world helps us have that perception. Our world puts subtle agency together, in ways we can understand. The methods of our universe apply to many different species of subtle agency, not just the human species. The methods of our universe help us understand subtle experience in a more general way.

ALL SUBTLE AGENTS ASSIGN HIGHER VALUE TO HIGHER SUBTLETY

If an agent has too little appreciation for subtlety in experience, then the agent is a spider. It cannot take care for the subtlety-potential of other agents. It cannot have moral status. As we saw in the last chapter, its existence descends to spider-style imperatives.

Moreover, all possible subtle agents implicitly assign higher value to higher subtlety. If they did not, again they could not take care to *improve* the subtlety of others. They would be spiders.

THE WORLD with the Best Possible Collection of Subtle Experience, Is Finite in Size and Has a Finite Number of Inhabitants, Each with a Life of Finite Extent.

These key assertions are the topic of the next part. We will look at the limits of subtle experience. Any story can go on too long, and the subtlety in any experience can be overdone.

THE BEST POSSIBLE STATE OF EXISTENCE IS ONE WORLD ALONE.

Would the best possible state of existence consist of just one possible world, or some number of separate worlds having no causal interaction?

Segregation into separate worlds makes isolation too rigid, inflexible, unsubtle. Better to put all the agents together into a single, finite, but very large world. That way, both interaction and isolation have subtle degrees.

The actual world appears to have 250 billion galaxies or more. The actual world is large. Astronomers tell us that our universe is expanding. All the various groups of galaxies are moving away from each other. And the rate of expansion is accelerating; the galaxy groups are flying apart faster and faster. Due to relativistic effects, humans will never be able to visit or even communicate with most of the actual world. We can deduce that a big world is out there, we can see some of it, but most of it we will never contact.

Our universe already has "separate worlds." Each group of galaxies is in effect a separate world. Our universe has some ten million isolated galaxy groups or more. None of these groups can communicate with any of the others. That's very much like ten million separate worlds, with each world averaging 25,000 galaxies.

(Our own Milky Way Galaxy, possibly a bit larger than average for a galaxy, has 400 billion stars. According to Carl Sagan, the stars in our universe outnumber all the grains of sand on Planet Earth.)

Astrophysicists now say that our universe is flying apart faster and faster. In ten or twenty billion years, they say, perhaps only the Virgo Supercluster will remain within view from our own galaxy. All the other parts of our universe will be so far away, that no one here will be able to detect them, much less interact with them. They will just be gone. In ten or twenty billion years, we are told, our universe will literally be a billion subworlds completely separate from each other.

You and I are members in good standing of the Virgo Supercluster, which appears to contain between ten and forty thousand luminous galaxies. Perhaps ten million superclusters or more populate the universe. In the gigantic reaches between superclusters, a few isolated galaxies wander like strays from the herds. Even after our universe has fragmented into subworlds, the entire Virgo Supercluster might remain within our own subworld. Other subworlds will range from single galaxies to several hundred thousand galaxies, according to current theory. Apparently our universe will fragment into subworlds both large and small.

Our universe already has colossal size and huge empty spaces. It already does isolation well. Surely our universe doesn't need further help with isolating agents from each other. Surely the isolation we see is already enough.

Our universe, though finite in size, might very well be big enough to express subtle experience fully. After all, the best possible world expresses subtle experience fully, and the best possible world is large but finite, just like our world.

One last loose end needs tying down, this one from the last chapter.

THE UNITED OPINION PREFERS
GENUINE FREE WILL TO FAKE.

To discover what state of existence ought to obtain, we looked to the ghostly convention of all possible subtle agents. We found an implicit but unanimous consensus, that the highest subtlety is best.

A parallel consensus obtains among the same agents, that genuine free will betters fake. The parallel consensus works like this:

All subtle agents have moral status. All subtle agents feel moral imperatives. Among these are a sense of justice. Feebly or strongly, any subtle agent has a standard of goodness, a moral sensibility, implying that justice ought to obtain, consistent with the highest subtlety. Like high subtlety, justice is a coherent notion to which all the standards point, strongly or feebly.

The possible world where the inhabitants experience the best proportion of justice to injustice—is incoherent, as we saw. But genuine free will appears to be coherent. If it is, then the united opinion wants the justice of genuine free will.

Fake free will would cause us to feel responsible for decisions, good and bad, that we don't actually make. Fake free will is unjust. The united opinion wants the most subtle world and in that world it wants genuine free will.

Not all the subtle agents attending the ghostly convention, know that their standards of good experience have those implications, but you and I can know.

All possible agents have an addiction to subtle experience, with higher subtlety more valuable than low. They have an implicit but united opinion, that the most subtle state of existence possible, ought to obtain.

Is the united opinion impossible to satisfy? Or does it pick out exactly one unique world in all its detail, as the best world and the best state of existence? I'm about to tell you.

Part Eight

THE UPPER LIMIT
TO THE VALUE OF
POSSIBLE WORLDS

One Unique Best World

Some people say that *no* possible world is the best. For every possible world, however good it is, some other world is better. No world rises above all the others.

Thus, suppose we think world A might be the best possible. We find it cannot be the best. Some other world B betters A. Still another world C betters B. World D betters C. And so on to infinity.

We wind up with a never-ending series of better and better worlds. Every world falls short of another world. No possible world is the best—some people say.

This claim has a useful function. It gets God off the hook. God can't be blamed for failing to create the best world possible. No such animal.

Next chapter, we will look at why some people hold that view. But in its simplest form, the never-ending series works like this:

A universe with ten billion people enjoying their lives, is inferior to a larger universe with twenty billion people enjoying their lives, which in turn is inferior to a still larger universe with forty billion people enjoying their lives, and so on to infinity. The series never ends with a best universe, or best world.

By contrast, I assert that exactly one possible world betters all the others. The underlying reasons are simple. They go like this:

Subtlety can be overdone. Any story can go on too long. The

world with just the optimum components of collective subtle experience, is unique.

Philosophy can seem complicated when it isn't. As you read the next three chapters, keep in mind the simple preceding paragraph.

The next three chapters address these assertions:

The quality of subtle experience has an upper limit.

The value of possible worlds has an upper limit.

Exactly one unique world stands at the upper limit.

The Upper Limit
to the Value of
Possible Worlds

Does one possible world better all the others?

Contemporary arguments against that notion are diverse. Philosopher Stephen Grover described them to me. They divide broadly into four kinds: qualitative, quantitative, the paradoxes of mere addition, and incommensurate value.

The first two kinds claim that possible worlds have no upper limit to their value. For any particular world, some other world is better. No particular world stands above all the others.

The last two cast doubt that the values of possible worlds can be usefully compared at all. One possible world bettering all the others, becomes incoherent.

All four kinds of argument talk about conscious beings in worlds finding value in their lives. All four kinds of argument fail, I claim, when we consider the characteristics of subtle agency.

"Opinions and Spiders" (p. 107) made this point: The value of a world is just the collective value of the lives of its *subtle* inhabitants.

The lives of spiders have no value—except as the spiders add value to subtle lives. Only the value of its subtle inhabitants counts toward the value of a world.

Good reader, you and I have traveled far together. We have discovered much about the character of subtle agency. In this chapter we have an application for all that knowledge. We can use it to refute the arguments that no possible world is the best. Here we go.

A quantitative argument, in which I very roughly paraphrase philosopher Richard Swinburne: Suppose that at least one element of the goodness of world W, consists in it containing conscious beings who enjoy their lives. Then W can be improved by "merely adding" more beings who also enjoy their lives. The new beings are "merely added" in this sense: They are placed far away in space from the original beings, so that the two sets of beings have no causal interactions that create social injustice, or alter the enjoyment experienced by either set. If any world with conscious beings can be so improved, then no world is the best possible.

We can refute this argument, by considering worlds that contain pigs and no other agents.

Different kinds of agent enjoy their lives at different levels of subtlety. Pig subtlety has less value than human subtlety. A pig's life, at a good level of subtlety for pigs, has less value than a human life, at a good level of subtlety for humans.

A world containing an infinite number of pigs enjoying good pig subtlety, is inferior to a world containing only one hundred billion humans enjoying good human subtlety.

The pig-world is inferior because the subtlety of its agents has distinctly inferior value. True, the pigs far outnumber the humans. But their subtlety has strongly inferior value. Even a large collection of pig-subtlety has inferior value. Some finite number of humans can best their collective subtlety. I think one hundred billion humans is enough.

But the value of subtlety for a finite number of humans, is finite. Therefore, the value of subtlety for an infinite number of pigs, must also be finite.

If we start with a world containing no agents and add a few

pigs with good pig subtlety, the value of that world has increased. But as we continue to add more and more pigs, the value approaches a plateau which cannot be surpassed. This pig-plateau lies at a level somewhere below the finite value of the world containing one hundred billion subtle humans.

Conclusion: the value of worlds containing only pigs, does have an upper limit.

When we begin with a world containing no agents and place more and more subtle pigs into it, the value of that world approaches a plateau. Even if each new pig always adds to the world's value, the successive added values must approach zero, as in the series

$$1/2 + 1/4 + 1/8 + 1/16 + \ldots = 1$$

At some point, the value reached by a finite number of pigs, becomes indistinguishable from the value reached by an infinite number of pigs.

In other words, a world containing ten trillion subtle pigs, is just as good as a world containing an infinite number of subtle pigs. The upper limit to the value of pig-worlds is reached by a world with a finite number of pigs.

By analogous reasoning, a pig has a life of finite value, even if he is immortal.

The analogous reasoning goes like this: The finite value of one hundred billion mortal human lives, exceeds the value of a single immortal pig's life. Human lives unfold at a higher level of subtlety. Therefore, the immortal pig's life also has finite value. As the pig's life continues, its value increases, but at some point that value reaches a plateau. And it reaches the plateau after a finite time.

Conclusions: The value of all worlds containing only pigs, has an upper limit. This upper limit is reached by a world containing a finite number of pigs, each having a life of finite extent.

If worlds capped by a pig's level of subtlety have values that plateau, then surely worlds capped by any other particular level of subtlety have values that plateau.

Therefore, if the level or quality of subtlety has an upper limit for all possible subtle agents, then all possible worlds have an upper limit to their value.

Moreover, this upper limit to the value of possible worlds, is reached by a world containing a finite number of subtle agents, each having a life of finite extent.

Our own world fits that description.

Next chapter we will examine why the level or quality of subtlety has an upper limit. I will make this claim: All possible subtle agents have an upper limit to the subtlety of discrete episodes of experience they can have. Subtlety can be overdone. And as we just saw, this upper limit entails another: an upper limit to the value of possible worlds.

When talking about worlds containing only pigs, I should mention this fact: Our own world benefits from having agents at various levels of subtlety. Uniform levels of subtlety are unsubtle.

Against the notion of a best among possible worlds, the mere addition argument fails, because the value of subtle experience doesn't accumulate in a straight line. More and more subtle experience eventually begins to taper off in value.

Indeed, more and more subtle experience eventually goes negative. Each new pig added to the pig-world, would not always increase value. A pig-world can have too many pigs. And a pig can have a life that goes on too long.

A world with an infinite number of subtle pigs, has clearly overdone the experience of being a pig. Were a balladeer to recite the entire history of the infinite pig-world, his ballad would eventually have nothing new to say. Once the pig-world reaches its plateau and no longer benefits from more and more pigs, the extra pigs become excessive.

More and more pigs becoming excessive to a world's subtlety, is a coherent concept, reflected throughout the united opinion. Therefore, according to the united opinion, only finite numbers of pigs may stand at the upper limit for pig-worlds.

By similar reasoning, the united opinion also decrees this fact:

only finite numbers of subtle agents, each with a life of finite extent, may stand at the upper limit of all possible worlds.

And that's a description of our own world.

Philosopher Derek Parfit has another way to attack the notion of a best among possible worlds. He points to paradoxes that arise when worlds are compared. Let's look at one of his paradoxes.

This particular paradox goes away when we consider the character of subtle agency.

Derek Parfit uses interesting reasoning to reach a "Repugnant Conclusion." He constructs a series of worlds A, B, C, ... World A has ten billion conscious beings enjoying their lives at a high level. World B has twenty billion conscious beings also enjoying their lives, but at a lower level than in A. World C has forty billion conscious beings enjoying their lives, but at a still lower level. This sequence approaches World Z, which has gazillions of beings with lives barely worth living.

Mr. Parfit carefully constructs this sequence in such a way, he claims, that World B is better than A, World C is better than B, and so on to World Z, which is the best of all.

(The construction goes like this:

(Suppose that world A has ten billion conscious beings, all enjoying their lives at a high level. To construct world A+, we *merely add* to these ten billion lives, another ten billion conscious beings also enjoying their lives, but each at a much lower level than the first group. World A+ seems at least as good as A, and perhaps better. Yet the average level of enjoyment in A+ has declined from the average in A. Now consider world B, containing the same number of lives lived in world A+: twenty billion. The conscious beings in B enjoy their lives at a lower level than the beings in A, but at a level higher than the average in A+. B seems better than A+, which seems at least as good as A. Conclusion: World B appears to be better than world A; the lower level of enjoyment in B seems more than compensated by the larger number of conscious beings having that enjoyment.

(By the same reasoning, a world C containing forty billion

lives, all lived at a lower level than the lives in B, is better than both A and B.

(We can continue this sequence indefinitely. To each of the worlds A, B, C, . . . , we can merely add new lives lived at some minimum level of enjoyment barely worth having, creating worlds A+, B+, C+, . . . , where $A \le A+ < B \le B+ < C \le C+$. . . . This sequence approaches world Z, where many, many billions of lives are lived at a level of enjoyment barely worth having. World Z is better than world A, which has ten billion beings living highly enjoyable lives. The enormous number of lives in world Z compensates for a far lower level of enjoyment.)

Derek Parfit's Repugnant Conclusion: A world containing gazillions of beings with lives barely worth living, is better than the world with only ten billion beings enjoying their lives at a high level.

The series of worlds A, B, C, . . . Z is a Repugnant Descent, Mr. Parfit finds. In this series, more and more agents compensate for less and less enjoyment by each agent. Enormous numbers of agents barely enjoying their lives, are better than only ten billion agents highly enjoying their lives. And that is a truly horrible conclusion.

This interesting paradox fails in two ways, when we consider the character of subtle agency.

First, Mr. Parfit's paradox relies on a straight-line accumulation of value. But we have seen that the value of subtle lives accumulates in a different way: the value tapers off to a plateau, then it goes negative.

Thus, World Z, with gazillions of agents barely enjoying their lives, has long since bumped up against its value-plateau. A world with one percent of Z's population would be at least as good as Z. The extra agents no longer compensate for the lower level of enjoying life.

Second, the character of subtle agency illuminates "higher" and "lower" levels of enjoying life. These can only be higher and lower levels of subtlety.

For subtle agents, and for a world's population as a whole, positive and negative experience must balance. They give size to each other. An individual can be relatively happy or unhappy, but collective happiness and unhappiness must balance. *All* the agents having lives barely worth living, can happen in just one way: All the agents have experience just barely subtle.

And *all* the agents enjoying their lives at a high level, also happens in just one way: Their lives are highly subtle.

The Repugnant Descent would actually work like this: World A has ten billion dolphins enjoying highly subtle lives. World B has twenty billion dogs enjoying less subtle lives. World C has forty billion mice enjoying lives still less subtle. And we are headed toward World Z, with gazillions of snails enjoying lives just barely subtle at all.

However, we have no Repugnant Descent. World A is already the best. The worlds are getter worse, not better as Derek Parfit feared. No matter how many barely subtle snails infest World Z, the ten billion highly subtle humans in World A have more value.

(Revealing to go through Mr. Parfit's argument as I have described it, substituting the notion "level of subtlety" for "level of enjoyment.")

Paradoxes give insight. The character of subtle agency shows why the Repugnant Conclusion is false. This attack on the coherence of comparing the value of worlds, ends up with a different conclusion: The notion of subtle agency is needed, to compare the value of worlds accurately.

The third argument arrayed against us, asserts that some alternate worlds have incommensurate value. Here I very roughly paraphrase William E. Mann as quoted to me by Stephen Grover:

Suppose that two worlds are identical in history up to the point where Teresa, present in both worlds, makes a decision. Teresa is torn between two callings. She is a talented soprano, and she also has the patience and compassion to care for the dying poor. Teresa believes that she cannot pursue both callings. In "Opera World," Teresa chooses to use her voice to enrich the lives of opera lovers. In "Hospice World," Teresa chooses to care for the dying poor. In each world she becomes an inspiration to others. Which world is better, Opera World or Hospice World? Or are they equal in value? How can we compare them?

If choices like Teresa's occur in the actual world, then surely the actual world has possible alternatives with incommensurate value. By what standard of goodness can we pick out a best among these alternate possible worlds?

Again, the character of subtle agency shows why this argument fails.

We do have blurry vision about the value of subtlety. We readily understand that Stalin had a more subtle life than a field mouse. We have more difficulty understanding whether Stalin or Picasso had the more subtle life.

I have argued that Stalin's and Picasso's experiences are not actually incommensurate in human perception. We are the product of a long and ruthless biological evolution. For hundreds of millions of years, we and our ancestors made choices, under the discipline of survival, among increasingly diverse alternatives. Under the discipline of survival, we evolved to make good choices, to find our alternatives commensurate. Our evolution made us each idiosyncratic, yet our evolution pounded together a profound commensurability within each human's experience. Diverse alternatives—walking the dog, visiting a friend, reading a book, painting a picture, issuing state directives—such diverse alternatives are commensurate in the view of each human.

Indeed, Teresa can be torn between the opera and the hospice, only because the two are commensurate. If she were really choosing between *in*commensurate alternatives, then she could never regret her choice. She would be unable to look back on her life and think, "I wish I had gone the other way." That feeling involves the commensurability of her alternatives.

Teresa is torn because she lacks information, not because her choices are incommensurate. We sometimes have blurry vision about subtlety, because we lack information about it.

If you and I interviewed both Stalin and Picasso for a year, we might be able to decide who had the more subtle life.

If Teresa had a twin sister who chose the opera, while Teresa herself cared for the dying poor, history might be able to render a judgment as to who made the larger contribution. Moreover, the two sisters, in conference near the end of their lives, might be able to decide who made the better choice.

But often in our world, we make decisions based on more limited information. Teresa, torn between two careers, and not wanting to feel regret for her choice, lacks enough information to be certain what to do.

Subtlety is complicated. Apparently we will never understand it all the way. Our world has persistent mystery. We don't always have enough information to make a reliable decision.

And that fact is part of the subtlety of our lives. That fact puts distance between us and spiders. A spider never regrets his choices.

William E. Mann's argument as described to me, fails in a second way, when we consider the character of subtle experience.

Suppose that two worlds really did have incommensurate value: (1) a world in which no one is tempted by a career in opera unless all the positions caring for the dying poor have been filled, and (2) a world in which no one wants to care for the dying poor unless he believes his prospects for joining an opera company are hopeless.

Those worlds would actually be commensurable to humans if we had enough information about them, but let's suppose otherwise.

Even if (1) and (2) had *in*commensurate subtlety-values, a well-composed mixture of the two worlds would have more subtlety then either.

The actual world, a well composed mixture where some people prefer careers as opera singers, some prefer to care for the dying poor, and some are torn between the two callings, is clearly more subtle than either (1) or (2). The actual world displays more subtle comparisons to its agents, including agents who merely observe choices like Teresa's.

If two possible worlds really did have incommensurate modes

of subtlety, they could still be blended together into a mixed world more subtle than either. The notion of a most subtle among possible worlds, remains unscathed.

To explore this conclusion a bit further, let's give Teresa a dilemma more obviously related to subtlety. Two worlds are identical up to the point where Teresa, present in both worlds, makes a decision. Teresa is torn between two plans. She can travel all over enormous Planet Earth, or she can remain at home and read all the books in her father's enormous library. Teresa has an intensely focused temperament. She believes she must pursue one plan or the other, but not a mixture. Each plan will differently affect not only satisfaction in the world, but also Teresa's subtlety as an agent. Which world is more subtle, Travel World or Library World?

Suppose that Travel World and Library World were somehow incommensurate. They aren't, but suppose they were. No matter. Clearly the more subtle world will be a well formed composition, in which some people travel, some read, and some do both. Even if travel-subtlety and reading-subtlety were somehow incommensurate, they could still accumulate to a higher subtlety-value than either form alone.

Asking which world is better, Opera World, Hospice World, Travel World, or Library World, has this analogous question: Which musical note is the best? Well formed compositions of the notes are better than any of them alone.

Often we do have difficulties choosing between alternatives. But these difficulties fail to confute the coherence of the notion of a most subtle among possible worlds. On the contrary, the persistent complexities attached to our choices, actually constitutes a small measure of evidence that our world's subtlety is the best possible.

And now for the fourth contemporary argument described to me, against the notion of an upper limit to the value of possible worlds. The qualitative argument goes like this:

A world containing conscious beings who enjoy it, might be

bettered by another world containing the same beings enjoying their world even more. If a world contains beings who do have an upper limit on their enjoyment, it might be bettered by other worlds containing different kinds of beings capable of more enjoyment. Why or if a highest possible level of enjoyment can be reached, remains unclear. But without this upper limit, any possible world can be bettered, and therefore no possible world is the best.

Again, this argument fails when we consider the character of subtle agency.

For all the subtle agents in a world collectively, negative and positive experience must balance. Happiness and unhappiness give size to each other. Enjoyment happens at a higher level in one world than another, in only one way: the enjoyment happens at a higher level of subtlety.

If the quality or level of subtlety has an upper limit, then the qualitative argument fails.

Next chapter I will argue that the quality of subtlety does have an upper limit. For all possible agents and all possible experience they can have, the subtlety of discrete episodes of experience never exceeds an upper limit.

As we saw, that upper limit entails another: an upper limit to the value of all possible worlds.

The Upper Limit
to the Quality
of Subtlety

The *quality* of subtle experience has an upper limit, because the *diversity* of subtle experience has an upper limit. Too much diversity defeats itself. It becomes too much the same.

Patient reader, you and I have already assembled most of the building blocks needed for this assertion: For all possible subtle agents and all possible discrete episodes of their experience, the level or quality of subtle experience has an upper limit.

In "The Human Style of Interpreting the World" (p. 65), you and I talked about the diversity in human experience, and the profound commensurability we find in our diverse satisfactions. Here's a quick summary:

A long biological evolution constructed humans. Our long and ruthless evolution pounded together the commensurability of our satisfactions. Under the discipline of survival, we evolved to make choices more and more complex. We evolved to find increasingly diverse alternatives commensurable.

In theory, could that process continue indefinitely? Could our commensurable alternatives become more and more diverse without limit?

At our leisure, good reader, let's journey toward the answer and its significance.

A subtle being might enjoy playing the familiar Western game of chess, with sixty-four squares and six different kinds of chesspiece. But only a spider can feel the monotonous satisfaction of chess strategy driven into the ground: a game with one million different kinds of chesspiece, one billion squares on the board, a typical game lasting six hundred trillion moves, yet the only object still to checkmate the opponent's king. A subtle being, even if he were sufficiently intelligent to play that game well, would find superchess repetitious.

Subtle beings face a bittersweet contradiction at our center. After a billion years of sipping ambrosia every damned morning, an enraged Hera would finally hurl her exquisite goblet against the nearest marble wall. After considering a trillion different strategies proceeding from the same interminable position at superchess, any subtle being would kick over the board. And yet, he might find the first five hundred or the first five million strategies absorbing.

During her first decade of sipping ambrosia, Hera enjoys herself, and casts sidelong glances at Zeus. But too much is too much. No subtle agent can relish repetitive experience endlessly. That kind of heaven must turn negative. Our own essential nature dooms us.

Nor does endless diversity help. That heaven also turns negative. Suppose the present typical diversity of a single human's satisfactions, were multiplied a trillion-fold. Then our satisfactions, and our strategies toward them, and how they change each other, and how they contradict each other, would resemble the intricacies of superchess. Their diversity would no longer be diversity. We could not perk up and take notice simply because a satisfaction happens to be new and different. Too many satisfactions are new and different. The game of something new has itself become old. In our trillion-fold diversity of satisfactions, they all become just about the same. But now they have a tedious, trillion-fold complexity.

When experience has too much variety, the variety loses its

size. Diversity blurs into sameness. The game of something new gets overdone. It becomes the same game repeated and repeated and repeated.

With too much diversity descended upon single agents, either we must be giant spiders playing superchess, or we must be subtle beings trapped by so much experience with so much relentless variety, that we long to put a bullet into our giant brain. Either way, the quality of any subtle experience has long since reached its upper limit.

Unlimited diversity in experience doesn't help subtlety. Could the subtlety of experience be increased, without limit, in some other way?

Let's think about subtle agents becoming more and more intelligent.

Does the intelligence of possible agents have an upper limit? Perhaps not. Would higher and higher intelligence increase the subtlety of experience without limit? No. Again, experience would have too much detail, too much diversity.

Consider an artificial intelligence that plays chess very well, and plays any board game very well. Because it has superior pattern-recognition ability and superior intelligence about the patterns, no human can beat it at chess, or Chinese go (a two-thousand-year-old board game, second only in popularity to chess worldwide), or any similar game of strategy. Indeed, the more the machine plays chess or go, the better it gets.

But suppose this artificial intelligence derives satisfaction *only* from winning at board games, and from contemplating the patterns in those games. Then it's a spider, reduced to mere calculation.

On the other hand, suppose the artificial intelligence enjoys food and drink, falls in love, waxes lyrical over a sunset, gets voted Miss Congeniality, works its way up to CEO of Gigantic Products Inc., scales dangerous mountain cliffs for the thrill of nearly dying, feels compassion for the victims of Alzheimer's disease, ponders its mortality, travels to exotic lands, fights for justice, feels both selfish and altruistic, feels moral dilemmas, rides the abortion issue into the US Senate, bargains at the flea market, writes a screenplay, raises children, and goes to the race track and screams for its horse to pay the rent. It does all this with high idiosyncrasy. And it finds a profound yet light commensurability among all its satisfactions.

Suppose we make our artificial being more and more intelligent. It applies its intelligence *not* just to board games and other calculation problems, as a spider does. No. Suppose this being applies its intelligence throughout the diversity of its experience.

As we increase the intelligence it applies to experience, without limit, this being finds its experience more and more diverse. It notices more and understands more. As we make this being increasingly intelligent without limit, at some point its experience becomes too diverse. With too much intelligence, it notices and understands experience in too much detail. The game of something new, gets played too much. It gets old. The game of innovation in experience, becomes the same game repeated and repeated and repeated. Diversity blurs into sameness.

Suppose the artificial being stops at some appropriate level of intelligence applied throughout its experience. But it discovers its experience having subtle commensurability—more and more commensurability without limit.

Same problem. At some point, the commensurability becomes too much. The game of noticing commensurability starts to resemble superchess. It gets too complicated. It descends into too much detail. The game of something new gets repeated too often. It becomes old and tedious.

Any method we try, to increase an agent's subtlety without limit, will eventually make experience too detailed. Then the variety of experience becomes tedious.

For completeness, I should mention the lightness of experience. Within the right structure, better and better lightness makes for better and better subtlety.

But the lightness of experience has an upper limit.

Lightness is a measure of the quality of randomness within a specified structure. Lightness corresponds to shuffling the deck. A perfectly light structure of randomness presents only a specified pattern, and contains no contaminating traces of any other pattern.

Perfect lightness in any given finite structure of randomness, requires only a finite amount of shuffling. At some point, further shuffling becomes superfluous. Shuffling the deck of cards one billion times, fails to improve its lightness after shuffling it one hundred times. Lightness has an upper limit.

Lightness in the actual world's subtle experience has a *high* upper limit, that may have required 13.7 billion years of shuffling to reach, but lightness in any finite structure of randomness reaches a point of no further improvement.

For the experience of any subtle being, an upper limit governs the value of diversity. Too much detail defeats itself. And too much subtlety makes experience too detailed. The level or quality of subtlety can be overdone.

Apparently the inhabitants of our universe will never completely understand subtlety. But we understand it partway. We understand enough to see an upper limit. Thus:

For all possible discrete episodes of subtle experience, the level or quality of subtlety has an upper limit to its value.

It follows that all possible worlds have an upper limit to their value. This upper limit is reached by worlds, at least one, with a finite number of inhabitants, each with a life of finite extent. Rather like our own world.

The mere logical fact that the quality of subtlety has an upper limit, and the logical consequences of that fact, and the evidence for perfection based on that fact—all these are the bones and not the flesh.

The upper limit to the subtlety of experience, has some complications.

We know that the quality of subtle experience has an upper limit, because the detail and diversity of subtle experience can be overdone. But *some* kinds of subtle agent bump up against other kinds of boundaries. Some subtle beings find their existence unworthy of further elaboration, long before diversity begins to blur into sameness. Subtle experience can go too far in myriad ways.

The incoherence of endless diversity applies to any kind of subtle agent. Other boundaries apply only to some kinds of subtle agent. Apparently, the more complicated the style of subtlety, the more ways it has to defeat itself. Unique internal tensions appear to plague precisely the most ambitious forms of subtlety. In consequence, those tensions also figure into the upper limit on the value of any possible existence.

To show something more of the upper limit, I will talk now about the upper limit to *contemporary human* subtle experience. As a highly subtle cosmos would have civilizations both more successful and less successful, we humans might not be the crown jewel of our universe; we might not be the actual world's most subtle agents. Or more optimistically, we might not *yet* be the crown jewel. But human experience as it is now, still affords some glimpses into the upper limit to high subtlety.

When we examine specific human lives, we discover an upper limit more intricate and subtle, and far more difficult to describe, than the simple straightforward incoherence of endless diversity. We discover that human beings can see and feel too much, and find their existence unworthy of further elaboration, sometimes for reasons beyond human understanding.

The incoherence of endless diversity emerges as a simple first approximation to the upper limit on the quality of subtlety. But it is far from the whole story.

If the kind reader will indulge me, I will begin with a controversial opinion: Among the human beings known to history, exactly four exhibited a wide-ranging intelligence significantly superior to any other. These four had an existence closer than usual to the upper limit of individual subtlety. As it happens, each was a military and political leader with a life fairly well documented. No doubt many other humans experienced subtlety even closer to the upper limit, but attracted far less notice. However, with those documented four, we can watch the boundary that limits any possible existence, actually shape the lives of specific human beings. We can glimpse the subtle complexity of that boundary.

During a long period of human history—perhaps five thousand years—making war was a human endeavor that sometimes gave enormous scope to an individual's ability. Some conflicts presented relatively straightforward challenges to the participants. But many others were profoundly fluid and complex. Military success went far beyond the tactics of the battlefield. The most effective military leaders knew how to manage shifting alliances, exploit the superstitions of their friends and enemies, inspire all manner of human fear, respect, and loyalty, and influence the minds of those who fought and those who observed the fighting. They studied not just the minds of opposing leaders, but the psychology of every person involved or potentially involved. They understood both strategy and people—all kinds of strategy and all kinds of people. They understood the interrelated resources required by war. They knew how, when, and why to avoid battle, reduce the incidence of war, reduce the ravages of war, and govern a conquered people effectively. They knew when to be ruthless and when to be generous. Their thinking always extended years into the future.

Committees usually gave inept leadership in a complex war. For maximum effect, all those different kinds of knowledge had to be combined within a single decisive commander. Let's look at one of them.

Hannibal in Italy led a small army of malcontents and adventurers from dozens of tribes and nations. At times they could barely understand each other's speech. He held their fierce loyalty for thirty-six years. He selected the favorable topography near Cannae village months in advance. The Roman commanders had learned to fear Hannibal, but he spent two years working on the exasperation of the Roman people. They crowded their leaders into offering a decisive battle. Hannibal timed his moment for maximum military readiness. He lured the much larger Roman army toward Cannae by feigning disarray and retreat, and at the chosen place, annihilated that army to the astonishment of his own officers and troops.

And well they should have been astonished. The Romans sent 85,000 foot and cavalry, disciplined and courageous, defending their own families on their own soil, against Hannibal's 35,000 renegades and mercenaries of uneven ability. Hannibal watched the fighting from a hilltop, and signaled his various units by fire. They retreated and advanced at precise times. The battle developed exactly as Hannibal had planned six months in advance. The formidable Roman infantry, three men deep, wearing good Roman armor, and bristling with swords, spears, and long pikes, pressed forward against a single thin line of their enemy. Their fighting front extended just over a mile. They advanced into a shallow valley or depression between low ridges, the entrance also just over a mile wide. At first they did not perceive that the valley gradually narrowed. The Roman infantry, three men deep, began to crowd together. Some of them became so congested that they could no longer use their weapons. Their cavalry, trying to protect the flanks, found themselves disorganized by assorted natural obstacles. Hannibal's own cavalry spent two hours destroying them one small group at a time, until no mounted Romans remained. Then they rode up behind the Roman infantry and completed the circle around them. The eight Roman legions on foot, had pursued their enemy into the narrowing valley for two hours, advancing in the center but held back on both flanks. Now they found themselves surrounded on all sides and suddenly pressed together into a compacted mass. They could barely move their arms and legs. They still numbered by the tens of thousands, but they were penned up like a herd of cattle. On their perimeter, the tangled Romans could not fight effectively. In the interior of their compacted mass, each immobilized man could only wait his turn to die. Hannibal's small army needed the entire afternoon to kill them all. His soldiers grew arm-weary from killing them. Almost exactly within the number of daylight hours available, they put 55,000 Romans to death. The cavalry caught another 20,000 in scattered isolated formations, and captured them alive. They were sold as slaves to a pirate fleet. The remaining 10,000 Roman troops were mostly deserters—raw recruits who successfully hid themselves in a gully while their compatriots died. Under cover of darkness they crept away toward their city, which soon sent them into dishonorable exile. Thus the Roman army vanished almost to the last man. Hannibal lost no more than two or three thousand killed, probably fewer. Immediately he used his crushing victory to gain allies in Italy and all around the Mediterranean—allies that he had carefully courted during the six months before Cannae. The Roman people outnumbered Carthage six million to seven hundred thousand, but Hannibal managed to advance from nuisance to mortal threat in one day.

Rome was fortunate to find her own great commander, Scipio Africanus, less skillful than Hannibal but equal in ability to Napoleon. But Rome's greatest asset was her dogged persistence.

The legend about Hannibal, that he bore an implacable hatred toward all things Roman, is supported by Roman propaganda, and contradicted by his actions. Almost immediately after Cannae, Hannibal offered peace to Rome on generous terms, including the return of the 20,000 prisoners. Rome would lose nothing further to be rid of him, except her dreams of empire. In Hannibal's time, the greater Mediterranean region fairly sparkled with a diversity of independent city-states, more interested in trade than war, and many with beautiful languages soon to be extinguished by the rising new empire. By comparison, the Roman people then were superstitious, dour, and uncultured, and they had a ferocious code of military conduct binding on every citizen. The Roman Senate and the Roman people did not wish to receive their 20,000 compatriots who had surrendered alive.

Hannibal spoke perhaps thirty languages fluently, some of them learned late in life. He was renowned for his sense of humor. His actions displayed a wide-ranging intelligence.

Perhaps one final detail completes the picture of that man's mastery at Cannae, and the subtlety of his life. Early on the morning of battle, Hannibal stood on his observation hilltop. His principal officers were dispersed on the field, but he was surrounded by lesser officers, mostly couriers. At sight of the huge Roman army advancing on them, they were visibly nervous. They had the habit of speaking freely to Hannibal. An officer named Gisco said, "It's an amazing thing, to see that many men in motion." Hannibal replied, "I'll tell you something even more amazing." He paused for effect. "In all that number, not a single one is called 'Gisco.'" The officers were amused. They all knew that Gisco was not the brightest bulb on the tree. As they rode out among the troops, carrying Hannibal's last-minute instructions, the couriers told of his jest. Soon the entire army was saying to each other, "Aye, the Romans number themselves by the tens of thousands, but they have not a single Gisco among them!" Hannibal's multinational army went into battle with camaraderie and high hearts.

In the intricate and profound contests that war could sometimes be—even a joke could affect the outcome—historians generally agree on four great masters: Alexander the Great, Hannibal, Zhu Ge Liang, and Genghis Khan. Hannibal was finally defeated. Zhu Ge Liang neither won nor lost. Alexander's military position steadily improved until the end of his life. And Genghis Khan, from desperate beginnings, enjoyed the most complete military success given to any human.

When we talk about the upper limit to existence, we can go beyond the bare bones of logic. At least four human beings grappled with their existence at a level difficult for the rest of us to understand. And the final periods of their lives were similar. While still vigorous and in good health, all four withdrew into themselves. Each man began to refuse human contact. Apparently, they lost pleasure in being alive, lost interest in the affairs of men, lost the desire to have their names or their deeds recorded in history, and apparently each man in his own way deliberately chose to end his life.

Alexander was peeved when his army of ten years wanted to retire. They felt they were getting old. But Alexander at the height of his reputation, could easily have raised an enthusiastic fresh army of younger men in Greece and Macedonia. Instead, he went into his dark tent and rarely came out again. Eventually he sickened or stopped eating or both, and died—at the age of thirty-four.

Zhu Ge Liang, the amazing general who struggled to restore the Han Dynasty and the unity of China, died while still in his fifties, and the conflict unresolved. Rather abruptly he stopped giving audience to anyone, and stopped eating anything more than a handful of grain each day. When the physicians asked if he needed them, he waved them away.

Hannibal at sixty-five was healthy, physically active, and long accustomed to the ascendancy of Rome. He disliked the petty squabbling among the leading citizens of Carthage, and did not mind living in exile. He had considerable portable wealth at his residence in Bithynia. He had loyal servants. To evade eventual arrest by Roman agents, all he had to do was quietly join a caravan or board a ship, and find a more distant place to live in exile. During most of his life he had felt curiosity about regions of the world still unvisited. A variety of comfortable lifestyles were available to him in a variety of civilized places. But he chose to take poison. To the servants who tried to dissuade him, he spoke his last words: "It's time for a hated old man to die."

In the case of Genghis Khan, his followers begged him to stop brooding, come out of his tent, and be with them again. Patiently but firmly he refused. He gave no explanation. Genghis Khan, from three warriors and four horses, built the most extensive land empire in history. At age sixty-eight he took sick or stopped eating and died. Most of his last three years he spent alone in his tent.

All four men appear to have seen and felt too much. They definitely became moody. But the explanation that the diversity of their experience had gone too far, seems rather bland. Perhaps Genghis Khan achieved too much and, paradoxically, found it futile. Perhaps Hannibal suffered too much disappointment, and Alexander too little. Zhu Ge Liang—the most enigmatic—apparently made some truly strange discovery about existence. No one reported that any of these four people said, "Nothing we do matters" or "What difference who wins the war?" or "Life is empty." Whatever happened to them, they did not much talk about it. They may not have understood it. But all four appear to have seen and felt too much.

Ants and spiders can build forever without despair. Subtle beings lack a constitution suitable for triumph. Our world does better than answer our pedestrian hopes and dreams. Our world shows us wonders, and burns us to ashes.

Dynamics at the Upper Limit

G ood reader, you and I have figured out that no possible world exceeds a specific, finite upper limit to value.

Now I'm going to tell you that exactly one unique world stands alone at that upper limit.

We don't have a situation where multiple possible worlds, all of them equal in value, reach the upper limit. No. One particular world betters all the others.

The unique best possible world, I'm going to tell you, requires a human race. It requires an assassination of Abraham Lincoln by John Wilkes Booth at Ford's Theater on April 14, 1865. The best world requires that you, gentle reader, were born just about exactly a particular number of minutes ago. It requires that your life extend just about exactly a particular number of minutes from beginning to end. The best world probably requires that you have a particular number of hairs on your head at any given moment during your life. And it might even require that each hair have exactly a particular length at some particular moments.

In short, the best world is unique down to rather fine details. Only the details "thoroughly beneath notice" can be varied. Here is why:

For highly subtle beings in the best world, experience has "sparks": the ineffable and the sublime visited upon us against our expectations and outside our ambitions.

I'm talking only about the highly subtle denizens of the best world, near the human level or higher. I'm not talking about the inhabitants with medium or low subtlety, like mice or chickens.

For highly subtle beings, the sparks constitute our best moments. They constitute unusually high quality episodes of subtle experience.

In the value of subtle experience, higher quantity fails to compensate for lower quality. We talked about that two chapters ago (see "The Upper Limit to the Value of Possible Worlds," p. 323). This conclusion seems to follow:

Collective experience at the upper limit of value for experience, must have a collection of sparks at the upper limit of value for sparks.

And therefore, let's consider what the best collection of sparks would be like.

Sparks cannot be visited upon us in arbitrary ways. Instead, they fit together and support each other, like pieces of a jigsaw puzzle.

Let's consider a collection of sparks at the upper limit of value. All the needed varieties of sparks are present. The sparks have their strongest diversity without overdoing diversity. And the sparks fit together into an elegant, compact mosaic, such that they support and help each other in optimum ways. The sparks support and help each other because they fit a compact pattern, like the pieces of a jigsaw puzzle.

Could that jigsaw puzzle be taken apart and reassembled in a different pattern, equally compact and valuable? Obviously not. The original pattern has the supreme value, precisely because the pieces enjoy strong mutual support. They depend upon and facilitate each other in highly idiosyncratic ways. They use pivotal efficiencies in the experience that embeds them. Precisely their intensely individual shapes and acute mutual dependencies, make them valuable. If these sparks could be reassembled into a different pattern equally compact and valuable, then their shapes are too generic—and therefore too unsubtle to stand at the upper limit.

Our own introspection, at the human level of subtlety, shows us how idiosyncratic and fragile are the sparks. Those qualities limit the jigsaw puzzle to a single best solution.

Suppose we start over with a different master plan: a world with a different human race or no human race; a world with totally different events and a totally different arrangement of sparks. Then we never get back to the upper limit. Here is why:

Possible subtle worlds have subtlety-value on a scale from one to a billion trillion quadrillion gazillion, as it were. The actual subtle world has 250 billion galaxies, at least thirteen billion highly subtle beings living and dying in just one of those galaxies, and yet the particular color of your eyes affects the entire world's subtlety-value. The chances are vanishingly small, that any totally different master plan for sparks, would have exactly the same subtlety-value as the actual master plan for sparks. Chances might be higher that some alternate master plan would have *close* to the same value, but the odds are vanishingly small that the values would be equal exactly.

Consequently, the most valuable collection of sparks, the best mutual support among their highly individual shapes, is unique.

Any world at the upper limit must have the same unique pattern of sparks—a unique pattern of the ineffable and the sublime visited upon the inhabitants against their expectations and outside their ambitions.

This unique pattern already entails a universe much like ours, with the same individual humans, the same events in human history—and apart from human history, the same highly subtle individuals and their histories everywhere in the universe like ours.

If multiple possible worlds stand together at the upper limit to value, then all those worlds have the same highly subtle people with the same general history as our world has. Without the same people and the same general history, the highly subtle inhabitants would have a second-best pattern of best moments, and therefore a second-best subtlety below the upper limit.

Moreover, all the worlds at the upper limit, must have even further details in common. Below the level of sparks in our lives, are the "lesser astonishments." These also must follow a single unique pattern at the upper limit.

The value of our lives goes beyond the unpredictable sparks. Many of our pleasures we do anticipate with confidence— returning to the people and the places we love, listening to our favorite music, watching the reactions of a defeated enemy, attending our child's graduation ceremony, and so on.

By contrast to the completely unpredictable sparks, the "lesser astonishments" affect us in ways both predictable and unpre- dictable. Usually, as we are about to watch the reactions of a defeated enemy, we know how we will feel and we don't know.

Even these more predictable experiences still have the fascina- tion of the unexpected. In our Siren universe, at least a mild aston- ishment quickens every experience that interests us. Highly subtle lives are filled each day with "lesser astonishments." Such is the nature of subtle experience in the best world.

For the collection of highly subtle beings at the upper limit, the lesser astonishments also have constraints on their pattern. The lesser astonishments embed and facilitate the compact pattern of sparks. Within that constraint, they must themselves be optimized as contributors to subtlety.

Those constraints are strong when subtlety is high. High sub- tlety involves a robust facility to interpret experience based on comparisons. Lots of comparisons intensify the interdependence of experience.

A good crossword puzzle has only one solution, because the words interdepend in so many ways. The best world's highly subtle inhabitants, have only one best pattern of sparks and aston- ishments, because these interdepend in so many ways.

For the highly subtle beings in the best world, strong con- straints appear to fix the pattern of lesser astonishments down to fine details. The highest collective subtlety needs even the fine details to be just right.

The very tiptop highest subtlety seems to require that your life extends just about exactly a particular number of minutes, and perhaps that you have a particular number of hairs on your head during each of those minutes.

The highest subtlety might *not* require that the books on your bookshelf have a particular arrangement at each moment. If you reach for a book in an absent-minded way, without paying much attention, then perhaps finding *Cooking with Style* just to the left of *Cooking with Class*, or just to the right, might be immaterial to the best subtlety.

If the hairs on your head happen to be the object of scientific curiosity, if laboratory technicians in white smocks are carefully measuring the distribution of hair mass on your noggin, then the highest possible subtlety might require not just a particular number of hairs on your head at that time, but a particular length for each hair down to the angstrom.

The details of the best world can vary, if the highly subtle inhabitants don't notice the variations or barely notice them—if the variations don't figure into comparisons or barely figure. But otherwise, the lesser astonishments appear to have their own unique optimum pattern, within the unique optimum pattern of sparks.

We have been talking about beings highly subtle. When their collective subtlety reaches the upper limit, the details of their experience have exacting interdependence. They have ambitious styles of subtlety. For the highly subtle beings as a collection, only one pattern of experience reaches the upper limit.

The best world also has denizens with medium and low subtlety, like mice and chickens. Uniform levels of subtlety in the world, would be unsubtle. The best world has subtlety at many different levels, from high to low.

Camarasaurus was a plant-eating dinosaur who walked on four tall legs. From a large central body mass, a longish neck ending in a small head shot out in one direction, balanced by a longish tail in the other direction. The bulbous central body had neck, legs, and tail sticking out in three directions, like a big radish with toothpicks. Camarasaurus was endearingly ugly.

Camarasaurus is so-called because it had chambers, or cameras, in its head. Paleontologists aren't quite sure what the cameras did.

As an adult, this critter weighed about twenty tons. Its brain weighed a few ounces. Large body, small head, tiny brain.

Camarasaurus *may* have had experience at the dim boundary of subtlety, one notch above mere machine calculation. *Perhaps* it made just enough comparisons to see the world in terms of balances, to be happy and unhappy as a subtle being. Just barely.

The Camarasaur critters came in four species with few differences. They were numerous for ten million years, from about 155 million years ago to about 145 million years ago. They ranged the plains of North America, and a fossil was found in Portugal. Camarasauri may have numbered in the millions, for ten million years. During their history, perhaps one trillion individuals reached adulthood.

Our universe has surely overdone the Camarasaur style of subtle experience. Camarasaur experience does add to the variety of subtle experience. It benefits the diversity of collective subtlety. But surely this benefit could be reached with far less than one trillion individuals.

Yet the Camarasauri were key in evolution. They processed a lot of ferns and tree leaves. They fed a lot of predators and scavengers. For a time, the turning wheel of evolution needed them in large numbers.

At the dim boundary of subtlety, Camarasaur experience has a certain sameness. For each individual, what happens today compares in limited ways to what happened yesterday. Camarasaurus made fewer comparisons then we make. Experience at their level of subtlety has more disassociation than experience at our level. Camarasauri perceived the world in the same ways over and over, with limited modification from comparisons. All their experience has a certain sameness.

In the best world, evolution needs a trillion Camarasauri. The best world drives their experience into the ground. Still, Camarasaur experience does reach an upper limit consistent with the needs of evolution.

One trillion individual Camarasauri reach that upper limit, *without fixing the precise details of their individual lives.* At the upper limit to the value of subtle experience, for one trillion individuals as a collection, the particulars of their lives are somewhat interchangeable.

The analogy would be an interminable jigsaw puzzle, with only a few simple shapes for the pieces, and empty spaces allowed. The puzzle has many different solutions. Camarasaur numbers being excessive, and their simple feelings and thoughts being rather disassociated, they reach their upper limit in many different ways.

By contrast, the upper limit to value for high subtlety, corresponds to a jigsaw puzzle quite different. This puzzle is large but not repetitive. The pieces have complicated shapes, each different from the other. No empty spaces allowed. The puzzle has only one solution.

Not all the details of the best possible world, are fixed. Numerous worlds with different individual Camarasauri, all stand together at the exact upper limit to value.

By contrast, the experience of highly subtle agents can be best in only one way, down to fine details.

The possible worlds standing at the upper limit to value, do have variations at lower levels of subtle experience. As subtlety dips too low, experience starts to blur together from one individual to another. And at the very lowest levels, in a large population, subtle experience can blur together rather completely.

Nonetheless, possible worlds standing at the upper limit to valuable subtle experience, all have exactly the same highly subtle inhabitants, and almost exactly the same details in their experience. In that sense, the most subtle possible world is unique.

THE ARGUMENT FOR BEST WORLD

Is our world the best and most subtle possible? We are left with this reasoning:

1. On the evidence for highly subtle experience in the actual world, our very own world stands at the upper limit to collective subtle experience. The actual evidence indicates that no other possible world has higher subtlety than ours.

2. If our world does stand at the upper limit, then it stands there without peer, as we saw in this chapter.

3. Therefore, on the evidence for high subtlety in the actual world, one unique possible world—the actual world—stands alone and solitary at the upper limit to subtlety. Ours is *the peerless and unique* most subtle world.

4. The united opinion mandates the possible state of existence with the highest subtlety in experience (and with genuine free will). We successfully identify their mandate as the peerless most subtle world possible, alone and solitary. That possible state ought to be the actual state of existence.

5. On the evidence for high subtlety in the very large actual world, the united opinion gets what it wants: the entire most subtle world existing alone and solitary.

6. Therefore, on the evidence for high collective subtlety in the actual world, what ought to exist does exist. Ours is the best possible world.

The evidence for high subtlety in the actual world, is ingenious physical law, ingenious evolution of highly subtle agents who understand physical law, and human experience transcending physical evolution.

Actual evolution produces an agent with satisfactions highly idiosyncratic yet deeply commensurable. The subtle human agent stands as an example of what our universe can produce. Actual evolution has the potency to evolve highly subtle agents, yet a simplicity that the agents can understand and use; actual reflexive causality constitutes a difficult technical achievement. Evolution in our world infuses the agent's experience with both structure and lightness. A long, ruthless evolution produces the commensurable yet conflicting sensibilities that beget inner struggle, moral status, and high subtlety.

Toward the inhabitants' struggles for happiness, this world maintains a persistent and elusive neutrality—another difficult technical achievement. Our world's cunning neutrality sharpens our human dilemma and gives us better than we can strive to have. We make the motions of swimming, but the living sea around us carries us in its own mysterious directions. Because it finally defeats us and terminates us, our world can sometimes give us the unexpected, the ineffable, and the sublime.

Some of the evidence is a bit soft. Not everyone will perceive a persistent elusiveness in their experience, as I have been describing. For those people, said elusiveness would be a *consequence* of the best-world thesis, not evidence for it.

On the other hand, some of the evidence is diamond hard. The single most striking piece of evidence is physical law: its mathematical elegance, its helpful, rigorous simplicity, and its potency to generate subtle agents and their subtle experience. Right now on Planet Earth, the single most striking element of physical principle is the DNA molecule made from dead star ashes. I have never heard any suggestions for improving either the molecule or physical law generally. Both are masterpieces. Both contribute to high subtlety.

This world plays well on its inhabitants' facility to compare. In consequence, you and I are addicted rather profoundly to What happens next? Surely ours is the most subtle, and therefore the best, possible world.

We have another kind of evidence. The best-world thesis answers a number of metaphysical questions that would otherwise be intractable. Examples:

Do we have genuine free will? If yes, how does it operate as genuine?

Why do mental events correspond to physical events?

Why is our world's causality reflexive?

Why do we have moral sensibilities?

Why do we suffer and perish?

Why do we exist?

Only if our world is the best possible, do those questions have reasonable answers.

THE BIG PICTURE: WHY WE EXIST REVISITED

Only subtlety ranks worlds. That fact adds significance to actual physical law, which well facilitates subtle experience.

In the actual world, physical law is a masterpiece of overall design and in its details (the ATP molecule, the DNA molecule, their relationships to stellar life cycles, and so on). Gentle reader, do you have a better explanation than I do for the excellence of our physical law? My explanation: Existence is governed by a principle of goodness, *which can only be*, a principle of optimum subtlety. Our excellent physical law fits that principle.

For humans and for all possible subtle agents, only subtlety ranks worlds. In consequence, the Big Picture looks like this:

The state of existence just is all the contingent true propositions. To explain why all the true contingent propositions are true, we cannot use a contingent proposition as explanans. That would be circular. Nor can we use a necessary proposition, for necessity cannot explain the contingent facts of existence. In short, there can be no explanation for the contingent state of existence.

Thus, suppose that "a fundamental agent" accounts for the order and coherence in the actual state of existence. This agent, if contingent, itself requires explanation, and if necessary, would incoherently make a contingent world.

There can be no explanation for the contingent state of existence. Any contingent explanans gets absorbed into the explanandum, and a necessary explanans cannot account for the contingent facts of existence.

To explain why all the true contingent propositions are true, the best you and I can do is find a true contingent proposition that entails all the others, that provides a comprehensive description of existence. What could that proposition be? How about, "Existence conforms to a principle of goodness, namely, optimum subtlety." That one already seems to entail consciousness, causality, free will, the structure of physical law, the structure of the molecules in our bodies, the mixture of surprise and order in our lives, high subtlety in the human mind, and the prospect of still higher subtlety elsewhere in the universe and/or in our own human future. That's a lot of true contingent propositions to entail, and that's a lot of value and potential value displayed in our universe.

The strong coherence and high value of conscious experience in our world, cry out for explanation. We appear to have exactly one viable explanans: Existence conforms to a principle of goodness. Any alternative explanans would be contingent, and therefore absorbed into the explanandum, or necessary, and therefore unable to account for the contingent facts of existence. Only one explanans can be viable: the contingent explanans that merely sums up the contingent state of existence.

The strong coherence and high value of conscious experience in our world, cry out for explanation. One and only one explanans can be viable: Existence conforms to a principle of goodness.

Gentle reader, make no mistake. The principle of goodness we're talking about, brings suffering and death. Those are integral and necessary to high subtlety.

I don't like that relationship either, but there it is.

If sometimes we hate perfection, then how are we reconciled to the perfect, uncompromising terms of our existence?

The Alien Presence

People have often imagined God as a bigger and better version of ourselves: We have a little knowledge. God has all knowledge. We have limited powers. God has omnipotence. We make mistakes and screw things up. God is infallible. We love others to various extents from time to time. God has perfect love always. We have a certain amount of justice in us. God has perfect justice. We can be harmed and defeated. God is invulnerable. We exist in this world for a time. God exists beyond time and apart from the world. We are limited. God has no limits. We are made in God's image, and God is the perfect model of us. God's thoughts and feelings and actions are perfect versions of ours.

People have also imagined Satan as a more powerful version of ourselves. Satan takes some of our characteristics that God leaves behind, such as selfishness and resentment.

Sometimes we have wanted God to help us out of our mortal dilemma. We don't want to perish, and we do feel ashamed when we act badly. If we repent, if we believe, we hope God will not abandon us. If we play our cards right, maybe God will help us with some of our weaknesses and imperfections. We want God to end our suffering, give us bliss, give us infinite existence, and purge us of Satanic elements.

Such hopes are groundless. Only spiders can go to heaven. Subtle agency reaches its maximum potential when it is limited, vulnerable, flawed, conflicted, and doomed. These "defects" enable the subtle comparisons we make. They open us to the ineffable and the sublime, visited upon us against all expectation.

In an absolute heaven, without our defects, without our disappointments, we are spiders and nothing more.

In the absolute heaven we sometimes envision, we would have no occasion to feel shame. We would be spiders reduced to mere calculation.

As we often see them in our imaginations, neither God nor Satan feel shame. If they are agents, then they are unconflicted spiders who only calculate.

The absolute heaven we yearn to reach, collapses our predicament—the predicament that animates us as subtle beings.

We cannot go to heaven, because we are there already. We cannot go to hell, because there, too, we who perish dwell already. If the world is wonderful, it must also be horrible. The best coherent heaven, the worst coherent hell—these are the same place. They happen together or not at all. Escape from one is escape from the other.

When we look for God in our lives, we may be looking for the wrong kind of God, a God who will rescue us from hell on Earth.

Gentle reader, let's look in a different direction.

In its own strange way, the universe around us appears to be perfect. Apparently, what exists could not be more subtle than it is already.

The united opinion mandates what ought to exist: the most subtle world possible, the world with flawless collective subtlety.

On the evidence for flawless collective subtlety in our very own universe, actual existence conforms to the mandate.

If we are looking for God, we can locate God. We can identify a simple, coherent structure for God. Quite simply, God is the mandate of the united opinion.

If that's what God is, then God is not an agent. Yet a divinity does shape our ends.

If God is the mandate, then God has certain attributes we like God to have. For example:

God exists. The mandate exists. We are living in it.

God has a form of omnipotence. Everything that ought to happen, does happen.

God has a form of omniscience. All the true facts that constitute the highest and actual world, are part of God.

God is eternal. The mandate does more than exist. The mandate also resides in the realm of possibility, outside actual time and space. The mandate of the united opinion, always was and always will be their mandate.

God is perfection and God is infallible. The mandate has no flaw anywhere.

God is love. The *best* collection of lives is mandated, to our benefit.

God has a coherent structure. You and I are talking about it.

Actual subtle agents are images of God, in this sense: God is the most subtle world possible. We are its subtle inhabitants. God does not have agency as we do, but God has a form of subtlety related to ours.

God is elusive and mysterious. The best world tantalizes just outside *everyone's* reach. We can understand much of God's subtlety, but never all of it.

God moves in mysterious ways. The mandated best world prefers to outguess us. It toys with our pedestrian hopes and our plodding ambitions, finally clears them away—and gives us better. It gives us better against all our expectation.

God is elegant. God exists exactly as far as needed, and no further.

Quite simply, God is the mandate of the united opinion. That's a simple, coherent structure for God.

Could God have *two* structures?

Persistent attempts to find another structure have led to complication, convolution, and contradiction. And this outcome should not surprise us. The *simple* structure already has all the potency needed. Complications only add problems.

Surely we have identified the single coherent structure of God.

But God with this structure, has acute differences from you and me. This God has no "perfect" versions of our thoughts, feelings, and actions. It has no thoughts and feelings as we have. It does not love as we do, nor hate as we do. It pursues neither justice nor injustice as we do. We will never know how to play our cards right with God. It cannot be pleased or displeased as we can.

In many respects, God remains aloof. It declines to intervene in a world already perfect. God declines to rescue us from God.

To give its inhabitants the highest subtlety, our world walks a precision fine line. It ruins our hopes, yet gives us good reason to hope. It treats us to injustice, yet bestows the satisfaction of good deeds. It angers us, but teaches forbearance. It takes away, but fills us with anticipation. It hurts us, but justifies trust. It remains elusive, yet sounds us. It shows us wonders, and burns us to ashes. This is the agenda of an alien divinity.

In its own strange way, God loves us. Therefore let us love the world.

ONE HUNDRED THOUSAND WORDS

Intrepid reader, I'm bumping up hard against the word count. These are the fading moments.

I'm sixty-one years old. I wish I could live another hundred years. I've been talking about the world's perfection and the value of subtle lives. Gentle reader, with your own cunning future, Godspeed.

A Professional Philosopher's Postscript to *Hating Perfection*

or

How We Know that Other People Have Consciousness
and a Chinese Room[1] Would Not

Turns out we have only one viable explanation. Let's see why.

Many people believe that some collection of true but contingent causal laws logically entails all of the other true contingent propositions. Indeed, many physicists believe that some *single* mathematical equation expresses a single true but contingent causal principle that logically entails all of the other true contingent propositions. This proposed hypothesis was once called the "TOE" or "Theory of Everything." During the last ten years, views on what the master equation would look like have changed radically.

My own view is that a single true but contingent principle of goodness logically entails all of the other true contingent propositions, including our excellent laws of causality and where consciousness resides. *Hating Perfection* describes this principle of goodness in detail (starting on page 107). An extremely brief description would go like this: Collective experience in the actual world has the highest possible level of the right kind of subtlety. Because all other perceived goods and evils have a specific balance in human perception (and in the perception of all other possible agents sharing crucial properties with humans), the level of collective subtlety emerges as the final arbiter of the goodness of collective experience. On rather massive evidence, as the text elucidates, our world does offer its residents, as a collection, the most subtle experience possible. Our world conforms to that standard of goodness.

This book as a whole explains and argues these claims. This postscript has a more modest goal: Simply to show that *some* principle of goodness governs events in our world. I'm going to talk about four issues that principles of causality cannot explain, but an appropriate principle of goodness can.

Humans have some remarkable instances of knowledge. Although a tiny minority of the human race hotly denies it, in fact we do know that other people have consciousness. But *how* we know is a bit mysterious. And again, although some philosophers deny it, we know that Chinese rooms, as they have been described, would not have consciousness. But *how* we know has yet to be figured out.

Knowledge is true belief justified in the proper way, we are told. How does the human mind justify those two instances of knowledge? *What are we seeing in the world*, that tells us where consciousness does and does not reside?

To get at this question, we ask another. Humans are conscious in the actual world, but in many alternate possible worlds humans (or creatures much like them) have no consciousness. Chinese rooms, on the other hand, have no consciousness in the actual world, but in many Cartoon Worlds they can be conscious. And so we ask our question:

In a Cartoon World, the heads on Mt. Rushmore might converse with you in English and they might have consciousness. We see Cartoon Worlds represented in various cartoons as coherent spatio-temporal worlds that mimic the actual world in many ways.

Question: What properties does *our world* have, and certain Cartoon Worlds not have, that contradict consciousness in a Chinese Room?

If we find those properties of our world, then perhaps we can understand how the human mind is justifying our remarkable instances of knowledge. Let's consider two explanations for the relevant difference between the actual world and Cartoon World.

THE CAUSAL EXPLANATION

Q. What properties does our world have, and Cartoon World not have, that contradict consciousness in a Chinese Room?

A. Our causality differs from Cartoon World's. In our world, the laws of causality are such that no consciousness would attach to a Chinese Room (CR).

Q. How do we know that causality operates that way in our world?

A. We know that actual CRs would not have consciousness. Therefore, the laws of causality would not attach consciousness to them.

Q. How do we know that actual CRs would not have consciousness?

A. How we know remains unexplained. We don't know from the laws of causality, for that explanation would be circular. (We already explained that the laws of causality would not put consciousness into CRs because CRs are not conscious. To explain in the reverse direction now would complete a circle.) How we know doesn't get explained. But we know.

Q. Then we have not yet identified the properties of our world that contradict consciousness in a CR, for: appropriate amendments to actual causal laws surely could have accommodated that phenomenon, but actual causality in fact does not accommodate that phenomenon for reasons yet to be identified.

The causal "explanation" of the relevant difference between our world and Cartoon World fails to identify the properties of our world that contradict consciousness in a Chinese Room.

Thus, suppose we assert: In alternate worlds, the right causal laws give consciousness to CRs. Our world does not have those particular causal laws. Hence the difference between worlds. *Explanans:* Our world does not have particular causal laws that give consciousness to CRs. *Explanandum:* CRs are not conscious in our world.

But how do we know that our world does not have particular causal laws that would give consciousness to a CR? We know only as a result of a previous explanation in which the explanandum and the explanans above are reversed. The causal "explanation" of the relevant difference between worlds is circular.

Thus, the absence from our world of particular causal laws that would give consciousness to CRs, does not actually justify our belief that CRs would not be conscious in our world. Apparently some other property of our world justifies that belief.

THE PRINCIPLE-OF-GOODNESS EXPLANATION

Q. Why can CRs be conscious in a Cartoon World but not in the actual world?

A. In the actual world, consciousness goes where it *ought* to go, *where it has value*. In humans, for example. Except under extraordinary circumstances, the experience of an actual CR would be unworthy of consciousness; I'll tell you why in a moment. Thus, the actual world conforms to a principle of goodness that does indicate where consciousness does and does not reside. Some Cartoon Worlds follow a principle of organization that does not indicate where consciousness resides, or indicates a different residence plan for consciousness than the one followed in our world. But the actual world's principle of goodness contradicts consciousness in a CR.

Q. How do we know that the actual world puts consciousness where it ought to be?

A. Most everyone knows that the world does *something* good for us. Our experience is interesting, engaging, surprising, detailed, and coherent. Those are good things. The world most definitely doesn't do what we want it to do; it disappoints us often, but it doesn't disappoint us by taking away the fundamental coherence of our experience. Most everyone knows that the world does *something* good for us, and it does it reliably. Apparently, we humans have sufficient confidence in such "fundamental services" provided to us, that we know other humans have consciousness and CRs do not. Hence our remarkable instances of knowledge.

CONCLUSION

We know that other people have consciousness and we know that Chinese Rooms do not. Both instances of knowledge appear to have the same justification: a principle of goodness that we perceive in the world. Let's elaborate a bit.

Only a few philosophers deny that we know that other people have consciousness and CRs do not. So how do we know? How does the human mind justify these instances of knowledge? The laws of causality cannot be the justification, as we saw. We are left with this conjecture:

An individual human readily understands that her experience is interesting, engaging, surprising, detailed, and coherent. Experience often deviates from what she would like it to be, but it does provide such "fundamental services" or "basic virtues." She readily understands that other people's experience would have the same basic virtues, if *they* had consciousness. She lives in a society where such basic virtues would apply to most everyone who is conscious. Consciousness in others would add value to the world. (Moreover, she lives in an *interactive* society where sometimes she hurts others, where she would wrongly feel shame unless other people really are conscious. This volume argues that we are genuine moral players for value reasons.) Consciousness *ought* to be in others, and it readily extends to others. Apparently, the appearance of basic virtue in her own experience is sufficiently pervasive and coherent to justify the knowledge that other people really do have consciousness. Apparently, she knows that the world's coherent basic virtue would not contradict itself or leave itself incomplete. Except for a few philosophers and other strange people, we all appear to trust the world that far.

But how would the world provide basic services to a CR? It could only do so with ponderous inefficiency and/or tangled lines of moral responsibility. The causal sources of basic virtue in our own experience are commonplace but incredibly complicated. They include the evolution of life on earth and the evolution of earth from the big bang. The human brain and human society are causally produced by a long, long evolution that generates interest, idiosyncrasy, surprise, detail, and coherence in our experience—the basic virtues that help make our experience worthy of consciousness. By contrast, an actual CR as usually described, would be one fatal step removed from the commonplace, but very complicated, causal sources of basic virtue in human experience. A CR would not be intimately embedded within a large coherent evolution as we are; it would not be connected to natural evolution in the right way. In short, a CR does not hook up, in the same beneficial way, to the causal sources of the basic virtues that flow readily into us.

The simplest way to find a *substitute* causal source of basic virtues for the CR experience would involve creating an entire society of interacting CRs that genuinely help and harm each other, with motivation sufficiently complicated, sufficiently self-contradictory, yet sufficiently coherent. That enterprise is rather astronomically more complicated than it may seem at first glance.

But without sufficiently strong basic virtues, the experience of a CR would be unworthy of consciousness. The present work goes through these statements with more deliberation.

Tricking out a CR (or any other human artifice) to pass as human and to participate in human society, such that the CR deliberately and genuinely and with convoluted motivation harms and helps the humans around it would be even more impractical. *Hating Perfection* explains, but the basic difficulty is this: Our long evolution causes each human personality to be enormously idiosyncratic yet highly coherent. The human species, and all of our ancestor species before us, evolved to make effective choices among increasingly diverse alternatives. Those who did not make effective choices died out. After several hundred million years of that discipline here on earth, almost every human critter has a personality both enormously idiosyncratic yet highly coherent. How would we cause an artificial personality to have those virtues? Again we would be trying to find a substitute for the causal effects of evolution, and this time for perhaps its most remarkable causal effect.

How do we know that our world would not attach consciousness to a Chinese Room? We begin with the vague unease that it doesn't belong there. When we investigate, we find that the basic virtues we see in our own experience, along with their causal sources, do not apply to a CR. Our vague unease was spot on.

In the text I offer a more detailed discussion of exactly what it takes to be worthy of consciousness. Also, I look into the principle of goodness that appears to govern existence. This principle does have an unexpected consequence: Unless a world is painful, unjust, ruthless, and fatal, the value of the inhabitants' experience collapses. Not entirely wonderful news.

Nonetheless: We need a principle of goodness to explain how the actual world differs from coherent alternate worlds with conscious Chinese Rooms, to explain how we know that our friends are conscious, and to explain how we know that actual Chinese Rooms would not have consciousness. We have no other way to account for the difference between worlds or for our remarkable instances of knowledge. And now we have three issues that a principle of causality does not explain but a principle of goodness does explain.

HISTORICAL CONTEXT

Some two hundred thousand years ago, when our ancestors had animistic explanations for natural phenomena, they might have had animistic opinions about consciousness in a Chinese Room had the idea been presented to them. Many Cartoon Worlds might have seemed rather natural to our ancestors. Today we see ourselves as scientific and rational. For the natural phenomena around us, we look for explanations that have a certain rational economy—and our universe has rewarded this approach.

In a Cartoon World basic virtues in experience can be present by fiat. That arrangement offends our modern sense of rational economy (which can make a Cartoon World funny to us). In our own world, by contrast, basic virtues in human experience are the product of an enormous but intelligible causal process.

This modern insight shows us properties of our own world that Cartoon World does not have. It shows us how our universe step by step assembles agency worthy of consciousness. It shows us what standards we must meet when assembling an artificial agency worthy of consciousness. And it brings into focus a particular value present in almost every human life.

A fourth issue that only a principle of goodness can explain is this: Why do our laws of causality give surprise, detail, idiosyncrasy, high coherence, and fascination to our experience? Why do our laws of causality take a form that gives extensive idiosyncrasy yet high coherence to each human personality? Why does our universe give us valuable lives?

SUMMARY

This essay presents four arguments:

Our *knowledge* that others are conscious implies that some principle of goodness governs our experience. Otherwise, we couldn't have that knowledge.

Our *knowledge* that Chinese Rooms would not be conscious implies that some principle of goodness governs our experience. Otherwise, we couldn't have that knowledge.

The *fact* that Chinese Rooms would not be conscious also implies that some principle of goodness governs our experience. Otherwise, we cannot explain how our world differs from coherent alternate worlds with conscious Chinese Rooms.

The *fact* that our lives have value implies that some principle of goodness governs our experience.

FIVE CLARIFICATIONS

(1) In *Hating Perfection* I claim that our world is the best possible world. I deny that any agency made it so. I deny that our world is caused, willed, sustained, or designed. Any of those explanans would only add supernatural contingent propositions to the natural contingent propositions we were already trying to explain; they raise more questions than they answer. I claim that "the final explanans" (technical term) is a principle of goodness, not a principle of causality.

As final explanans for the state of existence, the principle of goodness would need no supernatural help. It's nothing more than a summation of the state of existence, I claim, a summation of all the other true contingent propositions. Why the explanation rests with the principle of goodness is explained in *Hating Perfection*.

(2) G. E. Moore and many others have cast doubt on the coherence of notions of value in a thing. The chapter "Opinions and Spiders," beginning on page 107, is my response to these concerns.

(3) By "best possible world" I simply mean this: the world best suited to habitation by agents, or more accurately, the world whose agents have the best possible conscious experience as a col-

lection of agents. If a world is good in a way that fails to improve its conscious agents' collective experience, then such goodness fails to help the value of that world in the sense I'm talking about.

Thus, if the agents in World A and in World B have exactly the same subjective experience, but agents in World A have genuine free will and in World B only the illusion of free will, then (as the text explains) collective experience has more value in World A. On the other hand, if World A has a gorgeous but enormously remote planet that has no effect on any agent's experience, and this planet is omitted from World B, then World A and World B remain equal in value in the sense I'm talking about. The goodness of the gorgeous planet fails to improve the agents' collective experience in World A.

If the value of a possible world is simply the value of the collective conscious experience of its inhabitants, then the rules by which those inhabitants perceive their world gain importance. For humans and for all possible agents sharing crucial properties with humans, goods and evils must conform to specific balances in perception. If we perceive our world as wonderful, we must also perceive it as horrible.

In human perception, and in a number of ways, fifty percent of conscious experience falls below average whether or not our world is the best possible one. If it did not, the value of experience in the human style would collapse. Consequently, humans and agents like us cannot evade disappointing experience no matter what world we inhabit, as the text argues and elaborates. For us, the best world is just the most subtle world, not the world with the least disappointing experience.

(4) I claim that a single true but contingent principle of goodness (a principle of optimized subtlety in experience for a world's

inhabitants as a collection) logically entails and is entailed by all the other true contingent propositions. In a somewhat similar manner, a true but contingent principle of physics entails and is entailed by all of its instances in the actual world.

That all of the other true contingent propositions conform to the principle of goodness is a giant coincidence. However, as explained in *Hating Perfection*, my argument does not actually introduce giant coincidence into human experience. On the contrary, a rather sizable coincidence among the contingent facts about the actual world around us is already observable whether or not my explanation for it is accepted. My explanation does extend the observable coincidence, but not very far. As my discussion explains, the actual contingent-fact coincidence open to our direct view is quite a bit larger than may have been previously appreciated.

This very large coincidence either happens for no reason or it happens for a reason. This book discusses and compares alternative explanations. The best-world thesis has the best explanatory power.

(5) Suppose that brain researchers a few years from now identify a particular feature or activity of our brains that always corresponds in some precise way to conscious thought. Would they have discovered a causal explanation for where consciousness resides? No. Their results might very well help us understand *how* brains are conscious in our world, but not why they are conscious in our world, and not why they are conscious in that particular way. We can still point to coherent alternate worlds where the correspondence doesn't happen, and then ask: Why does the correspondence obtain in our world, but not obtain in certain coherent alternate worlds? The causal "explanation" is still empty. But maybe our principle of goodness would account for yet another interesting difference between our world and particular alternate worlds. Let's take a look.

Chinese Rooms, as usually described, ought not to be conscious, because causing their experience to have basic virtues would be impossible in practice. Other people ought to have consciousness for a number of strong reasons. But why would it be true that the human brain ought to be conscious when and only when a particular piece of it buzzes just the right way?

Sometimes we can only guess. That particular correspondence, were it a true fact that we discovered, might help us see coherence in the world, might help us understand ourselves, might reveal some basic mechanics in consciousness, might lead to further discoveries and new technologies, might get grant money into good hands. But we don't know. The researchers' results would have consequences that we cannot foresee, including painful and unjust consequences.

Under my thesis, sometimes we can see exactly why and sometimes we can't. The best possible world is quite straightforward with the intelligible, coherent evolution that produced us. We can see how we were put together, what we are, what our prospects are, why our lives have a particular value. But the same world keeps our experience elusive and mysterious in many ways, as it ought to do, for that approach sustains the interest and value of our daily lives.

Our lives are subtle in a good way. Some of us win, some of us lose, but we all get to play. Although the best possible world is no picnic, almost all of us want to know: What happens next?

NOTE

1. A Chinese room at bottom is a digital computer that converses in Chinese, where significant portions of the computer's working parts consist of a human operator who understands no Chinese. In a Chinese room thought experiment, the human operator receives Chinese ideographs as an input. Each input serves as an entry point to an elaborate set of digital rules. By following the rules faithfully, the operator (alters the rules a bit here and there and) produces Chinese ideographs as output, such that the Chinese room participates in a *coherent* extended dialogue in Chinese. The human operator would have con-

sciousness, people think, but the communicating Chinese room she operates would not. Thus, for different reasons, neither the human operator nor the Chinese room would understand the Chinese room's coherent conversations in Chinese.

READER'S NOTES